FIFTY CLASSIC MOTION PICTURES

by DAVID ZINMAN

Fifty Classic Motion Pictures
The Day Huey Long Was Shot
Rapid Writing

50 CLASSIC MOTION PICTURES
The Stuff That Dreams Are Made Of

by DAVID ZINMAN

CROWN publishers, inc. new york

Acknowledgments

I AM INDEBTED to the staff of the Theater Collection of the New York Public Library, Astor, Lenox and Tilden Foundations, especially to Paul Myers, its curator, and his professional staff of Dorothy Swerdlove, Dorothy O'Connor, Avi Wortis, Donald Fowle, Betty Wharton, Rod Bladel and Maxwell Silverman. Thanks also to Fay Dale and Monty Arnold, and to Don Madison of Photographic Services. In addition, I am grateful to the Film Study Center of the Museum of Modern Art in New York City and the Hempstead, N.Y., Public Library.

I owe a special debt of gratitude to John Cocchi, who checked my material for accuracy and helped identify character actors (although I take full responsibility for any errors).

For helping me locate stills, I am thankful to Movie Star News for opening its vast collection in New York; and to Kenneth G. Lawrence, the Movie Memorabilia Shop of Hollywood; Cinemabilia, New York; Kier's Celebrity Photos, New York; Larry Edmunds Bookshop, Hollywood; Raymond Guzman, United Artists; Eric Naumann, Universal; Norman Kaphan, MGM; Mel Asch, 20th Century-Fox; Henry Strauss, Columbia Pictures; Hal Roach Studios; Screen Gems; Alan Barbour, *Screen Facts;* John R. Cooper, *Hero Hobby* magazine, Clarksburg, W. Va.; Jack B. Hardy, Roxboro, N.C.; Al Kilgore, New York; C. H. Edwards, Hazel Crest, Ill.; and Eleanor Knowles, New York.

Also thanks to Bert Gray, New York; James A. Stringham, Lansing, Mich.; Diane O'Brien and Yolanda Ryder, my hard-working typists; and to Richard Schotter, my astute and perceptive editor.

Fourth Printing, August, 1973

© 1970 BY DAVID H. ZINMAN

LIBRARY OF CONGRESS CATALOG CARD NUMBER: 72–108081

ISBN: 0-517-504774

PRINTED IN THE U.S.A.

PUBLISHED SIMULTANEOUSLY IN CANADA BY GENERAL PUBLISHING COMPANY LIMITED

For Sara, the stuff my dreams
are made of

Introduction

I MAKE NO PRETENSE about being a movie scholar, historian, pedant, expert, buff or whatever. Even a buff implies discrimination. I am purely and simply a movie bum, an addict, a guy who's been hooked so thoroughly he sometimes sets the alarm for 3 A.M. when *The Maltese Falcon* shows up on the late, late show.

What reason does some retread from the popcorn brigade have to do a book? Well, my answer is that the old movies were made for the general public and so I think it is fitting for a book on the movies to be written with them in mind. Instead, most of the recent film books seem to aim at a small group of intellectuals. These books have bathed us in a deluge of words discussing the "art" of the cinema in technical and aesthetic terms, terms that have no interest for the average moviegoer. The man in the tenth row who howls at Fields and at Laurel and Hardy couldn't care less about dollying, panning, baby spots and the significance of shadows in von Sternberg films.

So this is an ode to the old movies, written not with the careful and sometimes acid words of a critic but with the nostalgic and sometimes adoring pen of someone who seeks to recapture the glitter and fantasy of that make-believe world in darkness. And, of course, the dreams.

Readers will find a wide variety of film selections. They range from such universal favorites as *Gone With the Wind, Citizen Kane* and *City Lights* to pictures that are seldom if ever chosen on any list—such as *Nightmare Alley, Death Takes a Holiday, She,* and *Charlie Chan at the Opera*. There is even one serial, *Flash Gordon*.

In picking my fifty pictures I made only two stipulations. First, that they be made in the 1930s and 1940s, the movies' so-called "golden years." Second, that they be movies I thought were distinguished or unique or hilarious in the old days and that they held up on rescreenings today. This makes my choices purely personal. But, in the end, every list in some way has to be a personal one. Naturally there will be disagreement, but this is a reader's privilege. And didn't the feller say, "If we all thought alike, we'd all be married to the same woman"?

Table of Contents

"We are such stuff as dreams are made on . . ."
—Shakespeare, *The Tempest*

Ward Bond: It's heavy. What is it?
Humphrey Bogart: The stuff that dreams are made of.
—Final sequence from *The Maltese Falcon*

FIFTY CLASSIC MOTION PICTURES

Mae West in all her splendor. She could be cool or she could be calculating. Or she could spoof everything with a line like: "Beulah, peel me a grape."

(Photos by Paramount)

I

GRAND DAMES

MAE WEST • SHE DONE HIM WRONG
GRETA GARBO • NINOTCHKA
MARLENE DIETRICH • DESTRY RIDES AGAIN
BETTE DAVIS • THE LETTER
JEAN HARLOW • DINNER AT EIGHT

2

Mae West

She Done Him Wrong

(Released January 27, 1933)

A SCREEN DRAMA ADAPTED by Harvey Thew and John Bright from the play *Diamond Lil* by Mae West. Art director, Bob Usher. Photography, Charles Lang. Editor, Alexander Hall. Costumes, Edith Head. Sound, Harry M. Lindgren. Music and lyrics by Ralph Rainger. Songs: "I Wonder Where My Easy Rider's Gone," "I Like a Man Who Takes His Time." Director, Lowell Sherman. Assistant director, James Dugan. Presented by Paramount. Running Time, 66 minutes.

Lady Lou	MAE WEST
Captain Cummings	CARY GRANT
Serge Stanieff	GILBERT ROLAND
Gus Jordan	NOAH BEERY
Russian Rosie	RAFAELA OTTIANO
Dan Flynn	DAVID LANDAU
Sally	ROCHELLE HUDSON
Chick Clark	OWEN MOORE
Rag Time Kelly	FUZZY KNIGHT
Chuck Connors	TAMMANY YOUNG
Spider Kane	DEWEY ROBINSON
Frances	GRACE LA RUE
Steak McGarry	HARRY WALLACE
Pete	JAMES C. EAGLES
Doheny	ROBERT E. HOMANS
Big Bill	TOM KENNEDY
Barfly	ARTHUR HOUSMAN
Pal	WADE BOTELER
Mrs. Flaherty	AGGIE HERRING
Pearl	LOUISE BEAVERS
Jacobson	LEE KOHLMAR
Mike	TOM MC GUIRE

Hips sashaying, shoulders rolling, she struts into our adulating presence with one hand on her hip, the other primping her blonde curls. "When I'm good, I'm very good," she says with a wink. "But when I'm bad, I'm better."

The violet eyes are rolling. The voluptuous, milk-white figure is undulating. Beneath an ostrich-feather picture hat, that languid, nasal voice is trailing off with just enough inflection to impart a *double-entendre* twist to every crack. "It's not the men in my life," says Mae West. "It's the life in my men."

Mae West. Sex queen of the movies. Her figure was enshrined in Madame Tussaud's waxworks. Her name became synonymous with GI life jackets in World War II. She was *sui generis*, one of a kind, an indelible part of the thirties. "She is as much one of the major phenomenons of 1933," said Joseph C. Furnas, writing in the New York *Herald Tribune*, "as the N.R.A., the three little pigs, the University in Exile, and Huey Long."

Mae West. A Hollywood Legend. An American Institution. Bawdy, brassy and bosomy. She extolled opera-length corsets and the hourglass figure even when Irene Castle was converting the nation to bobbed hair and the boyish silhouette. Eventually, Miss West won out. The main thing about corsets, she said, is, "You got to have something to put in 'em. Know what I mean?"

Not everyone relished her saucy style. New York critic Percy Hammond called her the world's worst actress. Joseph Wood Krutch, Columbia's distinguished drama professor, said she had the lowest form of animal life for her patrons. The authorities tossed her in jail for running a Broadway show they thought was obscene.

But each of them failed to discern the essential Westian wit. Her humor was a play on the morals and manners of a dull and dreary world. In her world, the female was a free, bold spirit—no longer passive and timid but liberated and brassy—even bold enough to invite an attractive male to come and see her sometime. Yet, it was all so obviously self-mocking, it came out as a caricature of sex. Her croony voice and her feline wriggle inspired not passion but laughter.

"It isn't what I do but how I do it," she once said. "It isn't what I say. But how I say it. And how I look when I do it and say it."

Her dimensions actually were not as Amazonian as they appeared on the screen. Although she weighed a hundred and thirty pounds, she was only five feet three. But she wore five-inch heels and her superwoman proportions were created by padding and a specially built corset that brought her waist in, hips out, breasts up. Her vital statistics were 38-27-38.

Only eight years of Mae West's life were spent outside the theatre. They were her first eight years. She was born in Brooklyn in 1893, the daughter of Jack West, a prize fighter who she later said was "cruel. . . . I took a dislike to him." She made her debut at eight, imitating Eddie Foy and Bert Williams at an amateur show. During the rest of her childhood and adolescence she played in vaudeville and musical comedies. When most girls were just getting out of school, she was a featured performer in Ned Wayburn's *Demi-Tasse Revue* and *The Mimic World*.

She went on to the big-time Keith Circuit where she claims she invented the shimmy before Gilda Gray. When she tired of trouping, she turned to writing, producing a play she called *Sex* in the days when the word was used only in medical books. It made her famous overnight. The title alone created a sensation. Newspapers banned her ads. Editorials denounced the show. But the public flocked to see what it was all about.

After the play had run eleven months, police suddenly closed it. They charged her with damaging the morals of her audience, sent her to the Welfare Island workhouse for ten days (after a trial that gave her about a million dollars' worth of publicity). When she drove to prison in her $20,000 Isotta-Fraschini automobile, cheering crowds trailed her. When she came out (after a stay in one of the prison official's offices and two days off for good behavior), she donated a thousand books to the prison library.

Her next show, *Diamond Lil,* which she also wrote, became an even bigger hit. A lusty story of a flaming Bowery favorite, it ran on Broadway for ninety-seven weeks. In 1932, in the depths of the Depression, Hollywood called her and she debuted in *Night After Night*. Box office returns were so good, a debt-ridden Paramount asked her to play in a screen version of *Diamond Lil* called *She Done Him Wrong*. The movie was such a solid hit, it practically single-handedly bailed Paramount out of its financial slump.

Miss West plays bejeweled Lady Lou, a Bowery chanteuse—she sings the old ballad "Frankie and Johnny" in this one—who judges men by the size of the diamonds they give her. For openers, she announces, "I'm the finest woman who walked the streets." Lou has forgotten Chick Clark (Owen Moore), who went to prison for trying to get her diamonds, and is working in the plush saloon of Gus Jordan (Noah Beery). Gus has showered her with diamonds, and so she has become his mistress.

That is, until handsome Salvation Army Captain Cummings (Cary Grant) makes her forget about diamonds. "Why don't you come sometime and see me," she tells him. (The quote evolved into her most famous movie line.) "I'm home every evening. . . . Come up. I'll tell your fortune." Cummings says nothing. But it's obvious he is wilting under the collar. Miss West laughs. "Ah, you can be had," she says.

Then things get complicated. Chick breaks out of prison, threatens to kill Lou unless she runs off with him. Gus gets into trouble with the law for counterfeiting and running a white slavery racket. Lou gets involved in an accidental slaying. But it all works out in the end. The police catch up to Chick just as he is about to do Lou in because she won't rush off with him. Cummings, it turns out, is really a G-man known as "The Hawk" and he arrests Gus.

For a moment, it looks like Lou is headed for the cooler too. The Hawk has the handcuffs out. "Is that absolutely necessary?" Lou asks. "I wasn't born with them."

"A lot of men would be safer if you had," The Hawk says.

Miss West, playing Lady Lou, a Bowery beauty well versed in love and heavily weighted with diamonds, with her saloon boss Gus Jordan (Noah Beery).

"I don't know," Lou answers. "Hands aren't everything."

But The Hawk is only kidding. He wants Lou. She snuggles into his arms murmuring, "I always knew you could be had . . . tall, dark and handsome." (One could conservatively say The Hawk is one lover who has undertaken a great deal.)

Miss West went on to make *I'm No Angel* (1933), also with Cary Grant, *Belle of the Nineties* (1934), *Goin' to Town* (1935), *My Little Chickadee* (1940) with W. C. Fields, and *The Heat's On* (1943). In all, she appeared in ten movies—eight of which she wrote. In 1959 she also wrote her autobiography, entitled *Goodness Had Nothing to Do With It.* (The title was what she told a hat-check girl in *Night After Night* who, dazzled by Miss West's necklace, remarked, "Goodness, what lovely diamonds.")

Mae West was one Hollywood figure who did not squander her money or her health. She invested in real estate and friends estimate her fortune at over four million dollars. A masterwork of self-preservation, her picture adorned the cover of *Life* in 1969 when she was seventy-six. That same year she announced her return to the screen after a twenty-six-year absence to play a key role in the film version of *Myra Breckinridge*, Gore Vidal's controversial best seller. "It's a return, not a comeback," Miss West told reporters. "I've never really been away, just busy."

Ironically, off stage, Miss West was surprisingly unlike her movie image. True, she had a bed with mirrored wall and ceiling ("I like to know how I'm doing") and displayed in her plush Hollywood apartment a nude statue of herself, for which she posed in 1935. But she lived a quiet life. Neither drank nor smoked. Almost never went to night clubs or parties. And outside of her only marriage —which took place in her teens and lasted only briefly *—her name was rarely linked romantically with another man. Of course, it could well be that she has fooled us all. "It's not the men you see me with," Mae West once said. "It's the men you don't see me with."

---

* She was married to Frank Wallace, a song and dance vaudeville partner, in 1911 when she was seventeen, and stayed legally married to him until their divorce in 1943. But they split up during their first months of wedlock and Wallace went out of her life.

Lou meets Serge Stanieff (Gilbert Roland) and another male heart starts thumping faster. Jordan looks on with consternation.

Lady Lou and the guy who makes her forget about jewels—Salvation Army Captain Cummings (Cary Grant).

The psalm-singing Cummings turns out to be a federal agent known as The Hawk and he closes in on Jordan, who's been running a counterfeiting operation and a white slavery ring on the side.

The captain accepts Lou's invitation and comes up to see her.

Russian Rosie (Rafaela Ottiano) takes a jealous stab at Lou
when Rosie's beau Serge casts longing eyes in Lou's direction.

Ninotchka (Garbo) before she succumbs to capitalism. Wearing stark, military-style clothes, a sober-faced Ninotchka is not amused by Count Leon's (Melvyn Douglas) Western-style humor.

(Photos by MGM)

Greta Garbo

Ninotchka

(Released November 3, 1939)

ADAPTED FROM AN ORIGINAL screen story by Melchior Lengyel. Scenario by Charles Brackett, Billy Wilder and Walter Reisch. Film editor, Gene Ruggiero. Camera, William Daniels. Art director, Cedric Gibbons. Musical score, Werner R. Heymann. Produced and directed by Ernst Lubitsch for Metro-Goldwyn-Mayer. Running time, 110 minutes.

Ninotchka	GRETA GARBO
Count Leon	MELVYN DOUGLAS
Grand Duchess Swana	INA CLAIRE
Iranoff	SIG RUMANN
Buljanoff	FELIX BRESSART
Kopalski	ALEXANDER GRANACH
Commissar Razinin	BELA LUGOSI
Count Rakonin	GREGORY GAYE
Hotel Manager	ROLFE SEDAN
Mercier	EDWIN MAXWELL
Gaston	RICHARD CARLE

(In 1956 the film was remade as *The Iron Petticoat* with Bob Hope and Katharine Hepburn, and, in 1957, as the musical *Silk Stockings* with Fred Astaire and Cyd Charisse. The latter version was based on the Broadway show.)

One day in 1938 a young Scotsman was arrested in Glasgow for stealing a photograph of Greta Garbo from a movie theatre. When police brought him to court, Magistrate Robert Norman Macleod looked over the charge, raised his eyebrows and muttered curiously, "Who is Greta Garbo?"

The incident was thought unique enough for the Associated Press to file a cable story. In the fourth decade of the twentieth century, it was world news that there lived a man who had not heard of Garbo. She was then, as she is now, the most celebrated actress the screen has yet known.

At the peak of her twenty-year career Garbo was not only considered Hollywood's most famous star, but possibly the world's best-known woman. She was her era's symbol of feminine beauty. To describe her sublime looks, writers used the phrase "the face of the century." It was a serene, detached face with classic features that in pensive close-ups seemed to reflect everybody's own fantasies and desires.

"As a love object, she combined the sensual with a spiritual appeal, femininity with a mannish quotient," Norman Zierold wrote in his *Garbo.* "She was as attractive to women as to men."

Physically, she was far from a sex goddess. She was flat-chested, gangly and broad-shouldered. And yet, without trying, her unorthodox appearance set a whole new style. Before Garbo, the trend was toward short bobbed hair, heavy eyebrows, robust features and coy manners. During Garbo's reign, actresses did their best to imitate her plain, pageboy cut, penciled eyebrows, long eyelashes, sunken cheeks and languid expression.

But no one could compare with Garbo. Her mystique was deeper than mere surface qualities. No one has ever totally succeeded in defining it. Perhaps the best that can be said—or suggested— is that the Garbo manner was a blend of fluid, graceful motion with a world-weary attitude, a woman who seemed tragically caught in the web of an ill-fated love. Her face in closeup was spellbinding. Her presence, hypnotic.

"Garbo had a sense of the mood, of the texture, of the instinct, without perhaps being very bright," said Billy Wilder. "Others can act their ass to shreds and nothing happens. But Garbo has a sixth sense, like Marilyn Monroe, a sense for what is appropriate."

Greta Gustafsson came to Hollywood in 1925, the protégée of Mauritz Stiller, Sweden's foremost movie director. The daughter of simple country people who had a hard time adjusting to life in Stockholm, she left school at fourteen to work as a lather girl in a barbershop. She soon got a job in the millinery department of P. U. Bergstrom's department store. It led to her appearance in a short advertising film for the store, an experience that convinced her she wanted to be an actress.

She enrolled in the Royal Dramatic Academy, then auditioned before Stiller for a part in *Gösta Berling's Saga*. Against his colleague's advice, he gave her the role. It had been said that Stiller was seeking a girl whom he could mold into a great actress. He apparently saw his dream in Garbo. When Louis B. Mayer offered Stiller a contract to come to Hollywood he accepted on condition that Garbo come with him.

But when they got to Hollywood they found MGM had no idea what to do with them. Studio executives were turned off by Garbo's stills and screen test. However, after a second test, they gave her a part in the film *The Torrent*. The public responded immediately. Her unusual presence struck some invisible, responsive chord. *Variety* hailed her as the find of the year.

Oddly, as Garbo's stock soared, Stiller's began sinking. He never completed a picture for MGM, although he did some for rival companies with mixed success. Stiller coached Garbo for her early roles. But he eventually despaired of enhancing his own career and returned to Sweden.

Left on her own, Garbo blossomed as an actress. Her reputation grew with each picture. Some say *Queen Christina* (1933), in which she played the unhappy Swedish ruler, marked the zenith of her popularity. Others say she reached the peak in 1936 when she played *Camille* opposite Robert Taylor.

Whichever it was, it is a fact that after *Camille*

she was in box office trouble. For one thing, her tragic roles made her too remote, too austere for average audiences. For another, her $250,000 salary —paid before she even stepped on the set—made her pictures fabulously expensive. Only her European popularity compensated for sagging domestic returns.

There are conflicting stories about how *Ninotchka* was chosen. But in his biography of Garbo, John Bainbridge says she had always wanted to do comedy and she felt now was the opportune time. MGM reneged, wary of putting their star in an unknown medium. However, Garbo reportedly forced the issue, hinting at retirement. The studio relented and under the sure hand of German director Ernst Lubitsch, she put her reputation on the line. She was, in effect, playing herself—the cool, distant beauty besieged by a romantic, debonair suitor.

The movie opens as Russia, starved for cash after a poor harvest, sends a committee of three (Sig Rumann, Felix Bressart and Alexander Granach) to Paris. Their mission—sell "legally confiscated" imperial jewels so Russia can buy tractors.

The gems once belonged to the Grand Duchess Swana (Ina Claire), a White Russian living in exile in the French capital. She puts her boy friend, Count Leon (Melvyn Douglas), on the trail of the Soviets.

He proves more than their match. First he gets an injunction that stops the sale of the jewels and throws the question of ownership into court. Not content to rely solely on the law, the resourceful Leon entertains the comrades so lavishly they soon cease to care if they ever go back to Russia. (Lubitsch shows their gleeful introduction to the corrupt pleasures of capitalism by training his camera on the doors of their suite. Mounting roars of acclaim bellow forth each time waiters pass in and out with food and drink. The noise reaches a crescendo when three cigarette girls prance in.)

To corral the wayward trio, Moscow promptly dispatches Comrade Ninotchka. She is an unsmiling, no-nonsense Soviet who wears severe clothes and is totally dedicated to the Communist credo. She tells Leon love is just a chemical reaction, that he is merely a decorative remnant of a doomed society. But he is persistent, escorts her through Paris—she wants to know how much steel the Eiffel Tower has—and then to his apartment.

When he kisses her, she says promisingly, "That

was restful." But she adds that she has also kissed a Polish lancer she killed in battle. However, Ninotchka's icy exterior slowly begins to thaw and Leon finally gets her to laugh when he takes her to lunch the next day. Cupid has prevailed over the Kremlin.

Losing interest in the case of the grand duchess' jewels, Ninotchka swaps her Russian garb for the latest Paris fashions. She even buys a silly hat she had scoffed at on arrival. Leon, who has fallen in love with her, takes Ninotchka to a night club where she gets gloriously drunk, calls all the patrons "comrades" and urges the washroom women to strike.

Later, when she goes to sleep in her evening gown, leaving her safe open, the grand duchess secures her jewels. The next morning the duchess has a sporting proposition for Ninotchka. She will sign over the jewels if Ninotchka takes the next plane back to Russia. Outmaneuvered, Ninotchka reluctantly leaves. However, Swana finds that she has lost more than her jewels. She can't get Leon back.

Leon tries to follow Ninotchka to Moscow but he's denied a visa. Then, the three comrades, on the strength of their Paris mission, are sent to Constantinople to sell furs. Again they flounder. Again Ninotchka is dispatched to straighten them out. (The commissar who gives Ninotchka her orders is Bela Lugosi in one of his rare non-monster roles.) What does she find when the three comrades meet her? They have opened a Russian restaurant. And there, instigator of their new rebellion, stands Leon, waiting with open arms.

The studio ballyhooed the film with the slogan, "Garbo Laughs." And the critics unanimously hailed her transition to sophisticated comedy. Frank S. Nugent, the New York *Times* reviewer, said the audience laughed so loud and long in Radio City Music Hall that he had to see *Ninotchka* twice to hear all the lines. "The great actress reveals a command of comic inflection that fully matches the emotional depth of the tragic power of her earlier triumphs," said Howard Barnes in the New York *Herald Tribune*. "It is . . . the year's most captivating screen comedy."

Despite the favorable critical response, Garbo's box office still dropped. She could have continued in less expensive vehicles. But she made only one more picture, *Two-Faced Woman*, a failure. Then she apparently lost interest in her career and retired in 1941. She was only thirty-six.

Unique as she was on the screen, the great mysteries of her career revolved around her off-screen life. She lived a secluded existence, rarely signed autographs, never married—although her romances with John Gilbert, Leopold Stokowski and Gaylord Hauser, among others, were widely publicized.

After Garbo became a star she answered no fan mail, attended no premieres. For a while she did not even disclose her address to her studio. In public she often appeared in floppy, face-concealing hats, low-heeled shoes and dark glasses.

Newspaper pictures showed her frantically hiding her face as she got on a plane, hopped into a car or boarded a train. Once asked why she was so publicity-shy, she said, "Being in the newspapers is awfully silly to me. It's all right for important people, who have something to contribute, to talk; I have nothing to contribute."

Garbo has had many movie offers. But for the past thirty years she has been content to drift and become the world's most intriguing lady in retirement. She has lived in Europe and in New York City where she has occasionally been seen window-shopping on Fifth Avenue or browsing in a Third Avenue antique store.

Ironically, she never won an Oscar—although she had three nominations. They were for *Anna Christie* (1930), *Camille* and *Ninotchka*. Of her twenty-four films, only a handful—perhaps half a dozen—could be called worthy of her acting ability. And yet today, three decades after her last movie, fans still flock to her pictures whenever they are revived. Nobody has taken her place. The Garbo legend is a strong as ever.

"She stood alone," said Lewis Stone. "She was Greta Garbo and that said it all."

The jolly comrades with French hotel manager (Rolfe Sedan).

Ina Claire, playing the Grand Duchess Swana, persuades boy friend Leon to win back her crown jewels from the Russians.

Ninotchka after the transition. Garbo has donned a low-cut Parisian evening gown and holds hands with Leon in a swanky night club.

Garbo laughs. Tossing her severe, disciplined attitude to the winds, Ninotchka gets uproariously drunk on champagne and calls all the formally dressed patrons "comrades."

Garbo puts her arms around her three Soviet musketeers—from left, Felix Bressart, Sig
Rumann, and Alexander Granach.

Marlene Dietrich as Frenchy, the bad girl of the Last Chance Saloon, with her boss, Kent (Brian Donlevy).

Mischa Auer, playing a henpecked Russian cowboy, seems to have his eye on a full house as La Dietrich ambles by.

Marlene Dietrich

Destry Rides Again

(Released December 29, 1939)

FROM THE NOVEL by Max Brand. Screen play by Felix Jackson, Gertrude Purcell and Henry Myers. Cameraman, Hal Mohr. Editor, Milt Carruth. Songs by Frederick Hollander and Frank Loesser: "Little Joe the Wrangler," "You've Got That Look That Leaves Me Weak," and "See What the Boys in the Back Room Will Have." Directed by George Marshall. Produced by Joe Pasternak for Universal. Running Time, 94 minutes.

Frenchy	MARLENE DIETRICH
Thomas J. Destry, Jr.	JAMES STEWART *
Wash Dimsdale	CHARLES WINNINGER
Boris Callahan	MISCHA AUER
Kent	BRIAN DONLEVY
Janice Tyndall	IRENE HERVEY
Lily Belle Callahan	UNA MERKEL
Gyp Watson	ALLEN JENKINS
Bugs Watson	WARREN HYMER
Loupgerou	BILLY GILBERT
Hiram J. Slade	SAMUEL S. HINDS
Lem Claggett	TOM FADDEN
Jack Tyndall	JACK CARSON
Clara	LILLIAN YARBO
Rockwell	EDMUND MAC DONALD
Eli Whitney Claggett	DICKIE JONES
Sophie Claggett	VIRGINIA BRISSAC
"Sister" Claggett	ANN TODD

* Four actors have played Destry in the movies. In addition to Stewart, the others were: Tom Mix, Joel McCrea and Audie Murphy. A musical version appeared on Broadway in 1959 with Andy Griffith in the title role.

Age cannot wither her . . .
—Shakespeare

Dietrich.

In 1930 she took the movie world by storm as Lola—Lola, the sultry cabaret singer who leads a university professor astray. For the next two generations she was the classic *femme fatale,* a world-weary seductress whose cold, masklike beauty fascinated all men. Exotic. Aloof. Ageless. She became a legend in her lifetime.

Yet Dietrich the artist and Dietrich the woman were two different persons. In private life she was the unaffected, loyal, down-to-earth woman. Her marriage, albeit an unorthodox one, has lasted over forty years. She was a doting mother—she had one child, actress Maria Riva—then a doting grandmother. And she has never had any grand illusions about fame and the so-called Dietrich mystique.

"I am not proud of being a film star," she once said. "I have no reason to be. Compared with other professions, what I am doing is so unimportant." What, then, was her greatest accomplishment? "I have a child."

It is one of the paradoxes of her career that Dietrich, the internationally famous glamor queen, can take pride in strolling with her two grandsons in Central Park. There is a story that she used to help Maria with her laundry after her daughter had married. One night, as she left Maria's apartment in New York at 3 A.M. lugging a bundle of wash, a cab driver stopped her. "He took me for a Third Avenue washerwoman," Dietrich said. "He was most sympathetic about the long hours I worked. I hadn't the heart to explain to him that I was then living at the Plaza Hotel. So I got him to drop me several blocks away in a poor quarter and walked back to the Plaza when he was out of sight."

If she deigns to perpetuate her legend, she usually does so with a touch of wryness. In a book called *Marlene Dietrich's ABC,* she commented on such matters as:

Kisses: "Don't waste them. But don't count them."

Sex: "In America an obsession. In other parts of the world, a fact."

Seduction: "Anyone who was seduced wanted to be seduced."

Tact, she once said, is man's greatest asset. After looking at what she considered unflattering close-ups, Dietrich once told a cameraman: "When you were filming *The Garden of Allah,* you made me look gorgeous. Why aren't these shots so good?" The cameraman thought a moment, then replied: "Well, Marlene, I'm eight years older now." That, she said, was the essence of tact.

Born Maria Magdalene Dietrich in Berlin, she was believed to have been the daughter of an imperial German cavalry officer who died when she was three. That is, until authorities uncovered a birth certificate that showed her father was actually a lieutenant in the romantic old Royal Prussian Police. (It also said that she was born in 1901, three years earlier than the year her studio listed.)

She decided on an acting career while still a teen-ager. But because her mother opposed the idea she took the name Marlene Dietrich when she enrolled in Max Reinhardt's drama school.

The German cinema was attracting world attention and Marlene got a job as an extra in a film studio. There she met Rudolf Sieber, an assistant casting director, whom she married in 1924. They had a daughter the next year.

The marriage has been called the strangest in show business. Sieber, a pleasant-faced, sandy-haired man, whom hardly anyone knows, has remained her husband all these years although they live apart. While she is escorted to posh supper clubs by socialites, actors, writers and statesmen, he runs a chicken farm in California. Still, they are together a couple of times each year and each speaks cordially of the other. "Our lives became so different," Dietrich said. "That is all. He preferred

to stay. I worked all over the world. It is best this way. There is no ill feeling."

After her baby was born, Marlene returned to films. She struggled in bit parts until director Josef von Sternberg spotted her in a revue. He was looking for a temptress to play a cheap but beautiful night club slut. He found what he sought in Dietrich's curvaceous body, shapely legs (later to be her most famous attribute) and chiseled features.

He cast her opposite Emil Jannings in *The Blue Angel.* What happened is now film history. Who can forget Dietrich slinking around the smoky cabaret stage, singing "Falling in Love Again," in husky, almost masculine tones.

When Paramount saw the movie it prevailed on Von Sternberg to bring her to Hollywood. In America, Dietrich quickly established her individuality. She candidly told the press she was a mother. And she created the stylish mode of wearing slacks and mannish attire.

Moving Svengali-like under Von Sternberg's hand—she refused to work for any other director —she glided like a mysterious vamp through such films as *Morocco* (1930), *Shanghai Express* (1932), and *Blonde Venus* (1932). Von Sternberg looked on movies as a great visual adventure. "The image is everything," he said. Though his pictures were creative photographically, their plots were often dull and static. Dietrich came through as an intriguing beauty but a lifeless character.

In 1935 she and Von Sternberg broke up. Dietrich did three pictures for Ernst Lubitsch. But she was still the silken siren and she emerged as the same exotic statue.

In 1937 Paramount dropped her contract. She made no movies, and her popularity waned. In 1938 she, along with other stars, was listed as "box office poison" by an exhibitors' trade journal.

Dietrich was about ready to consider her movie career over when Universal convinced her to try a comeback. The picture was to be a brawling Western in which she was to have a chance to come to life on the screen by displaying her talents as a hellcat. Her co-star was James Stewart. The story came from a popular Max Brand shoot-'em-up novel about the mild-mannered son of a fearless two-gun sheriff.

Bottleneck is the wildest frontier town in the West. Anyone who doesn't take orders from Boss Kent (Brian Donlevy), a gambler who runs the

Last Chance Saloon, is headed for an early grave. When the local sheriff comes in to protest Kent's switching cards in a poker game, the lawman is pumped full of lead.

As a joke, Kent appoints Wash Dimsdale (Charles Winninger), the town drunk, as the new sheriff. To everyone's surprise, Wash takes the job seriously and sends for Thomas Jefferson Destry, Jr. (Stewart) to help him clean up the town.

Meanwhile La Dietrich, smoking a cigar, belts out some lively numbers in her whiskey voice: "Little Joe" and "See What the Boys in the Back Room Will Have." She's playing Frenchy, the painted thrush, gyp artist and saloon bad girl. Wherever she roams, there's hoopla, hi-jinks and guffaws galore. When she slips some earrings into her bosom, Allen Jenkins delivers the celebrated line, "Thar's gold in them thar hills." The critics loved it. But the Hays Office ordered it out after the film had been released.

The most memorable scene is Frenchy's knock-down-drag-out battle with Una Merkel, playing an angry wife whose husband has lost his trousers to Frenchy in a card game. Both gals refused stand-ins. It was one of the roughest female film fights ever shot. The brawl, which lasted two minutes in the picture, took five days to film. Dietrich pulled hair, punched, wrestled, kicked, rolled on the floor and finally got doused with a bucket of water.

It is Destry who tosses cold water on the cat fight. But he turns out to be a soft-spoken young man who whittles napkin rings instead of toting guns. For the moment, Destry is a laughingstock. Kent and his rowdies return to their lawless ways.

But they have underestimated Destry. When he borrows a gun and puts on a dazzling display of target shooting, the town toughs suddenly stop laughing. Nevertheless Destry tells Wash that shooting isn't the answer. "You shoot it out with them and for some reason they get to look like heroes," Destry says. "But you put 'em behind bars and they look little and cheap."

Before he can take action, Destry has to find the slain sheriff's body. He tricks Gyp Watson (Jenkins), one of Kent's bullies, into digging it up, then slaps him in jail. But Kent and his gang break in and kill Wash.

That ends Destry's peaceful ways. He slaps on his shootin' irons and rallies the townspeople to battle the gang. In the ensuing hubbub Kent gets a bead on Destry with his rifle from the saloon balcony. Frenchy, who has fallen in love with the quiet deputy, tries to warn him.

He doesn't hear her and she throws herself in front of Destry as Kent fires. Destry brings Kent down with a hip-slinging shot. But Frenchy is mortally wounded. "Kiss me, good feller," she tells Destry in the script version. The marvelous curtain line is transformed in the movie to simply, "Would you mind?" And Destry kisses her lifeless lips as she dies in his arms.

Just as *Ninotchka* gave Garbo a new lease on life, so *Destry* proved the elixir to Dietrich's ailing career. *Time* called her performance the best since *The Blue Angel*. "To the thrilling question—could Dietrich come back via the western trail—. . . the answer [is], Dietrich has."

She did a dozen more pictures through the forties, fifties and early sixties. But except for a superb supporting role as a German general's wife in *Judgment at Nuremberg*, she never topped her performance in *Destry* and *The Blue Angel*.

In 1960 she went back to sing in Berlin after a twenty-nine-year absence. She half expected rotten eggs because she had marched through Paris with the victorious Allies. But although there were minor incidents—a girl spat in her face in Düsseldorf— she scored a personal triumph. West Berlin audiences demanded a half hour of encores. At Munich she got dozens of curtain calls. At Wiesbaden the audience pelted her with flowers.

Today, at sixty-eight, her beauty remarkably preserved, her film immortality assured, she goes on and on like an eternal fountain of youth. "If she had nothing more than voice, she could break your heart with it," said Ernest Hemingway. "But she also has that beautiful body and the timeless loveliness of her face."

Frenchy and Lily Belle Callahan (Una Merkel) have a go at it in one of the roughest Hollywood female fight sequences filmed. It took five days to shoot the scene, which lasted two minutes in the movie. Neither actress used a stunt girl.

Frenchy has a job for the new sheriff (James Stewart) and Boss Kent approves.

Things seem to be friendly for the moment at the Last Chance Saloon. That's crooked Mayor Hiram J. Slade (Samuel S. Hinds) in the top hat. At left is Edmund MacDonald, one of Kent's associates.

Frenchy has coffee at her place with the young, gunless sheriff.

La Dietrich and Stewart in close quarters.

Holding a gun she has just emptied into her lover, Leslie Crosbie (Bette Davis) stands over his body in the opening scene of *The Letter*. The murder takes less than a minute on the screen. But on the set, actor David Newell had to roll down those veranda steps in ten takes before director William Wyler was satisfied.

Mrs. Hammond (Gale Sondergaard), a Eurasian, stares stonily at Leslie Crosbie (Bette Davis), the planter's wife who has killed the Eurasian woman's white husband.

(Photos by Warner Bros.)
(Courtesy United Artists Corp.)

Bette Davis

The Letter

(Released November 23, 1940)

FROM THE SHORT STORY and stage play by W. Somerset Maugham. Screen play by Howard Koch. Cameraman, Tony Gaudio. Editor, George Amy. Orchestral arrangements, Hugo Friedhofer. In charge of production, Jack L. Warner. Executive producer, Hal B. Wallis. Producers, Warner and Wallis. Associate producer, Robert Lord. Director, William Wyler. A Warner Brothers Picture. Running time, 97 minutes.

Leslie Crosbie	BETTE DAVIS
Robert Crosbie	HERBERT MARSHALL
Howard Joyce	JAMES STEPHENSON
Dorothy Joyce	FRIEDA INESCORT
Mrs. Hammond	GALE SONDERGAARD
John Withers	BRUCE LESTER
Adele Ainsworth	ELIZABETH EARL
Prescott	CECIL KELLAWAY
Ong Chi Seng	VICTOR SEN YUNG
Mrs. Cooper	DORIS LLOYD
Chung Hi	WILLIE FUNG
Head boy	TETSU KOMAI
Fred	LEONARD MUDIE
Driver	JOHN RIDGELY
Bob's friends	CHARLES IRWIN, HOLMES HERBERT
Well-wisher	DOUGLAS WALTON
Geoffrey Hammond	DAVID NEWELL

(Warner Brothers made another version of *The Letter*, called *The Unfaithful*, with Ann Sheridan in 1947. Paramount produced an early sound film, also called *The Letter*, in 1929. Jeanne Eagels starred in the latter.)

A sexpot she wasn't.

The day she arrived in Hollywood the Universal representative sent to greet her couldn't find her.

"No one faintly like an actress got off the train," he said. Years later, producer Carl Laemmle, Jr., shrugged: "I can't imagine any guy giving her a tumble."

If Hollywood held a popularity contest, she'd probably come in last. She never was hot copy for the movie columnists. The fan magazines all but ignored her. If anything, she made her mark as a favorite target of caricaturists. They loved to spoof her great rolling poached-egg eyes, her birdlike movements, and her nervous, intense way of smoking.

Poor Bette Davis. All she had going for her was her talent. But no amount of sex appeal or publicity or fan polls could accurately measure the dazzling magic she displayed before the cameras. In her long career she starred in pictures running the gamut from heart-choking romances to sophisticated comedy. But she also had the fire and spunk and sagacity to play mean little vixens and selfish, vile-tempered shrews, parts that sent other Hollywood glamor pusses scurrying to their agents. And these roles became her trademark.

She was so hateful on the screen, *Time* coined the word "cinemeanness" to describe her bitchiness. She has made over eighty films, won two Academy Awards (a feat duplicated by only six other actresses *) and received ten Oscar nominations †

---

*Luise Rainer, Ingrid Bergman, Elizabeth Taylor, Olivia de Havilland, Vivien Leigh and Katharine Hepburn, who won two Oscars and shared a third.

† In addition to her Oscar-winning films *Dangerous* and *Jezebel*, they were for *Dark Victory*, *The Letter*, *The Little Foxes*, *Now, Voyager*, *Mr. Skeffington*, *All About Eve*, *The Star* and *What Ever Happened to Baby Jane?*

(more than any other actress, except Katharine Hepburn). Some call her the greatest actress of the 1930s and 1940s. Even if that's debatable, certainly no list of stars from that golden era could be complete without her.

Her real name was Ruth Elizabeth Davis, daughter of a Lowell, Massachusetts, lawyer who was divorced from her mother before Bette was out of grammar school. She was a precocious child and showed an early interest in acting. At eight, she romped naked in the snow to attract attention.

A year after she graduated from Cushing Academy in Ashburn, Massachusetts, she went to New York and tried to join Eva Le Gallienne's Manhattan Civic Repertory Company. Miss Le Gallienne turned her away, proclaiming that Bette's interest in the theatre was not sincere. Besides, she struck the great lady of the drama as a "frivolous little girl."

But Bette persisted. She enrolled in John Murray Anderson's Dramatic School and got a part in George Cukor's stock production of *Broadway.* Her mother advised her to learn the leading lady's part as well. Sure enough, the star sprained an ankle on opening night and Bette went on to play the lead.

She went on to appear in two successful plays on Broadway. Then Hollywood called. Almost immediately she had her first of many skirmishes with studio officials. Universal wanted to change her name to "Bettina Davies." The name conjured up nicknames that somehow didn't appeal to her. "I refused to go through a career as 'Between the Drawers,'" she said. And that was that.

For the first year she played a succession of dreary roles and Universal failed to renew her contract. She was about to go home when George Arliss picked her for a part as a dignified young actress in *The Man Who Played God.* Later, Arliss said she came on the set with a self-confidence and proficiency he had rarely seen before.

However, it wasn't until she played Mildred, the detestable hussy in *Of Human Bondage* in 1934, that she established herself as an actress of stature. There was an electric intensity about her that excited audiences. Some criticized the Academy for passing her up in the Oscar competition. But she won one the next year for her performance in *Dangerous* opposite Franchot Tone.

The award, she expected, would lead to bigger money and better roles. When it didn't, she went

on strike, sailing to England while a costly legal battle ensued. She lost. But Warner Brothers raised her salary anyway from $3,000 a week to $3,500 a week and began giving her meatier roles.

They included starring parts in such pictures as *The Petrified Forest* (1936), *Dark Victory* (1939), *The Old Maid* (1939), *Now, Voyager* (1942) and *The Corn Is Green* (1945). The title role in *Jezebel* brought her a second Oscar in 1938. It was during this string of films, at the peak of her career, that a newspaperman dubbed her "The Fourth Warner Brother." Another press sobriquet was "Popeye the Magnificent."

While she was reeling off one soap opera after another, she was busy on the domestic front with a parade of four husbands. She started with old school chum and orchestra leader Harmon Nelson in 1932. She divorced him in 1938. Then came two others, Arthur Farnsworth and William Grant Sherry, followed by actor Gary Merrill, whom she wed in 1950 and divorced in 1960. She has two adopted children—Margo and Michael—and a daughter, Barbara, with Sherry, husband number three.

Through the early 1950s her screen successes kept coming as she scored triumphs in *All About Eve* (1950) and *The Star* (1953). But late in 1953 she suffered a bone disease called osteomyelitis and surgeons had to remove nearly half her jaw. She retired to Maine to recover her strength and allow the bone to grow back, then launched a comeback. But she had been out of the limelight and could play only mature roles. And so she went along unspectacularly until 1962 when she teamed with Joan Crawford in the horror film *What Ever Happened to Baby Jane?* It was a box office hit and led to such similar macabre ventures as *Hush . . . Hush, Sweet Charlotte* (1965), and *The Nanny* (1965).

However, to me the one movie that best shows off her most creative screen trait—bitchiness—is *The Letter.* The film, a superb adaptation of Somerset Maugham's classic short story and play, had already provided a dramatic vehicle for Katharine Cornell on the stage and for Jeanne Eagels in an early talking screen version.

In the Davis movie, director William Wyler fills the picture with a brooding, tense, tropic atmosphere. Everywhere there are reminders of the oppressive heat—whirring fans, clinking ice-filled glasses, palm leaves and lacelike shadows through which the pale haunting moonlight streams.

The movie opens as the bright light of a Singapore moon floods the rubber plantation of Robert Crosbie. A rubber tree drips slowly. Coolies sleep in a thatched hut. A pigeon drowses beneath a long, sharp shadow. Suddenly, a shot disturbs the silence. The pigeon flaps away. Geoffrey Hammond (David Newell) staggers out onto the veranda of the Crosbie house, then down its five steps. A woman follows, pistol in hand. She fires into the prone body until the chambers click empty.

A few hours later Leslie Crosbie (Bette Davis) explains why she killed Hammond to her planter husband (Herbert Marshall, who played Hammond in the original movie version), their friend, attorney Howard Joyce (James Stephenson), and the District Officer (Bruce Lester). She says Hammond, a long-time acquaintance, came to the house, tried to make love to her, and attacked her. She says she shot him to defend her honor.

The men are sympathetic. But the District Officer tells her she still must go to jail and stand trial for murder. While they confer, Hammond's wife slips in to look at her husband's body. She is a Eurasian (Gale Sondergaard), with a face that is at once exotic, beautiful, inscrutable.

Before the trial, Joyce's law clerk, Ong Chi Seng (Sen Yung), discloses that Leslie had written a letter to Hammond imploring him to visit her on the night he was killed. The letter is so urgent that, if it were read in court, it would destroy her convincing story and probably convict her of premeditated murder. The Eurasian has the letter and will sell it for $10,000.

Under pressure, attorney Joyce gets Leslie to admit to him she wrote the letter. She says she loved Hammond and shot him out of jealousy after he married and ended their affair. Out of long friendship, Joyce agrees to commit the criminal act of buying the letter to suppress its use as evidence. He tells Crosbie some extra expenses are needed to prepare Leslie's defense. But he does not mention how much money is involved. And so a dramatic scene is set up in which Leslie has to kneel at the feet of her lover's wife to pick up the letter from the floor.

At the trial, no evidence is submitted against her

and Leslie is acquitted. Crosbie, elated, tells her he plans to take her away. He says he will buy a plantation in Sumatra with his savings of $10,000. Caught in their web of lies, Leslie and Joyce tell Crosbie that his money is gone. And they must explain the damning contents of the letter.

Crosbie is broken spiritually and financially. But he still is willing to go on with Leslie. "Leslie, tell me now, this minute, do you love me?"

"Yes, I do," she tells him, and he embraces and kisses her.

Suddenly, she tears herself away. "No, I can't, I can't, I can't . . . ," she shrieks. "With all my heart, I still love the man I killed."

Maugham's play ended here with Leslie condemned to this life in death, a fitting oriental revenge for the Eurasian woman. But the Hays Office required a retributive ending. Under its eye-for-an-eye doctrine, a woman can't shoot a man and go unpunished.

So, under the same kind of mysterious, compelling moon that opened the story, Leslie walks into the garden, moving through a wash of shadows, seemingly knowing that someone will be waiting for her. And someone is. The Eurasian woman stands there with a servant. As the two women look silently at each other, the Eurasian's servant pinions Leslie's arms and smothers her cry. A dagger flashes and Mrs. Hammond stabs Leslie to death. As the Eurasian leaves, a policeman spots her because, presumably, she too must pay the piper.

Many critics said the postscript did not ruin the film, but was unnecessary and added nothing to it. "Will somebody kindly tell us what the greater moral value is in that [the added ending]?" asked Bosley Crowther.

But the full irony was still to come. The Legion of Decency rose up in arms, complaining that the movie contained "no retribution for wrong-doing." It protested against what it called Miss Davis' apparent "suicidal intention in [the] finale."

Nevertheless, the film surmounts the contrived ending and remains to this day a tense, enthralling drama. It is a powerful example of Hollywood craftsmanship and Bette Davis at their best.

Leslie, weeping, clings to her husband Robert (Herbert Marshall) for comfort.

In an anteroom outside the court, Leslie knits while she and her husband await the jury's verdict.

Leslie stands in the dock during her trial for murder.

District Officer Withers (Bruce Lester) congratulates Leslie at a party after her acquittal.

Howard Joyce (James Stephenson), the Crosbies' attorney and old friend, tells Robert the shocking contents of the letter Leslie had written to the man she shot to death.

In the final scene, the servant (Tetsu Komai) of the Eurasian woman seizes Leslie as she takes a moonlight walk.

Kitty Packard (Jean Harlow) taking her afternoon exercise.

Jean Harlow

Dinner at Eight

(Released January 12, 1933)

A SCREEN DRAMA ADAPTED by Frances Marion and Herman J. Mankiewicz with additional dialogue by Donald O. Stewart. From the play by George S. Kaufman and Edna Ferber. Produced by David O. Selznick. Photography, William Daniels. Editor, Ben Lewis. Directed by George Cukor. Presented by Metro-Goldwyn-Mayer. Running time, 113 minutes.

Carlotta Vance	MARIE DRESSLER
Larry Renault	JOHN BARRYMORE
Dan Packard	WALLACE BEERY
Kitty Packard	JEAN HARLOW
Oliver Jordan	LIONEL BARRYMORE
Max Kane	LEE TRACY
Dr. Wayne Talbot	EDMUND LOWE
Mrs. Oliver Jordan	BILLIE BURKE
Paula Jordan	MADGE EVANS
Jo Stengel	JEAN HERSHOLT
Mrs. Wayne Talbot	KAREN MORLEY
Hattie Loomis	LOUISE CLOSSER HALE
Ernest De Graff	PHILLIPS HOLMES
Mrs. Wendel	MAY ROBSON
Ed Loomis	GRANT MITCHELL
Miss Alden	PHOEBE FOSTER
Miss Copeland	ELIZABETH PATTERSON
Tina	HILDA VAUGHN
Fosdick	HARRY BERESFORD
Mr. Fitch	EDWIN MAXWELL
Mr. Hatfield	JOHN DAVIDSON
Eddie	EDWARD WOODS
Gustave	GEORGE BAXTER
The Waiter	HERMAN BING
Dora	ANNA DUNCAN

She was the Marilyn Monroe of the thirties. They called her the blonde bombshell, the platinum-haired beauty, Hollywood's sex goddess. Like a goddess, she often wore no brassiere. She said it was an unnecessary garment. It was—at least for her. She was five feet three, weighed a hundred and twelve pounds and they were well distributed.

She had bright blue eyes, wore dark penciled-on eyebrows and bleached her hair—an act that was so widely imitated it almost single-handedly enabled the nation's beauty parlors to survive the Depression.

Because she was fair and her hair nearly white, she thought white set her off best. She decorated many of her rooms at her Bel Air, California, home in white. She wore mostly white dresses, white bathing suits, white negligees.

Sidney Skolsky wrote that she slept in the raw and smoked a cigarette first thing on getting up. She adored babies but looked quizzical when asked if she would like to have one. She never did.

Married at sixteen, by twenty-two, she had had three husbands. She had also made twenty-two movies, climbed to the pinnacle of Hollywood stardom and was earning $5,000 a week. She was dead at twenty-six.

Jean Harlow (34-24-35) was born in Kansas City in 1911. Her real name was Harlean Carpenter. Her father was a dentist. Her mother, a domineering woman who would always call her daughter "Baby," had wanted to be an actress herself. Her maiden name was Jean Harlow. She would see her dreams realized vicariously.

The Carpenters were divorced when Jean was a

little girl and her mother later married a former Latin waiter named Marino Bello. After Jean's first and unsuccessful marriage at sixteen to Charles McGrew, a wealthy young broker, she and the Bellos moved to Hollywood. It was 1928 and Jean got a job as an extra, using her mother's maiden name.

Her strikingly colored hair and physical assets brought her to the attention of Howard Hughes. Hughes put Harlow in the lowest-cut evening gown he could have designed and gave her a key role in *Hell's Angels*. "The climax was reached," *Time* said, "not in the million dollar uproar of 90 airplanes, but when Jean Harlow appeared in evening dress and said, 'Do you mind if I slip into something more comfortable?'"

Hughes later sold Jean to MGM, where she met Paul Bern, one of the studio's top executives. Their wedding on July 3, 1932, surprised Hollywood. She was twenty-one. He was exactly twice her age, a slight, balding man who was considered a confirmed bachelor.

Two months and three days later the marriage ended in tragedy. Bern's nude body was found in their bedroom with a bullet in his brain. He clutched a .38-caliber revolver in one hand. Behind he left a puzzling note to his bride, who had left him a short while before to spend the night with her mother and stepfather. The note read:

Dearest Dear—Unfortunately, this is the only way to make good the frightful wrong I have done you and to wipe out my abject humiliation. I love you.

PAUL

P.S.—You understand that last night was only a comedy.

Although Miss Harlow said she didn't understand the note, others have said Bern was impotent and had therefore ended the "comedy." His death was further complicated by the suicide two days later of Dorothy Millette, a woman in his past. Newspapers disclosed that Miss Millette, who had leaped from a steamer into the Sacramento River and drowned, had been Bern's common-law wife.

After Bern's death, Jean was seldom seen in public, but she continued her film work. Even before her marriage, her acting ability had been improving with every movie. Her second screen lover had been Johnny Mack Brown in *The Secret*

Six (1931). In quick succession, she had teamed with Lew Ayres in *Iron Man* (1931), James Cagney in *The Public Enemy* (1931), Spencer Tracy in *Goldie* (1931), and Robert Williams in *Platinum Blonde* (1931). When Clark Gable, her eleventh leading man, took her in his arms in *Red Dust* (1932), she catapulted to stardom.

Although she had first won notice for anatomical reasons, Harlow surprised the critics by developing into a first-rate comedienne. She usually played a hard-boiled, quick-tongued, gold-digging siren. And she carried it off so well, she became a box office sensation. Nowhere did she sparkle more brilliantly than in her next film, *Dinner at Eight*.

MGM bought picture rights to the Broadway stage play. Spurred by the success of their all-star line-up in *Grand Hotel* a year before, the studio mounted an even bigger-name cast. They recruited twelve stars—Harlow, Marie Dressler, John and Lionel Barrymore, Wallace Beery, Lee Tracy, Billie Burke, Edmund Lowe, Madge Evans, Karen Morley, Jean Hersholt, and Phillips Holmes. But it was Harlow who stole the show.

Who can forget Jean in her sleek silk negligee and her cyclonic exchanges with Beery, playing her self-made tycoon husband. "Go lay an egg!" Beery told her during one fiery argument. "When I tell about [your dirty business affairs]," Harlow countered, "you couldn't even get into the men's room at the Astor!"

Millicent Jordan (Billie Burke), wife of shipping magnate Oliver Jordan (Lionel Barrymore), plans a formal dinner in their New York home in honor of Lord and Lady Ferncliffe. Between the time the invitations go out and the guests file into the dining room, the lives of all have undergone radical changes.

Carlotta Vance (Marie Dressler), an aging star of the Gay Nineties, visits Jordan, her old beau, and asks him to help her sell her stock in his company. Although the firm is in dire financial straits, he agrees. He conceals from her—as he has from his wife—that he is dying from a heart condition.

Dan Packard (Beery) secures Carlotta's stock and also the majority of the stock in Jordan's firm. When his wife Kitty (Harlow) tells him about the Jordan dinner invitation, he refuses to go. But Kitty, a former hat-check girl with social ambitions, changes his mind by pointing out the advantages of a personal introduction to the wealthy and influential Ferncliffes.

When Packard leaves, Dr. Wayne Talbot (Edmund Lowe) arrives. It turns out to be something more than a professional visit to Kitty's boudoir. But he has tired of her. And when his wife discovers the affair and displays a tolerant attitude, he resolves to have done with it.

Meanwhile, another invited guest, Larry Renault (John Barrymore), a fallen matinee idol, is ending a secret affair with Jordan's daughter, Paula (Madge Evans). Penniless and a hopeless alcoholic, Renault fumbles his last chance for a part by insulting a theatrical producer (Jean Hersholt). Renault locks his hotel door, turns on the gas, then carefully positions himself under a lamp so that it illuminates his classic profile.

On the day of the dinner Mrs. Jordan learns to her horror that the Ferncliffes have suddenly left for Florida. She is frantic with anger. "Those miserable cockneys," she cries. But the dinner loses all its importance when she learns about her husband's condition.

Before they leave for the Jordan dinner, Harlow and Beery have another knock-down-drag-out tiff. She admits having a secret love affair and dares Beery to do anything about it. Furthermore, she threatens to expose all his crooked business deals unless he releases Jordan from the financial web he has spun around him.

And so, when the appointed hour arrives, the guests file into the dining room, the glitter of their put-on smiles covering the bitter experiences they have undergone. It remains for Harlow to set up the movie's memorable curtain line.

"I was reading a book the other day," she tells Marie Dressler. "It's all about civilization or something. . . . Do you know the guy said machinery is going to take the place of every profession."

"Oh, my dear," says Dressler, pausing to give Harlow a once-over. "That's something you'll never have to worry about."

The critics applauded the slick comedy although some felt the plot left the story at loose ends. But they were unanimous in praising the sterling performances.

Most gave Harlow their biggest bouquet. "Of them all, I think the amazing Miss Harlow gives the grandest show," wrote Richard Watts, Jr., in the New York *Herald Tribune.* "Among a congress of stars, she is quite the hit of the evening."

It would have been hard to believe then—the movie premiered August 23, 1933—that Harlow had less than four years to live. Her third marriage came in September of 1933 to Harold G. Rosson, thirty-eight-year-old movie photographer. It lasted eight months.

William Powell was her next romance and the two appeared devoted. Meanwhile, her movie career continued soaring. Then one day, as she worked with Gable in *Saratoga,* she was taken ill. The studio sent her home. Doctors discovered she had a kidney disorder that had deteriorated and developed into uremic poisoning. Harlow had slipped into a coma. An operation was required at once. But her mother, a Christian Scientist, refused.

Days passed before Jean was finally rushed to a hospital. It was too late. Doctors said cerebral edema (an abnormal accumulation of body fluids in the brain) had already set in. She died on June 7, 1937—nine days after her studio collapse.

Two hundred of Hollywood's most famous crowded the Forest Lawn Memorial Park chapel where a simple funeral service of the Christian Science Church was held. More than 1,000 fans stood around the chapel but they were orderly. Even after the rites started, truckload after truckload of flowers rolled up. Inside, women wept when Jeanette MacDonald opened the service singing "Indian Love Call." Nelson Eddy closed it with "Ah, Sweet Mystery of Life."

Harlow's body was put in a massive, $5,000 casket which had a silver nameplate that reproduced Jean's signature. She was entombed in a $25,000 crypt (paid for by William Powell), not far from where Rudolph Valentino, Marie Dressler, and other stars lay buried.

Despite the millions she made in her sensational eight-year career, Harlow's estate totaled only $41,000. She left it all to her mother.

Dan Packard (Wallace Beery) and his wife in one of their sizzling tiffs. "Go lay an egg," Beery tells her.

The host and hostess—Oliver (Lionel Barrymore) and Millicent Jordan (Billie Burke).

Fading matinee idol Larry Renault (John Barrymore) and admirer, Paula Jordan (Madge Evans).

Renault, drunk, insults theatrical producer Jo Stengel (Jean Hersholt), who has offered him a small part.

Dr. Wayne Talbot (Edmund Lowe) and wife (Karen Morley) make their entrance.

It's sweetness and light because the party's on. "Delighted," says Beery to his hostess Billie Burke. Harlow is on his arm.

II

HEROES and HE-MEN

HUMPHREY BOGART • THE MALTESE FALCON
CLARK GABLE • SAN FRANCISCO
GARY COOPER • MR. DEEDS GOES TO TOWN
JAMES STEWART • MR. SMITH GOES TO WASHINGTON
SPENCER TRACY • CAPTAINS COURAGEOUS
JAMES CAGNEY • THE PUBLIC ENEMY
FRED ASTAIRE • TOP HAT

Bogart

(Photos by Warner Bros.)

Humphrey Bogart

The Maltese Falcon

(Released October 18, 1941)

A SCREEN DRAMA by John Huston based on the novel by Dashiell Hammett. Music by Adolphe Deutsch. Photography, Arthur Edeson. Editor, Thomas Richards. Produced by Hal B. Wallis. Associate producer, Henry Blanke. Art director, Robert Haas. Directed by John Huston. Presented by Warner Brothers. Running time, 100 minutes.

Sam Spade	HUMPHREY BOGART
Brigid O'Shaughnessy	MARY ASTOR
Iva Archer	GLADYS GEORGE
Joel Cairo	PETER LORRE
Detective Lieutenant Dundy	BARTON MAC LANE
Effie Perine	LEE PATRICK
Kasper Gutman	SIDNEY GREENSTREET
Detective Tom Polhaus	WARD BOND
Miles Archer	JEROME COWAN
Wilmer	ELISHA COOK, JR.
Luke	JAMES BURKE
Frank Richman	MURRAY ALPER
Bryan	JOHN HAMILTON
Captain Jacobi	WALTER HUSTON

(Other versions: *The Maltese Falcon* (1931), and *Satan Met a Lady* (1936).)

"It's heavy," says Ward Bond as he lifts a black statuette of a bird in the final moments of *The Maltese Falcon*. "What is it?" he asks Humphrey Bogart.

Bogie doesn't answer right away. He's playing Sam Spade in the picture James Agee called "the best private eye melodrama ever made." There is a moment, a pause. And the silence, barely discernible, underscores what will become a memorable curtain line.

That tiny pause, that masterful touch, that extra something that Bogie brings to the part sets the tone of his flawless performance. Bogart *is* Spade. From the moment he appears, he dominates scene after scene. You are compelled to watch his every action even in the presence of such first-rate character actors as Mary Astor, Peter Lorre, Elisha Cook, Jr., and Sidney Greenstreet.

Probably no other actor of his era has fit a detective part so perfectly. Humphrey Bogart. Wry, detached, anti-Establishment, a man with the sure masculinity of whiskey straight. These were the qualities that Dashiell Hammett put into Spade in his 1930 novel. And these were the qualities that Bogart brought to the screen. These and more. Bogart was unflinching, outspoken, cynical and a realist: a tough guy in a trenchcoat, a man's man.

Twenty years later his cool style would intrigue a rebellious student generation and Bogart Festivals would spring up on campuses from Harvard to the University of California. In 1969 the durable Bogart mystique would inspire the Broadway comedy *Play It Again, Sam*, written by and starring Woody Allen.

"When you're slapped," he tells Lorre in the *Falcon*, "you'll take it and like it." Later, after he turns in the angelic-looking Miss Astor to the cops, he tells her he'll wait for her. "If they hang you," he adds matter-of-factly, "I'll always remember you."

Bogart was forty-two when he made the *Falcon*. He had gotten his big break as Duke Mantee, the killer in *The Petrified Forest.* But that had been in 1936, five years earlier. His career had since been mired in a succession of roles as hardened criminals. His performances were competent but the roles were generally one-dimensional.

Then, by a turn of luck, the Spade role came his way. Warner Brothers offered the part to George Raft. But Raft turned it down because it was to be the first movie for an untried director. That director turned out to be none other than John Huston, son of the distinguished actor Walter Huston. The younger Huston was later to make his own Hollywood mark directing the Oscar winner *The Treasure of the Sierra Madre* (with Bogie starring again), among more than twenty other films. But he was then only thirty-five and an unknown script writer who had drifted into directing when he tired of seeing what professional directors were doing to his scripts.

So in 1941, two months before Pearl Harbor, when the *Falcon* opened at the Strand in New York, it arrived as a sleeper. *Time* magazine didn't bother to review it. Others did, and it took them by surprise. "A knockout job," the New York *Herald Tribune* said. "Bogart is so good as Spade that it is hard to think of anyone else playing the part." Bosley Crowther, of the New York *Times,* called the film "the best mystery thriller of the year." "Huston," wrote Crowther, "is a brilliant new talent . . . a coming American match for Alfred Hitchcock." *Newsweek* said: "If half of Hollywood remakes turned out as well as *The Maltese Falcon,* the studios could stop buying stories for a while."

The movie was, in fact, a redo of the hard-boiled, fast-moving Hammett book. In 1931, Bebe Daniels and Ricardo Cortez starred in the first movie adaptation. Five years later, it was revived as *Satan Met a Lady* with Bette Davis and Warren William. But the third version—with Huston writing the script and his father doing an uncredited walk-on as a good-luck gesture—became the definitive picture.

The story opens in Spade's San Francisco office. Brigid O'Shaughnessy, an innocent-faced brunette played by Miss Astor, bursts in. She tells a vague tale of being followed by a sinister hood named Thursby and begs for protection. Intrigued by her beauty, Spade's partner, Miles Archer (Jerome Cowan), outmaneuvers Spade and gets the assignment. Within hours, both Archer and Thursby are shot to death.

Spade tracks Miss O'Shaughnessy down. She now tells him she's in danger of losing her life. But she still won't give too many details. "Trust me," she says, blinking her long dark eyelashes. She retains Spade for a kiss and an additional $500 (which he wrings out of her) to protect her name and interests.

Then, two odd Laurel-and-Hardy types materialize—Joel Cairo (Peter Lorre), an effeminate, scented little man with saucerlike eyes and spats, and Kasper Gutman (Sidney Greenstreet), a bald fat man with a waistcoat stretched across a great egg-shaped belly. (Greenstreet, a veteran British stage performer who had just toured the United States with a Lunt-Fontanne company, was making his screen debut at the tender age of sixty-one.) Cairo and Gutman are really members of an international gang of crooks, and they quickly recognize they have met their match in shrewdness in Spade. "Oh, gad, sir," the jovial Gutman tells Spade. "You are a character. There's never any telling what you'll say or do next. Except it's bound to be astonishing."

Gutman tells Spade he is searching for a black enamel Maltese falcon. The foot-high statuette is stuffed with jewels, Gutman says. It's worth a fortune. The falcon was a sixteenth-century gift from the crusading Knights of Malta to King Charles V of Spain. But it never reached Charles. After seventeen years, Gutman has traced it to San Francisco. He offers Spade $10,000 to help find it.

At first the hunt brings Spade only nasty business. He stumbles across a third corpse. He gets a Mickey Finn and a swift kick in the head from Gutman's itchy-fingered gunman, a little tough guy named Wilmer (Elisha Cook, Jr.) But in the end Spade finds the priceless bird.

The climax comes when Bogie delivers the falcon. The atmosphere reeks with greedy anticipation. Greenstreet can barely contain himself. Lorre is bug-eyed. Mary Astor is quivering. (It turns out she is a double-crosser, deeply involved in the intrigue. She has really been chasing the bird herself while professing her love for Bogart.)

The scene is Spade's apartment. Gutman cuts into the falcon. All at once, he grunts. With the consummate art of the great character actor he is, Greenstreet blinks vacant eyes. His body sags like a puppet let go. "You imbecile," Lorre shrieks. "You bloated idiot. You stupid fathead." Alas! The falcon is a fake.

Recovering, Greenstreet cranks out his patented belly laugh. He displays a *c'est la vie* attitude and leaves with Cairo to run down another lead on the falcon in Istanbul. But the last laugh is on them. Before they can blow town, Spade tips the police that they are involved in two of the three murders. Then, ice water flowing in his veins, Spade tells the cops to come to his apartment and pick up Mary Astor for the third murder, his partner's slaying.

While the police are on their way, she throws herself at him, hoping to melt his cool. "From the very first instant I saw you, I knew I loved you," she says. But it's no dice.

"If I do this [let you go] and get away with it," Spade tells her, "you'll have something on me that you can use whenever you want to. Since I got something on you, I couldn't be sure that you wouldn't put a hole in me someday. . . ."

Spade adds: "I hope they don't hang you, Precious, by that sweet neck. Yes, Angel, I'm sending you over. Chances are you'll get off with life. That means if you're a good girl, you'll be out in twenty years. And I'll be waiting for you. If they hang you, I'll always remember you."

And so, as the cops lead her off, Ward Bond takes the falcon and asks, "What is it?" For an instant Spade seems to run the whole weird case over in his head. Then, as the movie ends, he answers by paraphrasing Shakespeare in a line remembered by generations of Bogart fans. "The stuff that dreams are made of," Bogie says.

Brigid O'Shaughnessy (Mary Astor), a client, attracts the roving eye of Miles Archer (Jerome Cowan), partner of private detective Sam Spade (Humphrey Bogart).

After Archer is slain, Brigid tells Spade only that her life is in danger. The reason remains vague.

Spade meets Kaspar Gutman (Sidney Greenstreet), an international crook on the trail of a jewel-stuffed statuette of a falcon. It was Greenstreet's film debut at sixty-one.

Wilmer (Elisha Cook, Jr.), Gutman's tough little gunman, gets a steely-eyed look from Spade, who has spotted Wilmer following him.

The moment Gutman has been waiting for. He has the falcon and is about to cut it open to reveal its secret. Looking on are Bogie, Lorre and Miss Astor.

Wilmer has the drop on Spade. Brigid and Gutman watch.

Brigid and Joel Cairo (Peter Lorre) have just had a bitter scrap. But Spade saves Brigid from arrest by telling the police Cairo merely tripped. Playing the detectives are Barton MacLane, with scarf, and Ward Bond.

Bleeding from a head wound, Blackie Norton (Clark Gable) searches the San Francisco streets for Mary Blake (Jeanette MacDonald) after the earthquake has devastated the city.

Clark Gable

San Francisco

(Released June 26, 1936)

SCREEN PLAY by Anita Loos based on a story by Robert Hopkins. Musical director, Herbert Stothart. Editor, Tom Held. Photography, Oliver T. Marsh. Art director, Cedric Gibbons. Songs: "San Francisco" by Gus Kahn and Bronislau Kaper; "Would You?" by Arthur Freed and Nacio Herb Brown; "The One Love" by Kahn, Kaper and Walter Jurmann. Sound recording, Douglas Shearer.* Produced by John Emerson and Bernard H. Hyman for MGM. Directed by W. S. Van Dyke. Running time, 115 minutes.

Blackie Norton	CLARK GABLE
Mary Blake	JEANETTE MAC DONALD
Father Tim Mullin	SPENCER TRACY
Jack Burley	JACK HOLT
Mrs. Burley	JESSIE RALPH
Mat	TED HEALY
Trixie	SHIRLEY ROSS
Della Bailey	MARGARET IRVING
Babe	HAROLD HUBER
Sheriff	EDGAR KENNEDY
Professor	AL SHEAN
Signor Baldini	WILLIAM RICCIARDI
Chick	KENNETH HARLAN
Alaska	ROGER IMHOF
Tony	CHARLES JUDELS
Red Kelly	RUSSELL SIMPSON
Freddie Duane	BERT ROACH
Hazeltine	WARREN B. HYMER

He was the King. Spencer Tracy was the first to

---

* Academy Award winner.

call him that. And the name stuck although he never liked it.

He made movies for thirty years and, most of the time, he was among the top ten box office attractions. At his peak, he made $7,500 a week. But he was humble enough to remember his lean years when he was chucking lumber for $3.20 a day. He kept mementos of his earlier days in his dressing room and across some he wrote, "Just to remind you, Gable."

"You know this King stuff is pure bull shit," he said late in his career. "I eat and sleep and go to the bathroom just like everyone else. There's no special light that shines inside me and makes me a star. I'm just a lucky slob from Ohio. I happened to be in the right place at the right time, and I had a lot of smart guys helping me—that's all."

Nevertheless, during his long reign in Hollywood, he was one of the most colorful figures of the movie industry. He had five wives and played opposite virtually all the great leading ladies of his era. Caricaturists loved to poke fun at his big, jug ears. But women idolized him. Men admired him or envied him, or both. And movie-goers flocked to his pictures. Sometimes, theatre owners needed only to put on the marquee: "This Week—Gable."

It was his deep, rapid-fire voice, his tall, muscular body, his bright smile, his dark hair and dark eyes and elegant mustache. Most of all, it was his sure way with the women. He seemed to know just how to handle dames—particularly snooty society dames. If you had to define Gable's appeal with a single word, that word would be—masculinity. "He was consistently and stubbornly all Man," the New York *Times* said in an editorial the day after he died.

39

Gable's off-screen life was as rambling as some of the characters he played. Born William Clark Gable in Cadiz, Ohio, he was the son of a roving oil field contractor. His mother died before he was one. His stepmother, who was kind to him, and his grandmother also were to die in his youth. Some have attributed his marriages to older women to their early deaths.

When his father quit the oil fields for farming, Gable milked cows and pitched hay. But one of his dreams had always been to be an actor. And at fifteen, he left home to become a call boy in an Akron theatre, running errands and working for tips. Over the next eight years he acted in a traveling theatre troupe until it went broke, worked as a tool dresser in the Oklahoma oil fields, punched cattle, dug for ore, cut trees, sold neckties and repaired telephone lines.

Then in 1924 he joined a theatre company in Portland, Oregon, where he met Josephine Dillon, the group's director. Fascinated by his handsome he-man looks, she took him under her wing and taught him all she knew about acting. Eventually they married. She was thirty-nine. He was twenty-three.

When they went to Hollywood he appeared as an extra in a silent film with Pola Negri. But he failed to attract attention until he starred in a Los Angeles stage production of *The Last Mile* as Killer Mears—the same role that gave Spencer Tracy his big break in New York. His first talking film was *The Painted Desert* (1931) and it led to a contract with Metro-Goldwyn-Mayer. That same year he played opposite Norma Shearer in *A Free Soul*, a picture that called for him to slap her around. Letters poured in by the thousands from women who said they would love to be on the receiving end of one of Gable's punches.

Three years later he captured an Oscar for his sparkling performance in *It Happened One Night*. That really launched his career. During the rest of the 1930s he made such box office winners as *Men in White* (1934), *Mutiny on the Bounty* (1935), *Test Pilot* (1938), and *Gone With the Wind* (1939).

Also on the list, and not to be forgotten, is *San Francisco* (1936). The lusty, free-wheeling film somehow blended into one colorful story: a Barbary Coast love triangle, cabaret dancing, opera, religion and a breath-taking natural disaster. It gave Gable a chance to put on a virtuoso display of his virile charms and to use his fists too. Its big-name cast in-

cluded Tracy and Jeanette MacDonald. And, of course, it will be vividly remembered for its magnificently staged climax—the San Francisco earthquake—a scene so realistic, it had audiences mentally dodging the bricks from falling buildings.

The movie opens on New Year's Eve, 1906, with Blackie Norton (Gable), the dashing, raucous boss of the prosperous Paradise gambling house and beer garden. Into his wicked Barbary Coast palace comes Mary Blake (Jeanette MacDonald), a Colorado minister's daughter looking for a job as a singer. "Let's see your legs," Blackie says. "Hmmm, a little thin for down here." But when he auditions her, he concedes she has a "pretty fair set of pipes" and hires her.

The rest of the plot is pure hokum, but it's great fun. Mary's sparkling songs—one of them is the engaging "San Francisco"—attract a wide following. And it isn't long before she is discovered by Jack Burley (Jack Holt), a Nob Hill society man and Blackie's political rival.

When Burley offers Mary a chance to sing with the San Francisco Opera, she is torn between her infatuation for Blackie and her career. Blackie insists on holding her to her contract. But when Mary realizes he only wants her to be his mistress, she walks out. Father Mullin, a pal of Blackie's since boyhood, tells him Mary's talent is being wasted and prevails on him to give Mary her chance.

So Mary goes on to grand opera. Her debut as Marguerite in *Faust* wins her acclaim. However, when Blackie comes to the performance and then kayos his own process server, who had come to close down the house, Mary realizes she really loves Blackie. So the fickle singer returns to Blackie's dive.

It turns out to be only the start of a shuttle service. Father Mullin, disheartened to see that Mary has given up opera, tells Blackie he is merely cheapening her by exploiting her. Enraged, Blackie says, "You stick to your suckers and I'll stick to mine." And he stuns the priest with an uppercut. Mary, shocked, goes back to Burley, and accepts his marriage proposal.

However, Burley is no angel either. In an attempt to ruin Blackie, he gets the police to close up Blackie's joint. But Mary learns about it and tries to help Blackie in a cabaret competition. She sings for his dance hall and wins the $10,000 prize for him. Blackie, disgruntled because Mary is engaged to Burley, throws the money at her feet.

As she rushes from the stage in tears, there is a low rumble. Chandeliers tremble. The balcony sways, walls totter and the dance-hall crowd panics. In a few minutes buildings are toppling like dominoes. An avalanche of bricks pours down as fire spreads through the city.

Director W. S. Van Dyke's reproduction of the earthquake that devastated San Francisco on April 18, 1906, is so imaginatively done, some reviewers called it a climax without compare in the history of film-making.*

Van Dyke shot most of the twenty-minute scene inside the studio. He used outdoor shots only as background for montages. One of the most startling views shows the sidewalks splitting. This was done by building an elevated stage with two platforms. As cables pulled the platforms apart, hoses pumped water into the opening space. On the screen, it looked as if the earth had suddenly opened.

Blackie is buried by debris and, when he comes to, Mary is gone. He finds Burley dead, clutching a piece of Mary's gown and searches frantically for her. Days later he finds her in a tent settlement. Thankful, he kneels and prays, they patch up their differences and resolve to face the future together. (Some critics felt the last scene made Gable as uncomfortable as some in the audience. But studio heads saw Blackie's conversion to religion as a way to underscore a moral about sin and redemption, and so that's the way the film wound up.)

Six years later World War II interrupted Gable's career, which had reached its zenith with *Gone With the Wind*. In 1942, at the age of forty-one, Gable enlisted in the Army Air Force as a private. He went to Officers' Candidate School, got a commission and rose to major. During the war he flew

as a gunner on several bombing missions over Europe and won the Distinguished Flying Cross and the Air Medal.

When Gable returned from the war, he starred with Greer Garson in *Adventure,* and MGM papered the country with billboards and newspaper ads saying, "Gable Is Back and Garson's Got Him." He made twenty-one films during the rest of the 1940s, 1950s and early 1960s until *The Misfits,* his last, released in 1961. But none matched the style of his brawling, uproarious movies of the 1930s.

Certainly, the most publicized part of his private life was his marriages. In 1930 he divorced Josephine Dillon and married Rhea Langham, a Texas socialite who had a son nearly as old as Gable. But they were from different worlds, separated within three years and were divorced in 1939. Gable reportedly paid $250,000 for his freedom.

That same year he married actress Carole Lombard, the great love of his life. Less than three years later their marriage ended in tragedy when she was killed in a plane crash during a war bond tour. His fourth marriage in 1949 to Lady Sylvia Ashley, widow of Douglas Fairbanks, Sr., was a surprise. It lasted only sixteen months. But friends said it was over the moment she walked into his ranch house, replaced his servants with her own, and changed everything.

Kay Williams Spreckels, who had dated Gable when she was an MGM starlet, became his fifth wife in 1955. The marriage was apparently a happy one and in September 1960 she announced she was going to have a child. The baby, John Clark Gable, was born in the spring of 1961. But Gable never saw him. He suffered a heart attack on November 6, 1960, and died ten days later. He was fifty-nine.

Millions of words have been written to try to explain Gable's magnetic screen personality. But perhaps he summed it up best himself. "The reason they come to see me is because I know life is great. And they know I know it. They see me getting a kick out of all living. They know that even if I had known what was going to happen to Carole, for instance, it was worth it."

---

* Although he is not mentioned in the screen credits, James Basevi, MGM special effects man, is generally acknowledged to have done the major work in engineering the earthquake. For more on Basevi, who usually deplored notoriety, and on movie make-believe, see Chapter III, on *The Hurricane*.

Mary's flamboyant stage costume puts on display the shapely gams Blackie tells her look "a little thin for down here."

Blackie spars with Father Tim Mullin (Spencer Tracy), a boyhood pal who runs a mission near Blackie's Paradise Café.

Blackie takes to the stump to campaign for supervisor against his Nob Hill rival Jack Burley.

Burley (Jack Holt), a wealthy society man, introduces Mary, now his fiancée and a diva, to his mother (Jessie Ralph).

Blackie Norton, boss of the wicked Barbary Coast, ushers in 1906 with local liquor merchant Freddie Duane (Bert Roach).

43

Small-town bachelor Longfellow Deeds (Cooper) learns that he's just become heir to a multimillion-dollar fortune. Breaking the news is Cornelius Cobb (Lionel Stander), an apoplectic press agent, and John Cedar (Douglas Dumbrille), a scheming lawyer. Mrs. Meredith (Emma Dunn) pours the coffee.

Mandrake Falls, Vermont, says good-bye to its new hero. Deeds, a tuba player, joins the band playing farewell songs.

Gary Cooper

Mr. Deeds Goes to Town

(New York Premiere, April 16, 1936)

SCREEN PLAY by Robert Riskin based on the story "Opera Hat" by Clarence Budington Kelland. Camera, Joseph Walker. Special camera effects, E. Roy Davidson. Film editor, Gene Havlick. Art director, Stephen Goosson. Musical director, Howard Jackson. Produced and directed by Frank Capra.* Assistant director, C. C. Coleman. A Columbia Picture. Running time, 115 minutes.

Longfellow Deeds	GARY COOPER
Babe Bennett	JEAN ARTHUR
Mac Wade	GEORGE BANCROFT
Cornelius Cobb	LIONEL STANDER
John Cedar	DOUGLAS DUMBRILLE
Walter	RAYMOND WALBURN
Judge Walker	H. B. WARNER
Madame Pomponi	MARGARET MATZENAUER
Bodyguard	WARREN HYMER
Theresa	MURIEL EVANS
Mabel Dawson	RUTH DONNELLY
Mal	SPENCER CHARTERS
Mrs. Meredith	EMMA DUNN
Psychiatrist	WRYLEY BIRCH
Budington	ARTHUR HOYT
Farmer	JOHN WRAY
Mr. Semple	JAMESON THOMAS
Amy Faulkner	MARGARET MC WADE
Butler	BARNETT PARKER
Henneberry	EDDIE KANE
Brookfield	GEORGE MEEKER
A Writer	JAY EATON
Bailiff	LEE SHUMWAY
Mrs. Semple	MAYO METHOT
Walter	GENE MORGAN
Morrow	WALTER CATLETT
Jane Faulkner	MARGARET SEDDON

---

* Academy Award winner.

(A television series called *Mr. Deeds Goes to Town* debuted in 1969. It told the story of a small-town editor who became heir to a multimillion-dollar corporation.)

Gable made them squirm in the movies next to their wives or their Saturday night dates. With his handsome face, confident manner and lightning wit, he made every little man feel inferior.

But Cooper. Coop was one of them. He was taciturn and gangly. He was dusty and rumpled. And he said, "Yup." But he was not one to be messed with. He was one of the fastest draws in the great outdoors. He was an expert horseman and knew how to use his dukes, too. He gave the ineloquent little guy comfort and assurance as he left that dark world of make-believe.

Cooper, himself, was not unaware of his image. He knew that "identification" was his touchstone. Once asked to give his reason for success, Cooper replied: "Mostly, I think it's because I look like the guy down the street." He told many interviewers, "I'm just an ordinary Joe who became a movie star."

This ordinary Joe never took a formal acting lesson, never acted in a play, never passed a regular screen test. He made few broadcasts, fewer television appearances.

But his thirty-five years as a star were the movies' most durable success story. He ranked among the top ten box office names for more than fifteen years. In 1939, when he earned $482,819, he was America's highest-paid citizen. His total earnings as an actor have been estimated at over $10,000,000.

Howard Hawks, who directed *Sergeant York*, summed up Cooper's acting ability like this: "He's no Walter Hampden or Maurice Evans. He hasn't their range, their stagecraft, their technique. But that's less important in pictures than inner sincerity and conviction. The grand thing about Coop is that you believe everything that he says or does."

Cooper was born Frank James Cooper—an agent later made it Gary—in Helena, Montana, in 1901. His father was a British lawyer who had come to the United States, settled in Helena and married a Montana girl, also from England. The elder Cooper became a gentleman rancher and practiced law. He rose to become a justice of the Montana Supreme Court.

At nine, young Cooper and his brother Arthur were sent to England for four years at the Dunstable School. The boys returned with English accents and British-style suits. Both proved to be something less than permanent fixtures. The fancy clothes lasted only until their first day back at school. "All I remember for sure," said Cooper, "was that Arthur and I didn't run from the fight and that we didn't have any English duds when we got home." Cooper added: "We reverted to Western ways with relief."

Like most Montana boys, Cooper grew up learning to ride horses, shoot, fish and punch cattle. But his ambition lay in other areas. He studied at Iowa's Grinnell College for two years, then went to Los Angeles to find work as a newspaper cartoonist. He had no luck at that job. He also flopped as a door-to-door salesman for a photo studio and as a theatrical sign painter. Then he tried the movies.

It happened this way. One day in 1925, Cooper ran into three old Montana chums near Hollywood and Vine. They told him they were cowboy extras, making what they then considered the fantastic fee of ten dollars a day. They persuaded Coop to join them.

So for the better part of a year he worked as a trick rider, stunt man and saloon brawler in silent movies. "Some days I was a cowboy in the morning," Cooper said, "and an Injun in the afternoon."

In 1926, Sam Goldwyn spotted the lanky, six-foot-three, 175-pound Cooper and gave him the second male lead at $75 a week in *The Winning of Barbara Worth*. Cooper played with Ronald Colman and Vilma Banky, then publicized as the world's most beautiful woman. When it was released, Paramount signed him at $125 a week and gave him a part in *Wings*, the war-flying drama. It was a small role but the public took note of his performance.

At Clara Bow's urging, he was cast opposite her in *Children of Divorce* and Cooper was on his way.

In those days he was quite the gay blade and it was not unusual to see him on the town with Miss Bow, Lupe Velez, Tallulah Bankhead, Evelyn Brent or Countess Dorothy (Taylor) di Frasso, an international café socialite.

When talkies came, Coop played in *The Virginian*. In one scene Mary Brian, playing a school-teacher, tried to draw Cooper out. All his replies were "yup" or "nope." He blamed this scene for establishing him in the public mind as a man of few words. Actually, he was an articulate person with well-thought-out and reasoned opinions.

The 1930s saw Cooper get roles that he liked almost as much as the millions who watched his movies. Among other films, he starred in *Morocco* (1930) with Marlene Dietrich, *A Farewell to Arms* (1932) and *Lives of a Bengal Lancer* (1935).

That same year brought him together with Frank Capra, noted then for directing *It Happened One Night* (1934), winner of five Oscars. Capra's forte was social comedy. In *Mr. Deeds Goes to Town*, Capra splendidly satirizes the urban mind—so engrossed in dog-eat-dog existence it considers the small-town man who wants to live simply as either a charlatan or a nut.

Cooper plays Longfellow Deeds of Mandrake Falls, Vermont, a quiet, small-town bachelor who writes rhymes for birthday cards and plays the tuba to concentrate. His peace is disturbed one day when he falls heir to $20,000,000. When a slick New York lawyer (Douglas Dumbrille) arrives, Deeds receives the news without taking his lips from the tuba. But, at his lawyer's insistence, he departs for the big city to claim his fortune.

Once he reaches the city, Longfellow is surrounded by an array of moochers who want to cut in on his money. Deeds, though, comes from shrewd Yankee stock and proves no easy touch. He confides only in a pretty blonde (Jean Arthur), who faints at his doorstep. Deeds thinks she is a hungry, unemployed stenographer. Actually, she is Babe Bennett, a star reporter who has tricked him to get exclusive stories.

Deeds takes her to a sophisticated restaurant for dinner. There they join some famous New York poets who immediately start poking fun at Deeds, his homespun rhymes and his country-come-to-town speech. He stops them cold by saying: "I know I must look funny to you. Maybe if you came to Mandrake Falls, you'd look just as funny to us. . . . But nobody'd laugh at you and make you ridiculous —'cause that wouldn't be good manners." Then he proceeds to drop a pair of them with a couple of uppercuts.

Later, he tells Jean Arthur, "They work so hard at living, they forget how to live. . . . They created a lot of grand palaces here. But they forgot about the noblemen to put in them."

Bored by his constant fencing with smart-alecks, Deeds feeds doughnuts to hungry cab horses, chases fire engines, slides down a marble banister and tickles a statue's foot.

All this is duly reported by Miss Bennett. She dubs him "the Cinderella man." Her front-page stories make him a laughingstock. Then, suddenly, the hard-boiled newspaper dame realizes she's been taking advantage of a nice guy. What's more, she's fallen in love with her Cinderella man. "He's either the dumbest, silliest idiot," she says, ". . . or he's the grandest guy alive."

But it's too late. Before she can make amends, Deeds finds out her true identity. And he decides to give away his money. As he is figuring out how to do it, an unemployed farmer (John Wray) busts into his house and berates Deeds for feeding doughnuts to a horse while millions are going hungry in the Depression.

Then and there, Deeds decides to give away his fortune to unemployed dispossessed farmers. His lawyer and two relatives, shocked to see the money slip away, claim he is insane, forcing Deeds into a lunacy hearing.

In the movie's most brilliantly conceived scene, the lawyer argues that Deeds can't handle his own affairs because: (1) he plays the tuba to think, (2) he fed a horse doughnuts, (3) two old maids from his home town have testified that he is loony ("pixilated" is their word), and (4) he is irresponsibly proposing to spend his money restoring ruined farms.

Deeds, at first, won't defend himself. But Babe convinces him that he must and that she loves him. Deeds takes the stand and argues that: (1) His tuba playing merely assists his concentration, serving the same purpose as the psychiatrist's "doodles" in court. The judge (H. B. Warner), Deeds also points out, is an "O-filler" (one who fills in the "O" on printed matter in similar moments of abstraction). (2) Deeds says that when he fed the horse doughnuts he was drunk—just as the lawyer's own son had been recently and just as the judge had probably been in his youth. (3) Deeds argues that the two ladies who pronounced him pixilated considered everybody in Mandrake Falls to be pixilated

—except themselves. Finally, Deeds says that, by giving his fortune to needy farmers, he was doing what he could to help the government. Deeds climaxes his speech with another uppercut, this one descending on the lawyer. Farmers crowding the courtroom cheer.

"In my opinion," says the judge, "you are not only sane, you are the sanest man who ever walked into this courtroom." Whereupon farmers carry him out in triumph. Deeds scoots back a second later to kiss and make up with Jean Arthur.

The film, which added the words "doodle" and "pixilated" to American slang, lost out to *The Great Ziegfeld* in the Oscar balloting. But Capra won the Academy Award for best direction. And both the New York Film Critics and the National Board of Review named the movie the best film of the year.

Cooper, who made eighty-nine movies, went on to win two Oscars—for *Sergeant York* (1941) and as the determined sheriff in *High Noon* (1952). Most fans remember him best in this cowboy role. It made him a world symbol of the courageous, laconic pioneer of the American West.

Other outstanding Cooper movies include: *The General Died at Dawn* (1936), *Beau Geste* (1939), *Meet John Doe* (1941), *Pride of the Yankees* (1942) and *For Whom the Bell Tolls* (1943).

Cooper married the socially prominent Veronica Balfe, who had a brief screen career as Sandra Shaw. They had one daughter, Maria. Although they separated during the early 1950s, they eventually reconciled and their marriage was considered one of Hollywood's happiest. In 1959, Cooper, an Episcopalian, converted to Catholicism, the faith of his wife and daughter.

Cooper's last picture was *The Naked Edge*, a suspense story he made in London in 1960. Later that year he was stricken with cancer and underwent a series of unsuccessful operations.

His condition did not become known until he was unable to show up for a Special Oscar at the Academy Awards presentation on April 17. Reporters were told that Cooper was suffering from a pinched nerve. But James Stewart, a close friend who accepted the award for Cooper, knew the truth. And Stewart delivered a short, moving tribute. On his portable TV, Cooper watched as Stewart said, "We'll all very proud of you, Coop. All of us are tremendously proud."

Cooper, whom millions looked on as the all-American man, died twenty-six days later. He was sixty.

Editor MacWade (George Bancroft) persuades his ace reporter Babe Bennett (Jean Arthur) to try for an exclusive on Deeds.

The unsuspecting Deeds takes Bennett to a posh New York restaurant where the city's literati immediately begin ribbing his small-town ways.

A Depression-starved farmer (John Wray) storms with pistol into Deeds's mansion, berating him for feeding a horse doughnuts while millions are hungry. That's character actor Raymond Walburn next to Cooper, playing his valet. Next to Walburn is Barnett Parker.

48

Two old maids (Margaret McWade, left, and Margaret Seddon) tell a lunacy commission they think Deeds is "pixilated." The film added a fanciful term for "crazy" to American slang.

Deeds has a parting shot for lawyer Cedar, who has tried unsuccessfully to capture the Deeds fortune for his clients and himself. At right, behind Cedar, is character actor Arthur Hoyt. Bailiff (Lee Shumway) restrains Cooper.

Political babe in arms Jefferson Smith (James Stewart), head of the state's Boy Rangers, arrives at his Senate office.

Senator Paine (Claude Rains), left, and party boss Jim Taylor (Edward Arnold), who have appointed Smith, congratulate themselves on finding the perfect simpleton.

(Photos by Columbia)

James Stewart

Mr. Smith Goes to Washington

(Released October 19, 1939)

SCREEN PLAY by Sidney Buchman from a story by Lewis R. Foster.* Camera, Joseph Walker. Editors, Gene Havlick and Al Clark. Montage effects, Slavko Vorkapich. Musical director, M. W. Stoloff. Musical score, Dmitri Tiomkin. Art director, Lionel Banks. Assistant director, Arthur S. Black. Produced and directed by Frank Capra. Released by Columbia Pictures Corp. Running time, 126 minutes.

Jefferson Smith	JAMES STEWART
Saunders	JEAN ARTHUR
Senator Joseph Paine	CLAUDE RAINS
Jim Taylor	EDWARD ARNOLD
Governor Hopper	GUY KIBBEE
Diz Moore	THOMAS MITCHELL
Chick McGann	EUGENE PALLETTE
Ma Smith	BEULAH BONDI
Senate Majority Leader	H. B. WARNER
Senate President	HARRY CAREY
Susan Paine	ASTRID ALLWYN
Mrs. Hopper	RUTH DONNELLY
Senator MacPherson	GRANT MITCHELL
Senator Monroe	PORTER HALL
Senate Minority Leader	PIERRE WATKIN
Nosey	CHARLES LANE
Carl Cook	DICK ELLIOTT
Sweeney	JACK CARSON
The Hopper Boys	

BILLY WATSON, DELMAR WATSON, JOHN RUSSELL, HARRY WATSON, GARY WATSON, BABY DUMPLING (LARRY SIMMS)

Ragner	ALLAN CAVAN

---

* Academy Award winner.

Diggs	MAURICE COSTELLO
Schultz	LLOYD WHITLOCK

If you lived in Middletown, U.S.A., you might remember him as the lanky, wholesome kid from Shady Lane.

He was the lad who played the accordion, helped out in his dad's store and rented a tux to go to the Junior Prom. Later, he was the World War II hero who flew bombing raids over Germany and came home with a chestful of medals and only said, "Aw, shucks."

To millions of moviegoers, James Stewart fits to a T their idea of the all-American boy. Partly, it's because he's just being himself. It's also because, even at sixty, he looks the part.

Behind the crow's feet, you can still see the sparkle in his clear blue eyes. Neither divorce nor Hollywood scandal has touched his career. Everything he does, even the way he slouches when he sits down, somehow suggests solid homespun virtues. Most of all, it's the way he talks—that hesitant, whiny drawl—that makes you remember him as the boy next door.

Actually, Stewart, like Gary Cooper, is keenly aware of the way he achieved his effects on the screen. He nurtured his image, wearing a toupee when he reached middle age to conceal his thinning un-all-American hair line. But this is not to take away anything from the fact that he is a genuine product of mainstream America.

James Stewart—that's his real name—was born in the small town of Indiana, Pennsylvania (population 9,000). His father ran a hardware store that had been in the family for a hundred years. Later, when the younger Stewart became an actor, he would still come home during the busy Christmas season and clerk behind the counter.

Stewart went to Mercersburg Academy, then to Princeton, his father's alma mater. At college he acted in the famous Triangle Club productions and studied to be an architect. But young architects were not in demand during the Depression years. So after graduation Stewart joined a New England stock company. After a few months he forgot that he had once considered architecture as a career.

He went from one small acting role to another, rooming at one time with another aspiring thespian named Henry Fonda. At twenty-four, Stewart appeared on Broadway. Two years later he went to Hollywood. After playing minor roles, he was cast with Margaret Sullavan, an old stock-company friend and reportedly his girl friend at the time, in *Next Time We Love* (1936). Almost immediately, he headed for stardom.

The spindly, six-foot-three-inch, 167-pound Stewart played Jean Harlow's jilted fiancé in *Wife vs. Secretary* (1936), sang to Eleanor Powell in *Born to Dance* (1936), appeared in his first leading role opposite Simone Simon in *Seventh Heaven* (1937). In 1938 he made *You Can't Take It With You*, then *Vivacious Lady* with Ginger Rogers, and *Made for Each Other*, with Carole Lombard. But it was in 1939 that he reached the peak of his early career in Frank Capra's *Mr. Smith Goes to Washington*.

Ironically, Cooper was Capra's first choice for the movie based on Lewis R. Foster's "The Man from Montana." When Capra first read the story, he saw it as a natural successor to his whimsical *Mr. Deeds Goes to Town*. The title, of course, would be *Mr. Deeds Goes to Washington*. But Cooper had other film commitments. So Stewart was tapped for the part. Mr. Deeds became Mr. Smith. And Montana became an undesignated Western state.

Country bumpkin Jefferson Smith (Stewart), head of the state's Boy Rangers, goes to Congress to fill an unexpired term. His qualifications are zero—which makes him perfect as far as the state's political machine is concerned. Party boss Jim Taylor (Edward Arnold), Governor Hopper (Guy Kibbee) and Senator Paine (Claude Rains) need a simpleton who will do their bidding without asking questions. They have a bill in the hopper to give the state a new dam and, incidentally, return them rich real estate profits.

Washington awes Smith. The first thing he does is go out rubbernecking like a tourist at the capital's monuments and buildings. At his office, he meets his good-looking hard-boiled secretary, Saunders (Jean Arthur), as everybody calls her. "Is he animal, vegetable or mineral?" she asks bewilderedly after she's seen him.

But Smith shows he's no vegetable. Even before he's sworn in, he makes headlines. In his first news conference he eagerly demonstrates his repertoire of bird calls and sign language to the cynical, worldly wise Washington press corps. Their stories picture him as an "incompetent clown." Embarrassed, Smith wants to resign. But Rains, who knows Smith's pet idea is to build a national boys' camp, persuades him to stay and sponsor a bill for a camp on a site in their state.

As it turns out, Rains' advice backfires. Smith, enthused, gets Saunders to help him draft a bill. Weeks later Saunders finds she has, against her better judgment, fallen in love with Smith. She tells him the state machine's unneeded dam is going to be built on the same land he has unwittingly picked for his campsite.

Smith rushes to Rains. In a dramatic scene, Rains explains the facts of political life. "You've been living in a boy's world," Rains says. "This is a man's world. . . . You have to check your ideals outside the door like you do your rubbers. I've had to compromise. I've had to play ball. . . . That's how states and empires have been built since time began."

But Smith won't play ball. He decides to expose the fraud. Instead, the wily Rains beats him to the punch. Before Smith can make his charges, Rains tells the Senate that Smith owns the very land Smith has proposed for his boys' camp. Rains says that Smith is on the verge of making a huge personal profit from the deal. Later, Rains produces a deed to the site with Smith's forged name on it.

Smith says he's been framed. But the Senate won't believe him and his expulsion seems certain. Humiliated, he starts to leave. But Saunders stops him and convinces him to fight back.

Next day, his Senate desk crowded with books and food, he rises to defend himself. He tells the Senate about the corrupt dam scheme that Rains and the state machine have engineered.

In one of the great virtuoso scenes of the 1930s,

Smith launches a one-man filibuster, forcing the Senate to listen to him. The machine-controlled press and radio stations in Smith's home state won't carry what he says. But he keeps talking hour after hour, finally appealing to all that remains honest in Rains.

"You think I'm licked. . . . Well, I'm not licked," says Smith, barely able to stand after twenty-three hours. "I'm going to stay right here and fight for this lost cause. . . . Somebody will listen to me." Then he faints.

Conscience-stricken, Rains goes to the cloakroom and tries to shoot himself, but he is stopped. He bolts into the Senate. "Everything that boy said is the truth," Rains shouts. "Every word about Taylor and me and graft and the rotten political corruption of my state." The movie ends with the Senate and gallery applauding Smith.

The film, now considered a minor classic, got generally excellent notices, including a favorable review in the *Daily Worker*. However, as a footnote, it's worth mentioning that the Communist paper's Washington correspondent, Adam Lapin, was moved to take issue with his own publication's review. In a letter to the editor, Lapin said the film missed greatness because it dwelt on a "phony issue." It could have been a far more substantial picture, Lapin said, if Smith's boys' camp bill had, instead, been a bill calling for relief for the unemployed, pure food and drug legislation, a wage and hour law or a law limiting the munitions industry.

A more publicized broadside came from the Senate itself. Senator Alben Barkley (D-Ky.), then the majority leader and later Vice-President, dismissed the movie as "silly and stupid." He said it "makes the Senate look like a bunch of crooks."

Reviewers came to Capra's defense, among them Howard Barnes of the New York *Herald Tribune*. Barnes called Barkley "thin-skinned" and pointed out that Capra's story actually painted a conservative picture of the Senate compared to some of the real shenanigans that go on. William Boehnel added in the New York *World-Telegram:* "If it [the movie] says that graft and corruption can enter

its [the Senate's] sacred portals, it is saying no more than what facts have regrettably proved to be the truth."

The film was one of the also-rans in the Oscar derby to *Goodbye, Mr. Chips,* and the picture brought Stewart his first Academy Award nomination.

Equally important, it marked the real beginning of his rise to stardom. He followed it with the memorable *Destry Rides Again* with Marlene Dietrich, and *The Shop Around the Corner* and *The Mortal Storm*, both opposite Margaret Sullavan.

Then in 1940 he co-starred in *The Philadelphia Story* with Katharine Hepburn and Cary Grant. His performance as the crafty reporter won him an Oscar. The golden statuette is on permanent display in his father's hardware store.

In 1949, Stewart, long one of Hollywood's most eligible bachelors, was married, at the age of forty-one, to ex-model Gloria Hatrick McLean, ten years his junior. They have twin daughters of their own, and two sons by Gloria's former marriage.

After the war Stewart's acting matured and his roles broadened. Although he still exuded boyish charm, he played parts as varied as a detective and a headmaster involved with homosexuals.

He got Oscar nominations for his performances in *It's a Wonderful Life* (1946), *Harvey* (1950) and *Anatomy of a Murder* (1959). He also did such Hitchcock thrillers as *Rope* (1948), *Rear Window* (1954), *The Man Who Knew Too Much* (1956) and *Vertigo* (1958). Biographical performances came as the crippled baseball player in *The Stratton Story* (1949), as the ill-fated band leader in *The Glenn Miller Story* (1954) and in *The Spirit of St. Louis* (1957), in which he portrayed Lindbergh.

In 1969 when he was sixty, Stewart's career seemed to be still going strong. That was fine with him. "People ask me who's going to be the next Jimmy Stewart. Or the next Gary Cooper. And I say, 'Well, maybe there won't be.'" Then he added: "And what's the matter with me?"

Smith meets his secretary and aide Saunders (Jean Arthur), wise in the ways of Washington. She's not quite sure Smith is for real.

Smith gives out with some imitation bird calls at his first press conference. The next day he finds the Washington press has made him a laughingstock.

Enraged, Smith tries to hang one on the jaw of one of the reporters. Jack Carson, center, and Thomas Mitchell hold him back.

Smith has turned out to be his own man and Boss Taylor finds that he can't be bought off. Eugene Pallette is at extreme left. Other bosses are Allan Cavan (with cigar), silent-screen star Maurice Costello (Dolores' father) and Lloyd Whitlock.

In one of the great scenes of the 1930s, Mr. Smith holds a one-man filibuster.

Manuel (Spencer Tracy) sings a sea chanty, accompanying himself with a vielle, an ancient stringed instrument resembling both a mandolin and a piano-accordion. It was popular as far back as the sixteenth century. Harvey Cheyne (Freddie Bartholomew) looks on.

Spencer Tracy

Captains Courageous

(Released June 25, 1937)

FROM THE BOOK by Rudyard Kipling. Screen play by John Lee Mahin, Marc Connolly and Dale Van Every. Music, Franz Waxman. Songs, "Don't Cry Little Fish" and "Ooh, What a Terrible Man!" by Waxman and Gus Kahn. Marine director, James Havens. Art director, Cedric Gibbons. Photography, Harold Rosson. Editor, Elmo Vernon. Produced by Louis D. Lighton. Directed by Victor Fleming. Released by Metro-Goldwyn-Mayer. Running time, 115 minutes.

Harvey	FREDDIE BARTHOLOMEW
Manuel	SPENCER TRACY *
Captain Disko Troop	LIONEL BARRYMORE
Mr. Cheyne	MELVYN DOUGLAS
Dan	MICKEY ROONEY
Uncle Salters	CHARLEY GRAPEWIN
Long Jack	JOHN CARRADINE
Cushman	OSCAR O'SHEA
Priest	JACK LA RUE
Dr. Finley	WALTER KINGSFORD
Tyler	DONALD BRIGGS
Doc	SAM MC DANIEL
Charles	BILLIE BURRUD
Old Clemant	CHRISTIAN RUB
Tom	DAVE THURSBY
Burns	LEO G. CARROLL
Dr. Walsh	CHARLES TROWBRIDGE

The face was unforgettable.

It was craggy, freckled and roughhewn. It was tough and sturdy and sunburned and later seamed with a network of wrinkles. Someone once said the lines would hold two days of rain. He himself said his face reminded him of a beat-up barn door.

Even when he was young, Spencer Tracy was not handsome—at least, not in the Hollywood sense. But it was partly because he wasn't that he was able to make seventy-four movies in a career spanning thirty-seven years. When the studios dropped other leading men who had lost their looks, Tracy capitalized on his age. As his hair turned from red to brown to silver, his roles changed from tough guys, adventurers and brash reporters to elder statesmen, judges and fathers of the bride. In his last film, *Guess Who's Coming to Dinner*, he played a father whose daughter marries a Negro. That was 1967. It was his ninth picture with Katharine Hepburn, his favorite co-star and close friend of many years.

But it would be simplistic to credit Tracy's durable career just to his tousled looks. His weathered face was only one reason for his charisma. He was a distinguished character actor, a born talent whose performances seemed natural and effortless. With his calm but firm look and his steady blue eyes, he seemed to fit perfectly the role of the self-sufficient man. He was the guy who movie-goers knew would have the strength to prevail—no matter what the odds—if his cause was right. "Spence was like an old oak tree," Miss Hepburn said. "He belongs in an era when men were men."

Like his image, he was an individualist off screen. He felt his often stormy private life—he had black moods, a vicious temper and he often drank too much—was his own and he tried to guard it jealously. He rarely went to premieres, infrequently to cafés, seldom gave interviews. When he did, he

---

* Academy Award winner.

could be wry and brief, especially when he thought the questions were silly. Once asked what he looked for in a script, he snapped, "Days off." When a reporter asked him what makes a woman attractive, he answered: "Young man, I'll give you thirty seconds to think of another question." The reporter couldn't. That ended the interview.

But he was always honest and frank, especially when speaking about his own profession. He said he didn't think "anything an actor does is terribly important, except maybe to himself. Naturally, an actor's personality is part of his performance. All right, so you like mine. Big deal. Thanks." About actors going into politics: ". . . Just remember who shot Lincoln." About Academy Awards: "It doesn't mean a damn thing, except as a gesture. It is given to you by friends. More than an award for ability, it's likely to be a sentimental award." Nevertheless, Tracy was the only actor to win two straight Oscars —for *Captains Courageous* in 1937 and *Boys' Town* in 1938.*

Born into an Irish-American family in Milwaukee in 1900, he was a wild and carefree youngster whose early schooling was marked by truancy. Tracy, whose father was sales manager for a trucking firm, later showed a talent for acting at Ripon College in Wisconsin. But he was restless and impatient and left after three semesters to join his boyhood pal, Pat O'Brien, in New York and try his hand on Broadway.

While studying at the American Academy of Dramatic Arts, they roomed together in a seedy west-side apartment. Tracy's first part was a non-speaking bit in the play *R.U.R.* He got bigger roles in stock companies and it was while he was on the road in 1923 that he met and married a young actress, Louise Treadwell.

That same year Tracy got his first part on Broadway. But it took seven more years before Hollywood noticed him. He won plaudits for his portrayal of Killer Mears in *The Last Mile* and Fox offered him a contract. Ironically, his wife doubted much would come of it. She had seen him in a short subject that Tracy had made in New York earlier. "Spencer doesn't photograph well," she wrote to a friend, "so we are forgetting about the talkies."

He went to Hollywood anyway and made *Up*

---

* He also had six Oscar nominations for: *San Francisco* (1936), *Father of the Bride* (1950), *Bad Day at Black Rock* (1954), *The Old Man and the Sea* (1958), *Inherit the Wind* (1960) and *Judgment at Nuremberg* (1961).

the River with another comer, Humphrey Bogart. From then on it was films, except for one brief return in 1945 to star in Robert Sherwood's *The Rugged Path*. The play flopped, but the critics saluted Tracy.

In his early years in Hollywood, Tracy had his ups and downs. The studio was uncertain of his feminine appeal and failed to give him star build-up treatment. As a result, many of his efforts were in second-rate movies that squandered his talent. Tracy often fought against doing scripts he considered bad. But in the end he usually accepted whatever roles came his way.

After a while the good parts showed up. In 1936 he played in such first-rate movies as *Fury* and *San Francisco*. Then, in 1937, he was offered the part of Manuel, the simple Portuguese fisherman in *Captains Courageous*. He was hesitant about taking the role. It meant he had to talk with an accent, sing sea chanties and curl his hair. ("My God, it's Harpo Marx," Joan Crawford said when she saw him on the set.) But Louise read the script and encouraged him to do it. It turned out to be his favorite film of the 1930s and the one that catapulted him to the front ranks of stardom.

The movie, an adaptation of Rudyard Kipling's great sea story, is about a spoiled, rich boy swept off a luxury liner and rescued by the crusty crew of a Gloucester fishing schooner. Harvey Cheyne (Freddie Bartholomew) is the only child of a millionaire (Melvyn Douglas) whose wife is dead and who has not been able to spare enough time from business to know his boy.

At school, Harvey's burning ambition is to become a member of an exclusive club. He thinks his father's money can get anything he wants, and tries to buy his way into the club. When he is rebuffed and punished, Harvey smears ink over his face and clothes, runs away from school, and tells his father an exaggerated story of violent abuse. After a conference with the headmaster (Walter Kingsford), Mr. Cheyne despairingly withdraws his son and takes him to Europe.

On board ship, Harvey shows off to fellow passengers by downing six ice cream sodas. He becomes sick, heads for the rail, but leans over too far and, unseen by anyone, falls into the ocean. Luckily the liner is crossing the Grand Banks along the route of the New England fishing boats. Next thing Harvey knows, he is sitting in a bunk with the smell of fish deep in his nostrils. He is told he's aboard the schooner *We're Here* and that he owes his life to a fisherman named Manuel.

The gruff, kindly fishermen welcome him. But Harvey chooses to be obnoxious. He arrogantly orders Captain Disko Troop (Lionel Barrymore) to take him home immediately. The captain explains they can't sail back to shore until all the catch is in the hold, three months from now. When the captain's son Dan (Mickey Rooney) gives him some clothes, Harvey says, "This is a dirty rotten little boat, and these are the worst clothes I ever saw."

Harvey, at first, refuses to do any work. But the happy-go-lucky Manuel takes a paternal interest in his "leetle feesh" and gradually wins the boy's confidence. Harvey starts to mend his ways, goes to work in the galley, later is promoted to deck duty—cutting up cod and halibut. He learns to stand long night watches and to enjoy the stories and songs of Manuel, who plays the vielle, an old Portuguese instrument. These are tender and compassionate moments in which the lad learns the value of real friendship.

As the weeks pass he comes to worship Manuel. More than anything, Harvey longs to go fishing with him. But Manuel has never had a dory mate since his father died six years ago. Then one day Manuel takes him along and Harvey hooks a huge halibut. "My leetle feesh catch feesh beeg as he is," Manuel laughs. "Manuel and hees leetle feesh, they beat everybody." From then on Harvey is Manuel's dory mate.

At last *We're Here* is full and puts about for Gloucester, racing the *Jennie Cushman*, a rival schooner, for the honor of being first in port. *Jennie Cushman* has gotten a head start. But breaking out every inch of canvas and heeling until her decks are nearly vertical, *We're Here* overhauls the *Cushman*.

However, the strain is too much. Manuel volunteers to go aloft to furl the topsail. When he does, the mast cracks and he plunges into the water, caught in rope and canvas. The ropes have nearly sawed him in two. He shouts out—in Portuguese so Harvey won't understand—he is dying, imploring Disko to cut him loose. But crewmen row Harvey out in a boat for a tearful farewell. Then Disko takes an ax and severs the rope and Manuel slips beneath the waves.

At Gloucester, Harvey is reunited with his father. But the boy is heartbroken. He wants to stay with the fishermen. Out of his wages of nine dollars, he buys a candlestick for Manuel's father and one for

Manuel and takes them to their church.

Memorial services are held for those who have died at sea. When Manuel's name is called, Harvey throws a wreath into the water. Mr. Cheyne, understanding his son's deep loss, has brought one too. He throws it in and they drift entwined together. Harvey, for the first time, turns to his father for comfort. Mr. Cheyne puts his arm around his boy and they silently watch the two wreaths float away.

Critics hailed the film. *"Captains Courageous* belongs with the screen's few masterpieces," said Howard Barnes of the New York *Herald Tribune. Variety* rated it "one of the best pictures of the sea ever made." William Boehnel of the New York *World-Telegram* called it a "great picture." Tracy need not have worried about Manuel's dialect. "You may find Spencer Tracy's Portuguese accent a trifle startling at first," Barnes wrote. "But once he takes the little chap he fished out of the sea in hand, he gives an impersonation that can only be called perfect."

His performance brought his first Oscar. The parts that came to Tracy after that were all starring roles. The money was good, too, and it would seem that at last he had as much as any actor could hope for.

But if his career was going smoothly, his personal life was racked with problems. In 1924, a year after their wedding, Louise had given birth to a son, John, who was totally deaf. His son's affliction affected Tracy's disposition and eventually his marriage. Mrs. Tracy devoted herself to her son's care. But Tracy, though as anguished as his wife, lacked the patience to help teach John to talk and understand. They later had a daughter who was normal. Yet Tracy's guilt about his son festered.

His attitude became surly and he spent long hours after work drinking. He quarreled with his wife, left home and agreed to a trial separation.

Then Tracy had an affair with Loretta Young. Gossip spread and she decided to end it publicly. "Since Spencer and I are both Catholic and can never be married," she said in a brief statement, "we have agreed not to see each other again." Tracy returned to his wife, but he kept leaving home on and off from then on.

The one person who was always able to get along with him was Miss Hepburn. She met Tracy in 1941 when she played opposite him in *Woman of the Year*, their first movie. Thereafter, they were lifelong friends. She brought him into her circle of literary and society friends and introduced him to intellectual pursuits. He showed her how to relax, let down her hair and enjoy life. Their close relationship never became a Hollywood newspaper item. It was just accepted. Close friends felt they would have married except for Tracy's religion and his feelings about his family.

In June 1967, Tracy died from a heart attack at the age of sixty-seven. His funeral drew more than 600 persons, including his estranged wife, his son (who became an artist, married and had a son with normal hearing), his daughter, and most of the titans of the movie industry. Miss Hepburn was not present.

Monsignor John O'Donnell, the priest who had acted as technical director for *Boys' Town*, said the mass. But it was Clark Gable who had provided the most fitting epitaph years earlier. He said simply: "There's nobody in this business who can touch him."

Smearing his face and clothes with ink, pampered Harvey tells his father (Melvyn Douglas) that he was imprisoned and tortured at school. Dr. Walsh (Charles Trowbridge), examines Harvey's "sore" leg.

Opposite, top:
When Harvey has changed his manners, he works his way up to deck chores. Manuel shows him how to cut up fish. Harvey almost chops off his fingers. But by now he wants to be a great fisherman and become ·Manuel's dory partner.

Opposite, bottom:
The two dory mates together, Manuel helping Harvey sight through a telescope.

When the skipper's son Dan (Mickey Rooney) lends Harvey his clothes, Harvey cruelly tells him they're "the worst" he's ever seen.

In this famous scene Cagney, bored with his mistress, squashes a grapefruit half in Mae Clarke's face.

Tom Powers (James Cagney) and Matt Doyle (Edward Woods), two poor Irish boys from Chicago, start on a life of crime as bootleggers.

(Photos by Warner Bros.)
(Courtesy United Artists Corp.)

James Cagney

The Public Enemy

(Released May 15, 1931)

BASED ON A STORY by Kubec Glasmon and John Bright. Screen play by Harry Thew. Photographed by Dev Jennings. Editor, Ed McCormick. Directed by William A. Wellman. Produced by Warner Brothers. Running time, 83 minutes.

Tom Powers	JAMES CAGNEY
Matt Doyle	EDWARD WOODS
Gwen	JEAN HARLOW
Mamie	JOAN BLONDELL
Mrs. Powers	BERYL MERCER
Mike Powers	DONALD COOK
Kitty	MAE CLARKE
Jane	MIA MARVIN
Nails Nathan	LESLIE FENTON
Paddy Ryan	ROBERT EMMET O'CONNOR
Putty Nose	MURRAY KINNELL
Bugs Moran	BEN HENDRICKS, JR.
Molly	RITA FLYNN
Dutch	CLARK BURROUGHS
Hack	SNITZ EDWARDS

A young man and his mistress are having breakfast. The man is in a foul mood. He's grouchy, irritable, bored. "Maybe you've found someone you like better," the woman says. The man looks up. His face is screwed into a nasty grimace. He picks up a grapefruit half from his plate and pushes it into her astonished face.

No other scene from the gangster films of the early 1930s is more vividly remembered. The man was James Cagney. The woman was Mae Clarke.

Cagney is a different kind of movie hero. He is a good guy who is bad. Instead of using charm and wit and good looks to attract his women, he is blunt and daring and aggressive. He is not handsome like Barrymore and Grant. Nor tall like Cooper. But he is a man of action. His five-foot-eight-inch frame is muscular. His movements are quick and catlike. He is tough and cocky and assured.

Adventure is his business and his main interest. Women are not treated with flattery but with frankness. They are not pursued for who they are but for what they have to offer. And when they have no more to offer, or when the thrill of their bodies goes stale, they get fruit in the face and a shoe in the backside.

Gangster films brought a fresh excitement to the screen. They showed an underworld life previously hidden from America, a contemporary world of the big city, a world where ambitious men could quickly win power and money and respect. And in a Depression-bound nation, anyone who could scale the ladder of success fast became a popular hero.

Young girls longed to have boy friends treat them rough. Young boys dreamed of becoming brazen, bold men who carried guns, drove fast cars and swept women off their feet.

Cagney went on to play hoodlums for the next three decades, yet, ironically, he grew to detest underworld parts. He even formed his own production company after a bitter feud with Warner Brothers. "Movies should be entertaining, not blood baths," Cagney said at the time. "I'm sick of carrying guns and beating up women." But his own attempt at movie making was unsuccessful and he reluctantly returned to Warner Brothers.

Even away from the studio, the public's penchant for violence haunted him. Shortly after *White Heat* (1949) opened, a little boy walked up to him and shook his hand. "Gee, Mr. Cagney, I sure enjoyed the movie," the boy said. "You were great." Cagney looked at the youngster. "What does your mother think of your seeing a picture like this?" Cagney asked. The little fellow flashed a wide, toothless grin. "Oh, she liked it as much as I did." Cagney walked away talking to himself.

The redheaded Cagney drifted into acting by chance. As a teen-ager, he sold newspapers and shined shoes on the streets of New York to help support his poor Irish family of five. Cagney had ambitions of going to Columbia if he could save enough money. But one day a fellow newsboy told him about an opening for a chorus boy in a downtown vaudeville act. It paid $35 a week, $20 more than he made selling papers in the best of weeks. He raced downtown, tried out and got the job. He faked his way by using steps he had swapped on the sidewalks from other natural newsboy dancers and learned by sitting in the balcony watching the pros.

Vaudeville led to a Broadway show called *Pitter Patter*. In 1930 he got his first big break in *Penny Arcade*. Warner Brothers signed him for a movie based on this hit show. *The Public Enemy* followed and his no-nonsense walk, chip-on-the-shoulder stance and mercurial personality rocketed him to stardom.

The Public Enemy tells the rags-to-riches story of two poor Irish boys—Tom Powers (Cagney) and Matt Doyle (Edward Woods)—who grow up in the slums of Chicago. Tom, the son of a widowed mother, and Matt wander through the city streets where every store, saloon and poolroom is an adventure, an escape from their dreary neighborhood. Their introduction to petty crime comes when they shoplift in a department store. Putty Nose (Murray Kinnell), a barroom piano player who teaches them dirty songs, acts as their fence.

When they grow up, Putty Nose gives the boys their first guns. Cagney, sitting on a bed, looks down its barrel beaming with pride and delight. They pull a robbery at a fur warehouse, gun down a cop and the die is cast.

Bootleggers, who have watched their underworld career, offer the boys entrée into the liquor rackets. Posing as truck drivers, Tom and Matt steal beer by siphoning it from warehouse vats into a gasoline truck. With their fat wads of bills, Tom sheds his rough, slum clothes and outfits himself with tailor-made suits, smart snap-brim hats and camel-hair coats. He tells his mother he has contacts with influential people now. His brother (Donald Cook), who has come home wounded from the war, will have nothing to do with him. It only proves he is a sucker, Tom thinks.

With his new wealth and gangland connections come fast women. They are not girl friends who will become partners in love but mistresses who become objects of passion and who will change as frequently as Tom changes apartments. And we see the turn in Tom's personality in the famous breakfast scene. The tensions and violence implicit in his life have taken their toll. Drained of compassion and sensitivity, he has become hard and cruel. He squashes the grapefruit in Mae Clarke's face and we know he is beyond redemption.

Tom picks up a new mistress, a blonde siren (Jean Harlow), and, evening an old score, bumps off Putty Nose. Finally, exposing his soul at its most twisted extreme, he shoots to death a saddle horse that had accidentally thrown and killed Tom's big-shot pal Nails Nathan (Leslie Fenton).

Tom and Matt have turned to terrifying shopkeepers into buying their illegal booze. The enemy is not the police but rival gangs warring over territory. And finally their days of wine and roses run out. Matt goes down under a hail of machine-gun bullets as Tom runs for his life. To avenge his pal's slaying, Tom walks into a meeting of the gangster killers and shoots it out with them. He stumbles into the rain-spattered street, clutching his stomach and mumbling, "I ain't so tough." It's his first admission of vulnerability, but it comes too late.

He doesn't die and his rivals have a more grisly end in store. They kidnap him from his hospital bed, then call his mother and tell her that her son is coming home. When the bell rings, his brother answers the door. There stands Tom's bullet-ridden body, tied into a blanket like a mummy. He seems alive for a moment, then his body falls face first onto the floor, his feet bouncing into the air.

Little Caesar (1930) and *Public Enemy* touched off a cycle of gangster movies. Religious pressure groups fought against them and eventually won a compromise. The studios put Cagney and other crime heroes on the side of the law in such films as *G-Men* (1935), *Bullets or Ballots* (1936) and *I Am the Law* (1938). World War II made crime movies dated. They returned briefly in the post-war years before it became the fashion to spoof crime as in *Guys and Dolls* (1955), *Some Like It Hot* (1959), and *Never Steal Anything Small* (1959).

In between his crime roles, Cagney played Bottom in a film adaptation of the Shakespeare comedy, *Midsummer Night's Dream* (1935), a cowboy in *Oklahoma Kid* (1939) and George M. Cohan in *Yankee Doodle Dandy* (1942). The latter role won him an Academy Award. Other memorable non-crime Cagney pictures included *The Time of Your Life* (1948), *Mister Roberts* (1955), *Love Me or Leave Me* (1955), and *One, Two, Three* (1961).

Still, no matter how he tried, Cagney could never completely shake his image as the tough little guy with a gat under his vest, a left hook and a trigger temper behind his smile. Admirers who spot him dining out still send him grapefruit.

Mike Powers (Donald Cook), a wounded veteran of World War I, scorns his brother Tom, despite his new-found affluence. At left is Rita Flynn playing Molly, the boys' sister.

Fast money brings fast women. Matt meets Mamie (Joan Blondell) and Tom snuggles close to Kitty (Mae Clarke).

Dressed in a snazzy camel-hair coat, Tom meets Gwen (Jean Harlow), a dazzling blonde.

Tom has a fistful of knuckles for a bartender (Lee Phelps) who won't buy his illegal booze.

As their luck runs out, a hail of bullets from a rival gang cuts down Matt. Tom's days are numbered.

(Photos by RKO)

Fred Astaire

Top Hat

(Released September 6, 1935)

SONGS by Irving Berlin: "No Strings," "Isn't This a Lovely Day?", "Cheek to Cheek," "The Piccolino," "Top Hat, White Tie and Tails," "Get Thee Behind Me, Satan." Ensembles staged by Hermes Pan. Screen play by Dwight Taylor and Allan Scott from a play by Alexander Farago and Aladar Laszlo. Music director, Max Steiner. Art directors, Van Nest Polglase and Carroll Clark. Editor, William Hamilton. Photography, David Abel and Vernon Walker. Directed by Mark Sandrich. Produced by Pandro S. Berman for RKO Radio Pictures. Running time, 102 minutes.

Jerry Travers	FRED ASTAIRE
Dale Tremont	GINGER ROGERS
Horace Hardwick	EDWARD EVERETT HORTON
Madge Hardwick	HELEN BRODERICK
Alberto	ERIK RHODES
Bates	ERIC BLORE
Hotel Manager, Venice	GINO CORRADO
Flower Clerk	LUCILLE BALL

"Can't act. Slightly bald. Can dance a little." So said the report of Fred Astaire's screen test. Of course, it all seems laughable now. We can look back today and wonder how anyone in the business of judging talent could goof so badly about Hollywood's greatest dancer of the thirties.

But, in fact, he did have a high forehead. His face was too narrow. His build was slight—he was only five feet nine—his ears were too big, and he had no sex appeal. Secondly, although he showed a natural flair for banter and light comedy, he usually came across as a soft-spoken fellow with a kind of shy humor. Definitely not in the Hollywood he-man mold. But thirdly, and most important, the brilliance of his dancing was not immediately recognized because he was pioneering. He was smashing Hollywood idols.

The big spectacle musical was all the vogue until Astaire stepped out before the camera. In contrast to the long chorus lines, he glided across the silver screen alone or with a partner. And he made it look so easy. Watching his effortless grace and natural ease, you itched to jump up and take your best girl for a spin right then and there. He gave audiences a delightful sense of identification that they could never get from watching a hundred girls pirouetting and high kicking in a Busby Berkeley production number.

Simplicity in filming was another Astaire innovation. In earlier musicals, cameramen went to great pains to think up new angles for dance sequences. They shot through latticework, from high above the set, from low floor locations. The result was, the audience was often more aware of the camera than the dancers. Astaire always tried to run a dance straight, with camera at eye level. He insisted that the entire figures of the dancers be kept in view so the audience always saw the uninterrupted, full flow of movement. A perfectionist, Astaire often worked for weeks on a routine even before rehearsal. Then he would go over it as many times as necessary. Once he started shooting, he would do it again and again until he felt it was right.

His arduous preparations perhaps stem from his long apprenticeship. Born in Omaha, Nebraska, Astaire started dancing in public at five. His first partner was his sister Adele. They were already a sparkling team when they made their professional New York debut when he was only twelve.

However, child labor laws forced them off the stage and they had to seek bookings elsewhere for four more years. But in 1916 they were deemed mature enough to tour the United States and Canada in vaudeville. And the next year, when they appeared as bona fide professionals in New York, they were hailed as the best young talent in vaudeville. They soon took their snappy routine to the theatre, then to Hollywood.

But then Adele got married, and Astaire suddenly found himself without a partner. Hollywood wondered if he could replace her. He did better. He teamed with Ginger Rogers, a former band singer who had brief Broadway experience before going to Hollywood. The lithe, winsome blonde made moviegoers forget Adele.

They first appeared together in Astaire's second film, *Flying Down to Rio* (1933). The nation was soon tapping its feet to their lively "Continental" number. Then came *The Gay Divorcee* (1934). Their tuneful "Carioca" song and dance sequence immediately inspired ballroom dancers throughout the country. Later it became the first Oscar-winning tune.

But their biggest hit of all—the one most remembered throughout the years—came in 1935 when they did *Top Hat*. Astaire and Miss Rogers danced to sparkling melodies by Irving Berlin. Remember Fred and Ginger taking shelter from a thundershower in a park band shell and singing "Isn't This a Lovely Day?" ("Let the rain pitter patter but it really doesn't matter . . . It's a lovely day.") * Or "Cheek to Cheek" (". . . my heart beats so that I can hardly speak . . . when we're out together dancing, cheek to cheek").* There was also "Top Hat, White Tie and Tails" and the finale number, "Piccolino."

Like most of their films, the book was not the picture's greatest virtue. Jerry Travers (Astaire), a sensational dancer in Horace Hardwick's (Edward Everett Horton) London revue, is sharing his boss's plush hotel suite. Dale Tremont (Miss Rogers) happens to be staying in the suite below.

---

* From "Isn't This a Lovely Day" and "Cheek to Cheek." © copyright 1935 Irving Berlin; © copyright renewed. Reprinted by permission of Irving Berlin Music Corp.

Fred's tap routine keeps her awake and she storms up to his apartment to complain. She dislikes Travers so much, they fall in love.

But Miss Tremont mistakenly comes to believe that Travers is the husband of her best friend, Madge Hardwick (Helen Broderick), who is actually married to Travers' boss. The mistake throws a monkey wrench into their love affair. Through a script writer's labored efforts, the mixup manages to complicate matters throughout the rest of the picture.

Astaire pursues Ginger to Venice and gets slapped twice for his trouble. Ginger gets a Latin lover, Alberto (Erik Rhodes), who lunges all over the set with a bared rapier. When Ginger ups and marries Alberto, all seems headed for a sad ending. But she finally discovers Fred is really single, and Bates (Eric Blore), Hardwick's butler, saves the day. Bates discloses that he had turned his collar around and masqueraded as a clergyman to marry them. So Alberto and Ginger aren't legally married. And Fred and Ginger dance off together with the way clear for a second chance at love. (If you think twice about it, it seems like a cruel hoax on poor Alberto. But, as the man says, all's fair in love and Hollywood.)

The Astaire-Rogers team, who had, even at this early stage, made an estimated $10,000,000 for RKO, reeled off one successful musical after another for the next four years. *Follow the Fleet* (1936), *Swing Time* (1936), *Shall We Dance* (1937), *Carefree* (1938) and *The Story of Vernon and Irene Castle* (1939).

Ironically, the two reportedly did not get on well. The enthusiasm was so great for Astaire's work that Ginger felt overlooked. She thought her own talents as an actress couldn't be fully exploited until she made a go of it alone. And so she did.

Less than two years after she danced her last 1930s number with Astaire, she won an Oscar for her role in *Kitty Foyle*. Over the next three decades, she went on to stardom in her own right in such movies as *The Major and the Minor*, *Lady in the Dark*, and *Tom, Dick and Harry*. In 1949 she and Astaire were reunited for their last fling together in *The Barkleys of Broadway*.

Meanwhile, Astaire was developing a suave, cool air, polishing his blithe screen style to perfection. He danced his way through more than a dozen films, appearing with such nimble partners as Rita Hayworth, Ann Miller, Joan Leslie, Vera-Ellen and Cyd Charisse. His movies included *Holiday Inn*

(1942), *Blue Skies* (1946), *Funny Face* (1957) and *Silk Stockings* (1957). In 1949 he won a special Oscar for his "unique artistry and contribution to the techniques of musical pictures."

Later in his career he turned to non-dancing roles, appearing in such movies as *On the Beach* (1959) and *The Pleasure of His Company* (1961). But Astaire will be best remembered in motion —spinning, turning, leaping, tap-dancing—a light-hearted, light-footed forty-foot figure of grace.

Dale Tremont (Ginger Rogers) snuggles close to Alberto (Erik Rhodes), her volatile Latin lover.

Producer Horace Hardwick (Edward Everett Horton) raises apprehensive eyebrows when Alberto shows up with a bared rapier and a mean look in his eyes.

Hardwick with his resourceful butler Bates (Eric Blore), who, it turns out, saves the day for our heroes Jerry and Dale.

Two sequences showing the famous Astaire-Rogers duo doing their thing.

72

Hardwick seems to be having a hard time explaining his black eye to his wife, Madge (Helen Broderick), and dancer Jerry Travers.

Travers poses as a coach driver to be near his would-be sweetheart Dale Tremont.

III

ADVENTURE

MUTINY ON THE BOUNTY
SHE
BEAU GESTE
LOST HORIZON
VIVA VILLA
FLASH GORDON
THE HURRICANE

Clark Gable as master's mate Fletcher Christian.

(Photos by MGM)
(© 1935 Metro-Goldwyn-Mayer Corp.; © renewed 1962 Metro-Goldwyn-Mayer Inc.)

Mutiny on the Bounty*

(Released November 8, 1935)

FROM THE NOVEL by Charles Nordhoff and James Norman Hall. Screen play by Talbot Jennings, Jules Furthman and Carey Wilson. Musical score by Herbert Stothart. Song, "Love Song of Tahiti," by Gus Kahn, Bronislau Kaper and Walter Jurmann. Film editor, Margaret Booth. Cameraman, Arthur Edeson. Produced by Irving Thalberg. Associate producer, Albert Lewin. Released by Metro-Goldwyn-Mayer. Running time, 131 minutes.

Captain Bligh	CHARLES LAUGHTON
Fletcher Christian	CLARK GABLE
Roger Byam	FRANCHOT TONE
Smith	HERBERT MUNDIN
Ellison	EDDIE QUILLAN
Bacchus	DUDLEY DIGGES
Burkitt	DONALD CRISP
Sir Joseph Banks	HENRY STEPHENSON
Captain Nelson	FRANCIS LISTER
Mrs. Byam	SPRING BYINGTON
Tehani	MOVITA CASTANEDA
Maimiti	MAMO CLARK
Maggs	IAN WOLFE
Morgan	IVAN SIMPSON
Fryer	DE WITT JENNINGS
Muspratt	STANLEY FIELDS
Morrison	WALLIS CLARK
Hayward	VERNON DOWNING
Tinkler	DICK WINSLOW

(Another version of *Mutiny on the Bounty* was made in 1962 with Marlon Brando as Christian and Trevor Howard as Bligh. A previous version, *In the Wake of the Bounty*, was made in 1933 in Australia with Errol Flynn as Christian.)

---

* Academy Award winner.

"Here's to the voyage of the *Bounty*," says Midshipman Roger Byam (Franchot Tone), raising his glass at the start of the classic sea saga. "Still waters and the great golden sea. Flying fish like streaks of silver. Mermaids who sing in the night. The Southern Cross and all the stars on the other side of the world."

"Bless my soul," gasps elderly Sir Joseph Banks (Henry Stephenson), stirred by the exotic metaphors that have rolled off the young man's tongue. "To the voyage of the *Bounty!*"

The story that followed, perhaps the greatest sailing adventure of all time, was a director's dream. Its ingredients—a tyrannical skipper, a fearless first mate, beautiful Polynesian girls in a South Sea paradise, mutiny on the high seas, a shipwreck, and a cross-Pacific voyage in an open boat. There was a bonus, too. The story had the spellbinding lure that comes only from authenticity. The incredible, salty tale was fact, not fiction.

Charles Nordhoff and James Norman Hall had revived interest in the long-forgotten cruise in their 1932 novel, *Mutiny on the Bounty* (which grew into a trilogy). It became a best seller and MGM bought the screen rights.

Despite its potential, the decision to make a movie was not a unanimous one. Louis B. Mayer, the studio's head, thought the film would be a loser. Who ever heard of a hero who was a mutineer? Gable was reluctant to play Fletcher Christian because he didn't like the idea of competing with British actors. And Charles Laughton—who would always be remembered for the bitterness and malevolence he infused into the four words, "Mr. Christian, come here!"—bridled because, of all things, he thought the ship really had the leading part.

Nevertheless, once the studio decided to make

the film, it spared no expense. It built seaworthy replicas not only of H.M.S. *Bounty* but also of the *Pandora*, the ship that sailed in search of the mutineers. And it mounted expensive expeditions to Tahiti and remote Pitcairn Island (where mutineers settled after seizing the *Bounty*)—not to mention prolonged location trips to Catalina Island some twenty miles off Los Angeles. It took three years to make the picture at a cost of $2,000,000—a lofty figure in those Depression days.

Although MGM used poetic license to strengthen some parts of the story, the movie generally was faithful to history. The film opens in 1787 with the *Bounty*, refitted as an armed transport, setting sail from England on a scientific expedition. Her mission is to transport breadfruit trees from the South Seas to the British West Indies as a cheap food for slave labor.

In command is Captain William Bligh, a harsh taskmaster. He sees that every infraction, however slight, is punished, testing his iron will against his disgruntled crew, who have been pressed into service from jails and taverns. Christian, his mate, does what he can to stop the bestial treatment. His appeals are in vain.

"They [the crew] respect one law—fear," Bligh says. Every shading of his voice reeks with diabolical evil. At one point, he tells a shipboard visitor, "If you think there is no science in a cat-o'-nine-tails, you should see my bos'n." Whenever Bligh summons his mate to the bridge with the ringing shout, "Mr. Christian, come here!" you know there is darkness ahead.

But the strain of Bligh's relentless brutality is relieved when the *Bounty* drops anchor in picturesque Tahiti. Compared with the shipboard treatment, the island seems like a utopian dream. Officers and men go ashore and live with native families. Some take native wives. Christian falls in love with Maimiti (Mamo Clark) and Byam with Tehani (Movita Castaneda).*

(Because of the screen's racial sensitivity, their paradise revels had to be done with the utmost delicacy. Anthropologists consider Polynesians members of the white race. But, *Variety* pointed out, whether they are so held by the public is another matter. Nevertheless, the trade journal said

this part of the movie was handled "with diplomacy. . . . It's all done so neatly, the kicks won't be numerous.")

After six months the idyll ends. The *Bounty* is at sea again and Bligh's cruelty resumes. One day Bligh insists on ordering the ship's elderly doctor, an alcoholic who is sick, to witness a flogging. The old man struggles topside and dies on deck.

For Christian, this is the breaking point. He leads the men in mutiny, setting Bligh and eighteen loyal men adrift in an open boat. "You're taking my ship," says Bligh, incredulously. "The King's ship," Christian corrects him. "And you're not fit to command."

Bligh is given a limited supply of food and drink, a sextant and nautical tables, a few tools and four cutlasses. But he is still full of vinegar. "Cast me adrift," cries Bligh as the *Bounty* sails off. "You think you're sending me to my doom, eh? Well, you're wrong. . . . I'll live to see you hang from the highest yardarm in the British fleet."

In what has gone down in history as one of the greatest open-boat voyages, Bligh sails forty-nine days to Timor in the Dutch East Indies. The trip covers 3,618 miles and not a man is lost.

The mutineers return to Tahiti. But a year later when Bligh returns (in real life it was another British skipper, Captain Edwards), some flee with male and female natives to find a hiding place. After sailing for weeks, they come upon barren Pitcairn Island about midway between Australia and Chile, far from all sea paths. There, in 1790, they burn and sink the *Bounty*.

Bligh arrests all crewmen on Tahiti—even those who, like Byam, had remained loyal but had not been put on the boat for lack of room. Bligh then sails after Christian but wrecks the *Pandora* on a reef.

At the mutiny trial in England, Byam makes a full disclosure of the cruelties Bligh imposed. In a dramatic speech, he appeals for British skippers to call men to duty "not by flogging their backs but by lifting their hearts." This is, in fact, one of the repercussions of the voyage. The upshot of the mutiny helped moderate the harsh sea laws of eighteenth-century England.

Nevertheless, the crew is sentenced to death. But the King pardons Byam and he rejoins the fleet. Although no measures are taken against Bligh, he receives the contempt of his peers.

The movie, with its stirring action and exotic setting, immediately drew long lines outside

---

* Movita Castaneda, a Latin beauty, later appeared in John Ford films and married Marlon Brando when he did the 1962 *Bounty*. They were later divorced.

theatres all over the country. Many were fascinated by Laughton's portrayal of Bligh and wondered if Bligh was really as bad as he was depicted.

History tells us that Christian, who was twenty-four when he joined the *Bounty*, had sailed with Bligh on two previous voyages. They were good friends and often ate together. In fact, on the day of the mutiny, Bligh invited him to his cabin for dinner. Some historians feel that Christian and others had fallen in love with their Tahitian sweethearts and had probably decided that life in the South Seas would be infinitely better than the life to which they were returning in England. Supporters of this theory feel that Bligh's own account of the incident is probably correct. Bligh wrote that the crew "has assured themselves of a more happy life among the Tahitians than they could possibly have in England, which, joined to some female connections, has most likely been the leading cause of the whole business."

On the basis of Bligh's own log and other records, Owen Rutter and other English writers concede that Bligh was quick-tempered, overbearing, tactless, irritable and profane. But, they feel, he was not the tyrannical marine monster Hollywood made him out to be.

Despite the gamble they made, life on Pitcairn turned out to be disastrous for all the mutineers but one. Four years after landing, a quarrel erupted over a woman—there were more men than women in the exile group—and the natives murdered all but four of the crew. Two of the survivors drank themselves to death. Another was put to death to safeguard the lives of the others. In 1814, when H.M.S. *Briton* anchored off the island, it found only one survivor of the mutiny—John Adams. He was not arrested and lived on Pitcairn until he died in 1829. Today about a hundred descendants of the mutineers still live on the tiny, three-mile island. One of them is named Fletcher Christian.

The mutiny had little effect on Bligh's career. He visited Tahiti again and successfully transported the breadfruit trees to the West Indies. He went on to fight gallantly in two naval battles and Lord Nelson wrote him a personal letter of thanks. In 1805 he became governor of New South Wales in Australia. He was so severe that he was taken prisoner in a military mutiny and shipped to England. Here again, the mutineers were found guilty. Later, Bligh was elevated to vice-admiral, and died in London at sixty-five. Today he lies buried in the churchyard of Lambeth Palace, home of the Archbishop of Canterbury.

Along with its box office success, *Mutiny* received widespread critical acclaim. All three of its stars—Laughton, Gable and Tone—won Oscar nominations, a record that still stands. In the final balloting, they lost out to Victor McLaglen (*The Informer*), but the movie itself took the best film Oscar.

What lingers in memory most is Laughton's villainous portrayal of the inflexible, acid-tongued skipper. Bligh was the hallmark of Laughton's long and distinguished career, a role with which he was always identified. Years later, when directors called him to the set they would do so with the shout he made famous—"Mr. Christian, come here!"

A close-up of Christian's defiant face.

The crew has mutinied and Bligh is tied to the mast.

Opposite, top:
Captain Bligh (Charles Laughton) orders Christian to sign the doctored log of ship's stores issued.

Bligh and men loyal to him are cut adrift in an open boat. But he still roars defiance: "I'll live to see you hang from the highest yardarm in the British fleet."

Opposite, left:
Midshipman Roger Byam (Franchot Tone) with his Tahitian sweetheart Tehani (Movita Castaneda).

Opposite, right:
Christian and his native girl friend Maimiti (Mamo Clark).

"I am She-Who-Must-Be-Obeyed" (Helen Gahagan).

(Photos by RKO RADIO PICTURES)
(Courtesy Alan G. Barbour)

She

(New York Premiere, July 25, 1935)

FROM THE NOVEL by H. Rider Haggard. Screen play by Ruth Rose. Additional dialogue, Dudley Nichols. Camera, J. Roy Hunt. Special effects, Vernon Walker. Music, Max Steiner. Dance director, Benjamin Zemach. Produced by Merian C. Cooper. Directed by Irving Pichel and Lansing C. Holden. An RKO Radio Picture. Running time, 96 minutes.

She	HELEN GAHAGAN
Leo Vincey	RANDOLPH SCOTT
Tanya Dugmore	HELEN MACK
Holly	NIGEL BRUCE
Billali	GUSTAV VON SEYFFERTITZ
John Vincey	SAMUEL HINDS
Amahagger Chief	NOBLE JOHNSON
Dugmore	LUMSDEN HARE
Captain of the Guards	JIM THORPE

For every youngster, there is one fantasy that hooks him for life, an adventure story so awesome it leaves an indelible mark in his memory. For some, that yarn is *Twenty Thousand Leagues Under the Sea*. For others it is, perhaps, *Treasure Island* or *The Wizard of Oz* or *Buck Rogers*. For me, it was H. Rider Haggard's *She*, a magnificent tale of a two-thousand-year-old priestess-queen from a forgotten civilization who tries to induce the descendant of her murdered lover to join her in immortality.

Looking back, you wonder how childhood judgments would stand up today. Probably they would quickly crumble. There is no room in the adult world for fantastic stories in which heroines are all beautiful, heroes brave and something exciting is happening every minute. But in those lost and simple days of yesteryear those were the only things that mattered. Story was all. And *She* had the beguiling magic to carry you into a mystical world far beyond the humdrum city streets of New York's West Side.

She was the second successful novel of Haggard, a British government worker, lawyer and agriculturist who had begun writing in earnest to win a bet. In discussing *Treasure Island* with one of his brothers, Haggard remarked that Stevenson's book wasn't so exceptional. His brother wagered he couldn't write one half as good. That very evening Haggard started the novel *King Solomon's Mines*. It met with instant success. Two years later he followed it with *She*. It received even wider acclaim.

To a Victorian public used to dull, prudish novels, the idea of an immortal white goddess fired the imagination. She was the supreme *femme fatale*, the cold, heartless beauty, the eternal pitiless woman—a devastating contrast to the pale, fainting heroine of the time. The book even attracted the interest of psychiatrist Carl Jung. He said *She* represented man's unconscious ideal of what woman ought to be—an unchanging beauty, a woman of eternal youth and supernatural powers.

In his lifetime—he died in 1925 at sixty-eight —Haggard wrote fifty-eight works of fiction and seven of economic, social and political history. But he lacked the serious writer's dedication. He wouldn't revise and polish, and his stories, however spellbinding, wind along in long convulsive sentences. In the end, he failed to win a lofty place among England's distinguished men of letters.

Nevertheless, an estimated two million persons have read *She*. Since it first appeared in 1887, it has never been out of print. Hollywood has done the movie at least four times—silent versions in 1917 and 1925, and talking versions in 1935 and 1965. The latter was in color and starred sex goddess Ursula Andress. But it turned out to be a disappointingly weak and lifeless production.

RKO made the most famous movie in 1935, a picture produced by Merian Cooper, who had co-authored and co-directed *King Kong*. Cooper picked Ruth Rose, one of *Kong*'s screen writers, to do the scenario. For the title role, he chose Helen Gahagan, a stage star who had never made a movie. Her face was not well known to screen audiences, and this helped the illusion.

Still, the casting left something to be desired. Miss Gahagan, a dark beauty from Brooklyn, was a woman of Junoesque proportions. Heywood Hale Broun called her "the ten most beautiful women in America." Her leading man was Randolph Scott, an actor so stiff and humorless he might have inspired the term "wooden Indian"—except that he played cowboys almost exclusively. Nigel Bruce makes vague stabs at comedy, usually ending up muttering his key lines down his sleeve.

But so grand were the dazzling special effects that all else seemed upstaged. The movie showed the collapse of a gigantic ice barrier, eye-filling sets crowded with massive gongs, Roman-like centurions and dancing girls. It had weird incantations, ceremonial hocus-pocus and sacrificial scenes—spectacle à la Cecil B. De Mille. For adventure purists, there was also dialogue in an unknown tongue. Some samples were: *moja* (yes), *haddo* (hurry), *na miza zacu* (you say nothing), *no kali do ixta* (you tried to kill them).

The film, which opened in New York at Radio City Music Hall, generally paralleled the novel except that it transported She's empire from equatorial Africa to the arctic wastes, somewhere north of Manchuria.

Leo Vincey (Scott), at the request of his dying uncle (Samuel Hinds), joins English scientist Archibald Holly (Bruce) in a search for an element of eternal life. According to family legend, one of Vincey's ancestors had discovered a fountain of life-giving flame—a fire so hot it preserves instead of destroys—in the wilds of remote Muscovy.

The expedition pushes into bleak, uncharted mountains. There they find Dugmore (Lumsden Hare), a trader, and his daughter Tanya (Helen Mack), who agree to guide them to the Sugal Barrier. Days later they encounter glacial cliffs and come upon the original Vincey expedition—except for Vincey himself—frozen inside one of them. Against orders, Dugmore tries to cut through. He starts an avalanche and tons of debris bury everyone except Leo, Holly and Tanya. The survivors trudge on until a savage horde captures them. Billali (Gustav von Seyffertitz), a high priest, stops the tribe from killing them and leads them into a subterranean, tropical land, called the Kingdom of Kor. There he takes Holly before She, ruler of this strange world, a woman of ethereal mystery.

"I say," Holly gasps, wiping his sweating brow. "Who are you?"

"I am yesterday and today and tomorrow," She tells him cryptically. "I am sorrow and longing and hope unfulfilled. I am She-Who-Must-Be-Obeyed."

(The name "She" comes from an old rag doll of Haggard's nursery days—a fact which probably inspired several Freudian masters' theses. Haggard called the doll simply "She." When he wrote his novel, he felt an immortal queen should not have a mortal name. So, remembering *his* favorite doll, his goddess became "She.")

In this awesome city of enormous temples and halls the explorers learn that She long ago had loved the original John Vincey. The exotic ruler has been waiting all these centuries for him to return to her reincarnated. She, who achieved immortality by bathing in the Flame of Life, had killed Vincey in a jealous rage and has kept his embalmed corpse until Leo, a grandson centuries removed, has turned up.

Then She destroys the corpse and implores Leo to bathe in the Flame and spend eternity with her. But Leo, who has fallen in love with Tanya, tells She he prefers to live briefly and happily with a mortal woman.

She orders Tanya slain as a sacrificial offering. At the last minute, Leo saves her. Then She takes the explorers to the Flame and orders Leo to walk into it. When he hesitates, She steps in it for the second time in her long life to prove it will not destroy. Momentarily, She seems more beautiful than ever. Flames leap around her and She looks down on Tanya triumphantly. "Your hair will whiten," She says. "Your cheeks will wrinkle . . . while I defy the years."

But when She steps from the Flame, she falters. The things she has predicted for Tanya have begun happening to her. The divine beauty has turned into a shriveled old woman. Horrified, Tanya, Leo and Holly watch as She crumples at their feet. Lying on the ground, her mummylike head searches for Leo with sightless eyes. The blackened lips rasp two words—"My love." Then She melts into a mass of rotting flesh.

She received mixed notices. Most reviewers felt RKO had failed to achieve the novel's potential. For one thing, the production never changed pace to give contrast to its dead-serious theme. For another, RKO shot the tale amidst a background of stagy devices whose studio origin was all too obvious. Despite its faults, other critics said kids would love it.

Perhaps the most interesting footnote to the film is its star, Miss Gahagan. She had a remarkably versatile career. Before coming to Hollywood, she went to Barnard College in New York City for two years. In 1922 she went on the stage, appearing in many plays, including John Van Druten's *Young Woodley.*

At the peak of her career she astonished the theatrical world by announcing she was going to study opera. She later sang throughout Europe and in Broadway musicals before returning to the theatre. During her comeback, she met and married her leading man, Melvyn Douglas. They had three children.

Then, in 1944, Helen Gahagan Douglas launched her second career. She won election to Congress, starting a trend of actors in politics that twenty years later would be followed by Ronald Reagan and George Murphy. A liberal, she became known as a hard worker, a champion of the underprivileged and an eloquent speaker. She won re-election in 1946 and 1948.

In 1950 she ran for the Senate. Her opponent was another up-and-coming congressman—Richard M. Nixon. In a bitter campaign which politicians still discuss, Nixon circulated "pink sheets" describing the voting record of the "pink lady." These were the McCarthy days, and Nixon accused his opponent of voting the same way as notorious New York radical Vito Marcantonio 354 times. Little was said of the fact that many others in Congress had also agreed with Marcantonio that many times. Nixon won by 700,000 votes. But many feel it blemished his image as a clean campaigner.

The defeat marked the end of Miss Gahagan's political career and, in effect, her public career as well. Even her work in *She*—which some critics felt had amounted to an impressive screen debut—is no longer seen. The film appeared in a revival double feature with *The Last Days of Pompeii* (1935) in the late 1940s. But with the dissolution of RKO in 1953, all prints seem to have disappeared.

So *She* remains only in memory. Which is, perhaps, just as well. Seen from the adult world, the childhood illusion is certain to be cruelly shattered. But no youngster who marveled at the radiant guardian of the Flame of Life is likely to forget her.

In the awesome temple rooms of the Kingdom of Kor.

Holly (Nigel Bruce), Tanya (Helen Mack) and Leo Vincey (Randolph Scott) are captives of the Amahagger savages and their chief (Noble Johnson).

She and Tanya watch over an unconscious Leo.

Leo learns the story of his ancestor, John Vincey, from She.

The ageless ruler of this strange world asks Leo to join her in immortality.

Tanya is about to be offered as a sacrifice at the Ceremony of the Flame.

The Geste brothers in French Morocco as soldiers in the Foreign Legion.

Beau Geste

(Released July 24, 1939)

SCREEN PLAY by Robert Carson from the novel by Percival Christopher Wren. Art directors, Hans Dreier and Robert Odell. Musical score, Alfred Newman. Cameraman, Theodore Sparkuhl. Editor, Thomas Scott. Directed and produced by William A. Wellman for Paramount. Running time, 120 minutes.

Beau Geste	GARY COOPER
John Geste	RAY MILLAND
Digby Geste	ROBERT PRESTON
Sergeant Markoff	BRIAN DONLEVY
Isobel Rivers	SUSAN HAYWARD
Rasinoff	J. CARROLL NAISH
Major Henri de Beaujolais	JAMES STEPHENSON
Lady Patricia Brandon	HEATHER THATCHER
Augustus Brandon	GEORGE P. HUNTLEY
Beau Geste (as child)	DONALD O'CONNOR
John Geste (as child)	BILLY COOK
Digby Geste (as child)	MARTIN SPELLMAN
Isobel Rivers (as child)	ANN GILLIS
Augustus Brandon (as child)	DAVID HOLT
Lieutenant Martin	HARVEY STEPHENS
Maris	STANLEY ANDREWS
Renoir	HARRY WOODS
Dufour	JAMES BURKE
Schwartz	ALBERT DEKKER
Hank Miller	BRODERICK CRAWFORD
Buddy McMonigal	CHARLES BARTON

(*Beau Geste* was first made in 1926 with Ronald Colman as Beau and Noah Beery as the tyrannical sergeant. The third version in 1966 had Guy Stockwell and Telly Savalas in the roles, but much of the original plot was dropped.)

The closing scene of a great movie from the thirties and forties is often so dramatic, its last lines are remembered as long as the title itself. But few opening scenes of movies from these decades have been engrossing enough to stay in memory. Think about it. You probably can recall no more than a handful.

For obvious reasons, directors wanted their pictures to end with a socko finale, one that would stay with audiences long after they left the theatre. The job of the opening scene was merely to set the stage and get things rolling. And so its potential was generally overlooked and wasted. And, in fact, it was not until the 1950s that movie makers began hooking audiences with melodramatic starts bursting on the screen even before titles flashed.

One movie that upset this comfortable framework was *Beau Geste*. It begins, instead of ends, with a thrilling, hauntingly puzzling episode. The film grips the audience from the very first frames. The camera work is so resourceful that the picture packs more mystery and suspense in the first five minutes than other movies often achieve in an hour. The movie has, in my opinion, the most engrossing opening of any picture made in the 1930s.

The wind blows gently across an ocean of sand that is the vast Sahara. There is utter silence in the great African desert until a relief party of the French Foreign Legion is seen arriving at Fort Zinderneuf.

Through his field glasses, Major de Beaujolais (James Stephenson) sees a soldier in every embrasure, each with his rifle cocked for action. The tricolor flies. But the only response to his bugler's call is a shot that kicks up sand. Cautiously, the major rides close to the walls. There he finds the fort's defenders staring with blank eyes. They are dead to the last man.

He sends the bugler over the wall. But, strangely, he fails to return. When the major himself scales the wall, he discovers the dead body of Sergeant Markoff (Brian Donlevy), who had been in command. A French bayonet has been driven through his heart. Nearby lies the body of a legionnaire, reverentially laid out—his eyes closed, his hands folded on his chest.

The major opens the gate and calls for volunteers to make a further inspection. When he re-enters the fort, he is astonished to discover that the bodies of the sergeant and legionnaire are both gone. As he withdraws, intending to take a closer look in the morning, the fort bursts into flame. Suddenly, an alarm sounds. Arabs are attacking. The matter is forgotten as the troops fight for their lives.

Such is the mystery of Zinderneuf, the silent fort-tomb. Its unfolding is the theme of *Beau Geste*.

The story comes from the pen of Percival Christopher Wren, an English novelist who was a trooper in the British cavalry and served in North Africa with the French Foreign Legion. Wren, who retired with the rank of major in the British army, looked more like an officer than a writer. Tall and soldierly in bearing, he wore a monocle and had a military mustache. He made little impact on the literary world until he wrote *Beau Geste* in 1924. It was a smashing success as a book, play and movie—a success Wren never quite repeated.

The original film version, directed by Herbert Brenon in 1926, had Ronald Colman as Beau and Noah Beery as the cruel sergeant. It became a classic of the silent screen. Robert Carson's 1939 adaptation cast Gary Cooper in the title role with Brian Donlevy as Markoff, and paralleled the action of the old version almost sequence for sequence.

In fact, in a bold attempt to show how far movies had advanced in thirteen years, Paramount showed the first reel of the 1926 film to reviewers before screening *Beau Geste* number two. The plan nearly backfired.

Howard Barnes, critic for the New York *Herald Tribune*, said the talkie couldn't compare with the silent version. "Where dialogue might have been expected to strengthen the personal drama, the opposite is true," Barnes wrote. *Time* said *Beau Geste* II "follows its original so relentlessly, it resembles nothing so much as a talking mummy."

But *Newsweek* felt it was precisely because the 1939 edition so closely resembles the earlier film that it "graphically demonstrates the great strides made in screen techniques since the advent of sound." The New York *World-Telegram* also found the new product superior. "It seems to me that acting has improved," the paper said. "The over-emphasis of pantomime is not needed to establish a point or a thought. The action is more rapid. For where pantomime required minutes of silent explanation to convey its thought, one staccato command or two sentences of dialogue will suffice."

Whoever was right, it must be acknowledged that the talkie version made it possible to hear the stirring bugles, the bullets zinging against the old fort and the shrieks of the poor devils wincing under Markoff's heavy hand. And the mysteries posed at the outset are still every bit as intriguing. Who fired the shot from the fort? What happened to the bugler? Was Markoff bayoneted by one of his own men? Where did the bodies go? And how did the fire start?

The story flashes back fifteen years to Brandon Abbey, an English estate, where John (Ray Milland), Digby (Robert Preston) and Michael "Beau" Geste (Gary Cooper) are raised as wards of their aunt, Lady Patricia Brandon (Heather Thatcher). (None other than Donald O'Connor plays the twelve-year-old Beau, who, by the way, gets this nickname for his charm and good looks.)

The brothers are a close-knit bunch with strong all-for-one-and-one-for-all loyalties. Their favorite games are soldiers and sailors and knights in armor. Imbued with ideals of chivalry and honor, Beau asks his brothers to give him a Viking's funeral when he is dead—a pyre in the center of his ship, with his spear and shield laid beside him, his horse and hound at his feet.

Lady Brandon owns a magnificent sapphire, a family heirloom, called the Blue Water. One day Beau overhears her talking in low tones with a maharajah about the jewel.

The story jumps several years. The Geste brothers are now grown. Lady Brandon is married to a dissolute husband, Hector Brandon, and a day comes when he demands that she sell the sapphire to pay off his debts.

The stone is brought to the table. Suddenly the lights go out. When they come on, the gem is gone. Lady Brandon orders the room darkened again so the guilty person can replace the jewel. But the stone is still missing when the lights return.

Beau, Digby and John disappear, each leaving a note to say he was the thief. Each has tried to prevent the other from being involved in a family disgrace. Separately, they join the Foreign Legion and are reunited in French Morocco. But they come under the harsh Sergeant Markoff, who breaks up the trio. He sends Digby to a remote desert post. Beau and John he keeps at Zinderneuf.

Markoff lives up to his reputation as a cruel taskmaster. He beats and even maims his men to enforce his iron will. At one point he nails Private Rasinoff (J. Carroll Naish) to a table with bayonets after Rasinoff is caught snatching Beau's money belt. But Rasinoff also overhears the Gestes talking about the stolen sapphire and, to lighten his punishment, he tells Markoff about the fabulous gem. The sergeant determines to get it. In the meantime, his men have been driven to the brink of mutiny and Markoff is about to take stern measures to quell the impending revolt when Arabs attack the fort.

Most of Markoff's men are killed early in the battle. But he props them up in place and fires from behind each to bluff the attackers into believing the fort is still well defended.

Still the Arabs press the attack. One by one the legionnaires go down, including Beau, leaving only John and Markoff. Then the Arabs withdraw and Markoff sends the exhausted John down for coffee. John warns him not to touch Beau's body. But when John returns he sees Markoff rifling Beau's pockets. John pulls a bayonet. Markoff is about to shoot him when Beau, thought to be dead, clutches Markoff's feet with one convulsive movement. Markoff is off balance for an instant. And John runs him through with his bayonet.

At that point the relief battalion arrives at Zinderneuf. If he stays, John knows he will be court-martialed for Markoff's slaying. So he fires a shot to give him time to escape. The bugler sent over the wall is Digby Geste. He finds Beau dead, but no trace of John. Remembering Beau's childhood wish for a Viking's funeral, Digby hides while the major makes his first inspection. When the major leaves to get volunteers, Digby carries the bodies of Markoff and Beau into the barracks and prepares a bier. He puts a dog (symbolized by the body of Markoff) at the feet of the Viking (Beau) and builds a funeral pyre that also burns down the fort.

Digby then escapes over the back wall and finds John in the desert. They run into two legionnaires sent back for reinforcements. They become lost, and one of their two camels dies. Later, an Arab kills Digby.

The final scene is in England on the Brandon estate, where John hands Lady Brandon a letter from Beau.

When you get this I shall be dead. And I hope, forgiven for doing what I thought was best. I knew you had sold the Blue Water to the maharajah for our benefit. And when Uncle Hector's letter came, I knew things would be desperate for you when he discovered the substitution . . . so I stole the imitation. . . . I can only pray that I have helped you a little.

With sincerest gratitude for all you have done for us,

Your loving and admiring nephew,
"BEAU" GESTE

"If he had only waited . . . ," Lady Brandon says. "Sir Hector was drowned while on his yacht." She puts a handkerchief to her eyes and adds quietly, "A *beau geste* [beautiful gesture] indeed."

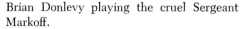

Brian Donlevy playing the cruel Sergeant Markoff.

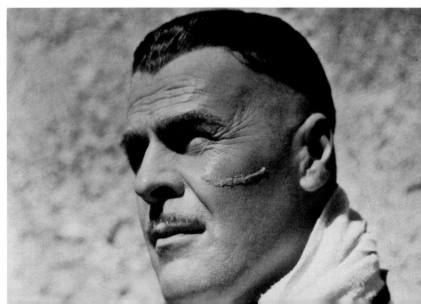

Gary Cooper as Beau Geste of the French Foreign Legion.

The three Geste brothers—Digby (Robert Preston), Beau and John (Ray Milland)— with Isobel Rivers (Susan Hayward) a pretty ward of their aunt, Lady Brandon.

Sergeant Markoff orders cowardly Private Rasinoff (J. Carroll Naish) to take lookout duty in the highest turret.

Fort Zinderneuf under attack by Arab legions.

Like a mirror image, a pool reflects night lights in the Valley of the Blue Moon.

Diplomat-writer Robert Conway (Ronald Colman) finds that the pilot who crash-landed their plane is dead.

(Photos by Columbia)

92

Lost Horizon

(Released September 1, 1937)

A SCREEN DRAMA by Robert Riskin based on the James Hilton novel. Musical score by Dimitri Tiomkin. Musical director, Morris Stoloff. Photography by Joseph Walker. Aerial photographer, Elmer Dyer. Special camera effects, E. Roy Davidson and Ganahl Carson. Technical editor, Harrison Forman. Film editing, Gene Havlick * and Gene Milford.* Art director, Stephen Goosson.* Produced and directed by Frank Capra. Presented by Columbia Pictures. Running time, 125 minutes.

Robert Conway	RONALD COLMAN
Sondra Bizet	JANE WYATT
George Conway	JOHN HOWARD
Lovett	EDWARD EVERETT HORTON
Gloria Stone	ISABEL JEWELL
Chang	H. B. WARNER
High Lama	SAM JAFFE
Maria	MARGO
Barnard	THOMAS MITCHELL
Lord Gainsford	HUGH BUCKLER
Prime Minister	DAVID TORRENCE

When General Doolittle bombed Japan from a secret base in World War II, President Roosevelt told the nation the planes had taken off from "Shangri-La." Although it was a name coined less than ten years before, the fictional locale needed no elaboration. Everyone knew FDR was talking about James Hilton's mythical hidden kingdom. First the novel and then the movie made this mountain paradise a household word.

Shangri-La. No other fantasy place so vividly captured the public's imagination. The High Lama. The timeless Valley of the Blue Moon. A garden of contentment. A serene lamasery where doves fly and the air is crystal clear and a man's life goes on

---

* Academy Award winners.

untroubled for hundreds of years. For millions, it fulfilled their fondest dream of utopia.

As soon as director Frank Capra read the book, he wanted to do the movie. "It held a mirror up to the thoughts of every human being on earth," Capra said.

It had taken Hilton six weeks to write his novel. It was to take Capra nearly two years to film it. The first challenge was the re-creation of Shangri-La. The set was one of the largest ever built in Hollywood. One hundred and fifty workmen labored two months. In a space more than 1,000 feet long and 500 feet wide they put up a huge lamasery surrounded by a great patio and distant mountains. Soaring flights of marble stairways glided to pavilions that stood amidst luxuriant gardens, sweeping terraces and lily-covered pools.

The smallest role—that of the High Lama—brought the biggest headache. He appears only once, but it is a crucial scene because the story's credibility rests on the two-hundred-and-fifty-year-old patriarch. Capra's first two choices—old screen favorites A. E. Anson and Henry B. Walthall—each died before they could go before the camera. For a time Charles Laughton was considered. Finally Sam Jaffe, a great character actor who two years later would portray Gunga Din, got the part.

Capra thought he played the part perfectly. But Harry Cohn, Columbia's president, said his make-up left him looking grotesque rather than a figure of fatherliness. So Capra reshot the scene with Walter Connolly in the High Lama's robes. When the picture was shown to preview audiences, they picked Jaffe.

The easiest task proved to be casting the leading role—Robert Conway, the courageous, debonair British consul. Capra had Ronald Colman in mind from the start.

With a certain sadness in his melancholy-tinged voice, Colman projected an aura of dignity. Someone said he left you wondering what secret sorrow lay deep in his heart. Suave, gallant, utterly charming, he was the very personification of an English gentlemen.

(Even in his middle years, women were to find his darkly attractive features irresistible. In 1935, fifty-one female stars voted for the handsomest man on the screen. Colman, who was then forty-four won with twenty-two votes. Gable was a distant second with eight. Fredric March had seven.)

The story centers around Robert Conway, British writer and Far Eastern diplomat. Caught in a Chinese rebellion, he and his brother (John Howard) are evacuating Europeans before an approaching horde of bandits. The two get out on the last plane along with a fugitive swindler (Thomas Mitchell), a fossil expert (Edward Everett Horton) and a consumptive girl (Isabel Jewell). They soon discover that their plane is going in the wrong direction. The pilot, an oriental, is taking them over mountainous Tibet, the roof of the world.

Deep in the snow-capped Himalayas, the plane crashes. The passengers are unhurt but the pilot is dead. Days go by in the bitter cold. Just when it all looks hopeless, a caravan appears led by an elderly Chinese named Chang (H. B. Warner), who seems to be expecting them. He takes them over miles of icy, treacherous cliffs. Incredibly, the rugged mountains give way to a magnificently beautiful land. Chang says it is called the Valley of the Blue Moon. Warm and fertile, the valley is the site of the lamasery of Shangri-La.

(Despite the care Capra gave the set, it received a mixed reaction among critics. *Newsweek* told its readers they might find Shangri-La's modernistic architecture jarring. Howard Barnes, reviewer for the New York *Herald Tribune*, felt that impressionistic backgrounds would have been more plausible. But *Time* called the re-creation "one of the most magnificent sets in cinema history.")

Conway and the others are given luxurious rooms and extended every courtesy. They find Shangri-La a land where greed, war and crimes are unknown. Instead, beauty and love and gentleness abound and people never seem to grow old. Chang, the High Lama's chief disciple, tells Conway that a Belgian missionary, a Father Perrault, founded Shangri-La in 1713 as a contemplative refuge. The peaceful valley's rule has become moderation in all earthly wants, Chang says.

As time passes, Conway meets and falls in love with Sondra (Jane Wyatt), a lovely girl who lives in the escapist enclave. But the new visitors find they cannot leave and one day the High Lama (Jaffe) calls Conway.

As the wise old man talks, Conway realizes the High Lama and Father Perrault are the same person. The elderly Lama is more than two hundred years old. He says he is dying and, impressed by Conway's idealistic writings, has chosen Conway to succeed him.

The ancient leader says Shangri-La's mission is to bring order to the world after its mad orgy of wars. "Against that time is why I avoided death and am here and why you were brought here," the High Lama says. "For when that day comes, the world must begin to look for a new life and it is our hope that they may find it here.

"For here we shall be with their books and their music and a way of life based on one simple rule—be kind. When that day comes, it is our hope that the brotherly love of Shangri-La will spread throughout the world."

Conway is won over. But his brother doesn't believe the High Lama is Father Perrault and plans to leave with Maria (Margo), a Russian girl who looks twenty but who Chang says is sixty. If she leaves, Chang says, she will quickly grow old. When Margo claims the High Lama and Chang are crazy and says she hates living in Shangri-La, Conway's faith is shaken.

Maria has bribed some porters and Conway slips away with her and his brother. But the expedition fails when the porters are killed in an avalanche. As the three survivors plod on, Maria's face begins to wither. The forced march across the wind-swept Tibetan slopes tires her and that night they find she is dying, a wrinkled hag. The sight of her horribly creased face is one of the picture's most memorable scenes.

In a fit of remorse, Conway's brother throws himself off a cliff. Conway trudges on to a native village. His memory fails and British officials start taking him to England. Suddenly he remembers Shangri-La and runs away to try to return.

The scene shifts to a London club where Lord Gainsford (Hugh Buckler), an explorer who has tried to find Conway, proposes a toast. "Here is my hope that Robert Conway will find his Shangri-La. Here is my hope that we all find our Shangri-La."

It is here that the book and the movie have a major point of departure. The book ends without

94

our ever knowing if Conway reaches Shangri-La. But the movie's final scene shows Conway struggling through snow and ice toward the entrance to the Valley of the Blue Moon.

The film received wide critical acclaim and got an Academy Award nomination although it lost out in the final balloting to *The Life of Emile Zola*. But Colman's career continued with even greater success. Among his many fine films were *The Prisoner of Zenda* (1937), *Random Harvest* (1942) and *A Double Life* (1948). For his performance as a schizophrenic actor in the latter, he won an Oscar.

Colman had one of Hollywood's most durable careers. In 1950, film workers, voting in a *Variety* poll, placed Colman and Laurence Olivier as runners-up to Charlie Chaplin as "best actor of the half century."

Two legends persist. One says that he insisted in his contracts that his name alone be given star billing above a film's title. The other was that he was frank, direct and eminently courteous in his dealings with the press. A man of good taste, culture and grace in private life, he died in 1958 after being hospitalized with a lung infection. He was sixty-seven.

Perhaps the most lasting monument to his career is the universality he helped give Hilton's mystic retreat. Today, Shangri-La has come into general usage. Webster's Third International Unabridged Dictionary gives it two meanings. It defines Shangri-La as (1) a remote, beautiful, imaginary place where life approaches perfection and (2) a place whose name is not known or not given.

The weary travelers arrive in the mountain paradise of Shangri-La, somewhere in the Himalayas.

Conway and Chang (H. B. Warner), who introduces Conway and his companions to the mysteries of Shangri-La.

Conway meets Sondra Bizet (Jane Wyatt), who has lived for years in this land of contentment where aging has slowed down.

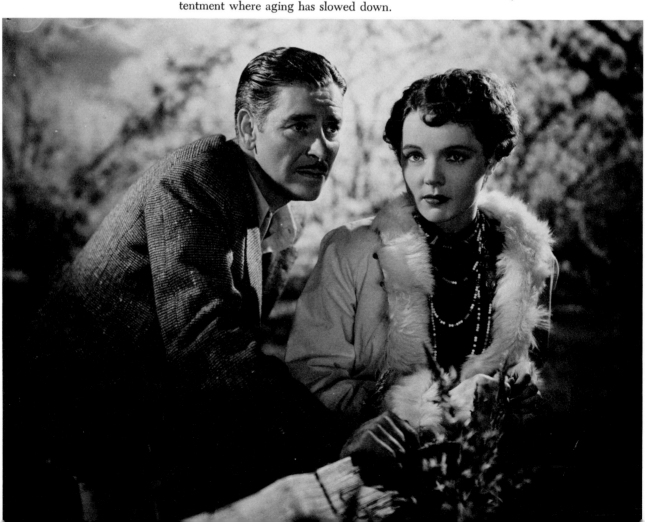

Chang tells the visitors they cannot leave. Partially obscured by Colman is Thomas Mitchell. Edward Everett Horton is third from left. At right, seated, is John Howard.

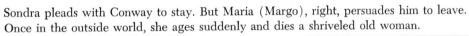

Sondra pleads with Conway to stay. But Maria (Margo), right, persuades him to leave. Once in the outside world, she ages suddenly and dies a shriveled old woman.

Pancho Villa (Wallace Beery) and his guerrillas gather round a fire in their mountain hideout. Sierra (Leo Carrillo), Villa's chief aide, is shaving. That's newspaperman Johnny Sykes (Stuart Erwin) without the belt of bullets. Next to Sykes is Chavito (George E. Stone) with melancholy expression.

Villa eyes Teresa (Fay Wray) suspiciously at a party at her hacienda.

Viva Villa

(Released April 27, 1934)

SUGGESTED BY THE BOOK by Edgcumb Pinchon and O. B. Stade. Screen play by Ben Hecht. Music by Herbert Stothart. Film editor, Robert J. Kern. Photography, James Wong Howe and Charles G. Clarke. Produced by David O. Selznick. Directed by Jack Conway. Assistant directors, Art Rosson, Johnny Waters.* Released by MGM. Running time, 115 minutes.

Pancho Villa	WALLACE BEERY
Teresa	FAY WRAY
Johnny Sykes	STUART ERWIN
Sierra	LEO CARRILLO
Don Felipe	DONALD COOK
Chavito	GEORGE E. STONE
General Pascal	JOSEPH SCHILDKRAUT
Madero	HENRY B. WALTHALL
Rosita	KATHERINE DE MILLE
Bugle Boy	DAVID DURAND
Villa as a boy	PHILLIP COOPER
Villa's father	FRANK PUGLIA
Pascal's aide	JOHN MERKEL
Staff	CHARLES STEVENS, STEVE CLEMENTO, PEDRO REGAS
Old Man	CARLOS DE VALDEZ
Majordomo	HARRY CORDING
Prosecuting Attorney	SAM GODFREY
Judge	NIGEL DE BRULIER
Grandees	CHARLES REQUA and TOM RICKETTS
Jail official	CLARENCE H. WILSON
Mexican officer	JAMES MARTIN
Dancer	ANITA GORDIANA
Villa's man	FRANCIS MC DONALD
Soldier	HARRY SEMELS

---

* Academy Award winner.

Telegraph operator	JULIAN RIVERO
Bartender	BOB MC KENZIE
Drunk	DAN DIX
Newspaperman	PAUL STANTON
Military attaché	MISCHA AUER
Wife	BELLE MITCHELL
Statesmen	JOHN DAVIDSON, BRANDON HURST, LEONARD MUDIE
Generals	HERBERT PRIOR, EMILE CHAUTARD
Mendoza brothers	HENRY ARMETTA, ADRIAN ROSLEY, HECTOR V. SARNO
Calloway	RALPH BUSHMAN (FRANCIS X. BUSHMAN, JR.)
English reporter	ARTHUR TREACHER
German reporter	WILLIAM VON BRINCKEN
French reporter	ANDRÉ CHERON
Russian reporter	MICHAEL VISAROFF
Wrong girl	SHIRLEY CHAMBERS
Butcher	ARTHUR THALASSO
Peons	CHRIS-PIN MARTIN, NICK DE RUIZ
Don Rodrigo	GEORGE REGAS
Man	LEON WHITE

An assassin's bullet rips through the body of Wallace Beery, playing Pancho Villa, the fiery Mexican revolutionary. Mortally wounded, the big guy lies in the arms of his lifelong pal, newspaper reporter Johnny Sykes (Stuart Erwin).

"I hear about big men what they say when they die," Beery says. "You write something very big about me."

"I'll write about how Pancho Villa died with a medal that had once been given him for the rescue of Mexico still around his neck," Sykes says, consoling the illiterate bandit hero.

"What else, Johnny?" Beery asks, his life slipping with every breath.

"The peons," says the newspaperman. "From north and south, the peons who had loved him came to see him . . ."

"That's fine, Johnny," says Beery. "You tell me more."

"Pancho Villa spoke for the last time. He said, he said . . ."

"Hurry, Johnny. Johnny. What were my last words?"

" 'Good-by, my Mexico,' said Pancho Villa. 'Forgive me for my crimes. Remember, if I sinned against you, it was because I loved you too much.' "

Beery isn't smiling. His brow is furrowed. His face has a puzzled look. "Forgive me?" gasps the marauder who has killed a thousand men. "Johnny, what I done wrong?"

Wallace Beery. Tough, but oh, so gentle. As Pancho Villa—the murderous but childlike guerrilla who cannot believe killing is sinful when the cause is just—he was at the crest of a long acting career. More than 250 pictures. They spanned four decades of silent and talking films.

For a six-foot-one-inch, 240-pound actor whose bearlike appearance set him distinctly apart, his versatility was remarkable. Beery played roles ranging from a servant girl to a pirate. He was a hardened convict in *The Big House* (1930), a washed-up fighter idolized by young Jackie Cooper in *The Champ* (1931), for which Beery won an Oscar.

In the memorable *Min and Bill* (1930) he teamed with Marie Dressler and played a waterfront ruffian. In *Grand Hotel* (1932) he was a German industrial magnate. He was a shrewd businessman in *Dinner at Eight* (1933), a harbor skipper in *Tugboat Annie* (1933), again with Marie Dressler, and Long John Silver in *Treasure Island* (1934). He played the title role in *The Mighty Barnum* (1934) and a cowboy in *Wyoming* (1940) with Marjorie Main, who became his latter-day co-star.

Beery was born in 1889 in Kansas City, Missouri, the son of a policeman. Wallace, who was big even as a boy—his friends called him Jumbo—never liked school. He got as far as the fourth grade where he stayed for two years. One day he ran away and became a corn shucker in Illinois. (He saved enough for a pair of yellow shoes and came home briefly just to show them off.) He was a railroad section hand and an elephant trainer with Ringling Brothers Circus.

But he had a fine baritone voice, and after a while, he joined his brother Noah, who had become a chorus boy in a Broadway show. In less than a year Beery replaced Raymond Hitchcock as the star in *The Yankee Tourist* and toured the country. It was in 1913 that he decided to try a movie career and signed with the Essanay Company. One of his earliest roles was, of all things, that of a Swedish housemaid in a series of shorts based on the "Swedie" character. It was a burlesque part and it became one of his nicknames among his intimates.

After a tour as a comedian in Keystone pictures, Beery married Gloria Swanson, an extra at the time. They were divorced two years later in 1918 but remained good friends. Beery was remarried in 1924 to Rita Gillman. They had no children so he adopted the eighteen-month-old daughter of a friend. He was devoted to the girl, Carol Ann Beery, and later willed her a generous portion of his estate. She appeared in a number of his movies, including *China Seas* (1935).

In 1917, Beery played a villain for the first time. That launched a series of bad-guy parts in such silent films as *The Lost World, The Three Musketeers* and *Robin Hood*.

When talkies began in the late 1920s, he returned to leading roles, generally cast as a kind of tame bulldog whose bark was far worse than his bite. His greatest pictures followed, including *Viva Villa!* a robust spectacle that included some of the most sadistic and bloodthirsty footage filmed to that day.

To get that footage, the film company had more than its share of trouble. In shooting on location in Mexico, Lee Tracy, originally cast as the reporter, drew the wrath of authorities when he had some drinks and shouted from his hotel window at Mexican troops parading by. This was bad business because the Mexican government was providing a guard of federal soldiers to escort the film expedition deep into the interior. Tracy was sent home and replaced by Stuart Erwin, noted for his comic but not his dramatic talent. And so the part was rewritten and weakened considerably.

Returning with thousands of feet of film, an airplane crashed, destroying weeks of work. Howard Hawks, the director, was replaced, apparently because of a disagreement over his interpretation of Villa's part. A second director took sick and a third, Jack Conway, rushed in to do the job.

Finally, Mexican officials objected to Beery,

whom they considered a comic actor, playing the role of their swashbuckling national hero. But here MGM stuck to its guns and refused to withdraw him.

The movie, largely fictitious, opens with a soldier whipping to death Pancho Villa's father. The elder Villa had protested the seizure of the peons' land by the tyrant Porfirio Diaz. The young boy watches and later he avenges his father by knifing the soldier and then fleeing to the hills.

There he grows up to lead a wild band of fighters who sweep down on the haciendas and towns, slaughtering and robbing landowners, but giving relief to the poor. On one of these raids the illiterate Villa runs into Sykes, an American newspaperman, and they begin a lifelong friendship.

Later, Villa is called to the hacienda of aristocratic Don Felipe de Castillo (Donald Cook) and his lovely sister Teresa (Fay Wray), who are sympathetic to the rebel cause. They introduce Villa to Francisco Madero (Henry B. Walthall), intellectual leader of the peon revolt, who persuades Villa to use his fighters as the élite core of an army to overthrow Diaz.

With his faithful lieutenant Sierra (Leo Carrillo)—who kills three prisoners with one bullet to avoid wasting ammunition—Villa unleashes a bloody campaign. He joins with General Pascal (Joseph Schildkraut). But Villa doesn't trust the ambitious, army-trained officer and won't take orders. Villa's savage warriors overrun the federal forces. Diaz abdicates and Villa proclaims Madero president. When he has assumed power, Madero gently tells Villa that he and his undisciplined men aren't needed any more. He advises Villa to disband his army and return home. Pascal will be Madero's adviser.

Once home, Villa quickly gets into trouble. Through ignorance, he thinks banks exist merely to hand out money. When a teller tries to stop him from helping himself, Villa blackjacks him, killing him. Pascal, seizing his chance to do away with a hated rival, orders a firing squad. Madero gives Villa a last-minute pardon on condition he leave the country. But before releasing him, Pascal humbles Villa by making him crawl on his knees.

When Villa goes into exile, Pascal assassinates Madero and takes over. However, Villa returns to launch a second revolution. This time there is no Madero to temper him and Villa's bloodthirsty peons run amuck.

Teresa and her wealthy brother refuse to join Villa this time. Stung, Villa attacks her, and she shoots him in the arm. He makes her bandage his wound. But she pulls it so tight, he grunts in pain. Furious, he strikes her a blow in the face that seems so powerful it could fell a man. Blood trickles from her mouth and she curses him. "Now I know why it was music to my people to hear the peons' cry," she says, recalling how the landowners whipped the peons mercilessly. Villa pulls out a heavy whip and lashes her. She only laughs scornfully. Seconds later, one of Villa's men accidentally shoots her and she dies.

In another sadistic scene, Villa captures Pascal and avenges himself by having his men pour honey on the general, then leaving him to be eaten alive by ants. "Pour it on his hair, his eyes, his nose," says Villa. "Put it every place on him. . . . He screams much louder and longer than I did."

Villa becomes President. But his crass ignorance makes his reign a short one. He retires to his ranch. One day he comes to the city and runs into his old chum Johnny Sykes. As they are talking, Teresa's brother spots Villa from a building across the street and cuts him down with a rifle barrage. In the arms of Sykes, Villa dies in a butcher shop, his childlike mind failing to understand that his well-intentioned life has also been stained by sins.

Beery received excellent notices. And the movie drew generally favorable reviews, although some critics took exception to the gore. The film was one of the nominees for the 1934 Academy Award, which was won by *It Happened One Night*.

In his later years Beery spent much of his time on his ranches in the Jackson Hole country of Wyoming and in Idaho. He died suddenly in 1949 at his home in Beverly Hills, California, suffering a heart attack.

Louis B. Mayer, head of MGM, served as a pallbearer at his funeral at the Church of the Recessional in Hollywood. "Perhaps Wally's most outstanding characteristics to those who knew him best," said the Rev. Ross Shaffer, "were his childlikeness, his enthusiasm and his great warmth."

Villa with Mexican President Francisco Madero (Henry B. Walthall) and General Pascal (Joseph Schildkraut).

Exiled in Texas, Villa reads that his friend Madero has been assassinated. Sykes looks on.

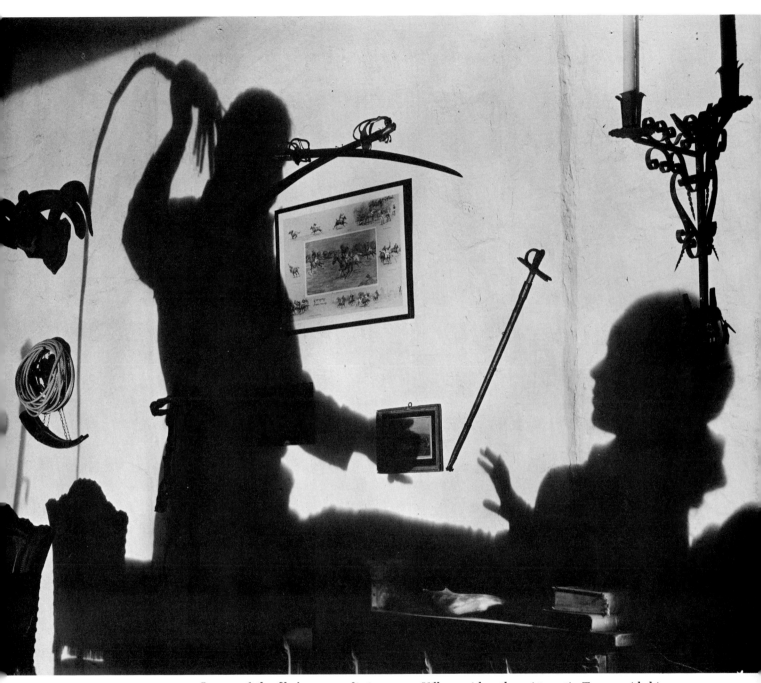

In one of the film's most sadistic scenes, Villa punishes the aristocratic Teresa with his bullwhip after she and her family have refused to help his rebellion. The lashing is shown through their shadows cast on the wall.

Buster Crabbe as Flash Gordon, hero of the Universe.

(Photos by Universal)

Flash Gordon

(Released April 6, 1936)

UNIVERSAL'S RELEASE of Henry MacRae's thirteen-part serial. Based on Alex Raymond's cartoon strip. Screen play by Frederick Stephani, George Plympton, Basil Dickey and Ella O'Neill. Art director, Ralph Berger. Electrical effects, Norman Drewes. Special properties, Elmer A. Johnson. Camera, Jerry Ash, Richard Fryer. Directed by Stephani. Running time each episode about 20 minutes.

Flash	LARRY (BUSTER) CRABBE
Dale	JEAN ROGERS
Ming	CHARLES MIDDLETON
Aura	PRISCILLA LAWSON
King Vultan	JOHN LIPSON
Prince Barin	RICHARD ALEXANDER
Zarkov	FRANK SHANNON
King Kala	DUKE YORK, JR.
Officer Torch	EARL ASKAM
Professor Hensley	GEORGE CLEVELAND
High Priest	THEODORE LORCH
Shark Man	HOUSE PETERS, JR.
King Thun	JAMES PIERCE
Zona	MURIEL GOODSPEED
Gordon, Sr.	RICHARD TUCKER
Soldiers	FRED KOHLER, JR., LANE CHANDLER, AL FERGUSON, GLENN STRANGE

Episodes: 1. The Planet of Peril. 2. The Tunnel of Terror. 3. Captured by Shark Men. 4. Battling the Sea Beast. 5. The Destroying Ray. 6. Flaming Torture. 7. Shattering Doom. 8. Tournament of Death. 9. Fighting the Fire Dragon. 10. The Unseen Peril. 11. In the Claws of the Tigron. 12. Trapped in the Turret. 13. Rocketing to Earth. (Feature version was entitled *Rocketship*.)

Holy Moley! Flash Gordon is racing through a tunnel to stop Ming the Merciless from marrying Dale Arden. Suddenly, there looms a Gocko, an eleven-foot, fire-breathing monster. The creature grabs Flash and starts to crush him in its huge claw. Just when it looks like the end, the screen blacks out. And three familiar words appear across it—"Continued Next Week."

Every boy who grew up in the 1930s and 1940s, even through part of the 1950s, can recall those thrill-packed Saturdays when *Flash Gordon*—or whatever the current serial was—flicked on the screen. Remember, there was no television during most of those years. There were comic books and radio—true. But to the genuine, red-blooded movie buff, they were distant seconds.

Serials go back to the days of the silent film. The first one was made in 1912. During the next two decades studios ground out another two hundred, including the famous *Perils of Pauline* starring Pearl White. Silent serial stars included Tom Mix, Warner (Charlie Chan) Oland, Anna May Wong, William Desmond and such non-actors as Gene Tunney, Jack Dempsey, Red Grange and Harry Houdini.

But the serials that grown-up kids of my generation remember were the talking serials that had their birth in the mid-1930s. They were usually divided into twelve to fifteen installments which ran once a week on Saturday afternoons. The dialogue was wooden. The plot mindless. But one thing they did have, boy, was action. Every chapter, which ran about fifteen or twenty minutes, had two to three knock-down, drag-out battles royal. And I'm here to tell you they were real humdingers. (We didn't know it then, but the truth is stunt men usually took over from our heroes. They even donned skirts and wigs and filled in for the lady serial stars when the going got rough.)

But it was the endings that we dug the most.

Who can forget those climaxes when our hero was left plunging off a cliff in an auto? Or dropping into a pot of boiling lava? Or locked in a warehouse with a time bomb ready to blow him to smithereens?

The problem was the studio writers apparently couldn't resolve all of these cliff hangers logically. So they resorted to cheating. When you came back the next week, some of the old footage was rerun and you found the hero had actually rolled out of the auto before it went over the cliff. Or, out of nowhere, someone had tossed him a rope just before he slipped into the lava. Or he had found a secret exit just before the warehouse went up into a thousand pieces.

But life springs eternal in the serial fans' breast. And we kept coming back for more. Hollywood obliged. During the 1930s, Republic, Universal and Columbia—the big three of the serial movie makers —cranked out a total of sixteen serials a year. There were more when you count those made by Mascot and the other independents. Some of the better ones include *The Lone Ranger, Dick Tracy, Zorro Rides Again, Drums of Fu Manchu.* Later, there were *Captain America, Spy Smasher* and *Tiger Woman.*

Surprisingly, big-name stars got their start, or put in some of their early work, in serials. These include John Wayne, Jennifer Jones, Carole Landis, Jon Hall, George Brent, Boris Karloff and Bela Lugosi. Actors who made a career out of serials were Kane Richmond, Ralph Byrd, Don Terry, Warren Hull, Bruce Bennett and Tom Tyler. There were serial queens, too—Linda Stirling, Kay Aldridge and Frances Gifford. Though their popularity never duplicated the silent serial heroines, their fetching shorts and blouses added a little spice to the robust fare. The Westerns (they made up the largest category of serials, with action thrillers next) had such heroes as Johnny Mack Brown, Buck Jones, Dick Foran, Bill Elliott and Clayton Moore.

But unquestionably the king of serials was Larry (Buster) Crabbe. He made nine hard-fisted, slam-bang adventure episodes. Some kids idolized Buster because he was an Olympic champion. He swam in both the 1928 and 1932 games and this proved there was nothing phony about his derring-do. Others admired him because he looked just like the comic strip hero he played. And at least one fan was attracted by the nostrils that quivered at the tip of his aquiline nose. "They could express anger, hatred,

fear, annoyance and lust," Charles Beaumont recalled in his book, *Remember, Remember.* In one scene with Dale Arden (played by Jean Rogers), "Flash's nostrils told us, in no uncertain terms, that holding hands was not all this wench had on her mind."

Of about 220 talking serials made through the mid-1950s, the 1936 *Flash Gordon*—first of a trilogy —stands supreme in my mind. Universal spared nothing in its lavish production. It was carefully cast and imaginatively written. Even today, more than thirty years after it was filmed, the plot seems timely for a children's science-fiction yarn.

The planet Mongo has broken out of its orbit and is headed toward Earth to destroy it. Panic spreads throughout the world. In a desperate effort to turn the planet from its course, Flash and Dale Arden embark for Mongo with Dr. Zarkov (Frank Shannon) in his rocket ship.

Their reception is anything but cordial. Ming the Merciless (Charles Middleton), who aspires to be Emperor of the Universe, imprisons the trio. Unexpectedly, Ming's daughter Aura (Priscilla Lawson) gets a crush on Flash and tries to steal him from Dale. Meanwhile, Ming takes a fancy to Dale and tries to kill Flash.

Then, for the next twelve chapters, Flash runs into stranger things than you'd find in the Congo. He outswims Shark Men, outmaneuvers Hawk Men, outwrestles Monkey Men, outroars Lion Men. He has to defeat fire dragons, tigrons, zebra-striped bears and Gocko, a fantastic beast with a head like a horse, a body like a dinosaur and a dragon's tail. Meanwhile, all sorts of amazing devices pop in and out of the story. Flash looks into a Spaceograph (a kind of television set that lets him see anything anywhere), travels underwater in a hydrocycle (a tiny submarine) and uses a new machine to turn invisible. It all ends happily in Chapter 13. Flash overcomes Ming, who in his haste to get away runs smack into one of his own hungry Gockos. Finally Flash, Dale and Zarkov return to Earth, happy in the thought that they have saved the world from destruction.

Universal produced two more Flash Gordon serials—*Flash Gordon's Trip to Mars* (1938) and *Flash Gordon Conquers the Universe* (1940)—and a *Buck Rogers* (1939) serial. But nothing could approach the first *Flash Gordon.*

World War II saw a rash of spy serials with heroes smashing Nazi and Japanese undercover rings. But with the end of the war, the rise of production costs and the emerging popularity of television, the serial started slipping. Studios tightened the budgets. Directors were forced to resort to stock footage, standard sets, quick shooting. Filming was so rushed, in fact, that little effort was made to reshoot badly done scenes. In *The Invisible Monster* (1950, Republic), the hero (Richard Webb) tails the crooks by watching them with binoculars from across the street. He follows their car from a distance of ten feet. They never spot him. Actor Webb wears a wide-brim, snap-down hat. It never comes off in more than two dozen fights in which he absorbs over a hundred blows over the course of twelve chapters.

While the serials were cheapening their product to survive, television showed free half-hour adventures that were as good as, or better than, their movie counterparts. As the serials deteriorated into a meaningless hodgepodge of chases and fights, TV began to display more and more fast-moving stories with crisp dialogue. (Eventually, in the 1960s, such programs as *Batman* were to acquire expensively mounted sets and move into prime time.)

In 1956, Columbia produced the last U.S. serial, a dull fifteen-chapter piece called *Blazing the Overland Trail*. And so the serial died not with a bang but a whimper.

Charles Middleton, archvillain of outer space, playing Ming the Merciless, who calls himself Emperor of the Universe and is bent on conquering the Earth.

Flash and Dale Arden (Jean Rogers) are captives in Ming's fortress on the planet Mongo. That's Dr. Zarkov (Frank Shannon) with the starlike emblem.

Flash battles for a death-dealing ray gun with guard (Al Ferguson) as Aura (Priscilla Lawson), Ming's attractive daughter who has a crush on Flash, looks on.

Flash stands before Ming's firing squad in Chapter 10. But before it can execute him, Zarkov pushes Flash into a machine that makes him invisible and the startled guards flee. Prince Barin (Richard Alexander) is at extreme right. Officer Torch (Earl Askam) is about to give the order to fire to his guards led by Glenn Strange.

King Vultan (John Lipson), ruler of the Sky City, has Flash's arms pinioned as Officer Torch points his sword menacingly. Aura, Dale and Ming stand alongside Flash. King Thun (James Pierce), the bearded one, is at extreme lower left.

Spec. 5

(Photos by Samuel Goldwyn)

Terangi (Jon Hall) and his wife Marama (Dorothy Lamour) feel the first stiff winds of the hurricane—"the wind that overturns the land"—as the storm approaches their South Sea isle.

The two lovers embrace watching the high winds roar in from the Pacific.

The Hurricane

(Released December 24, 1937)

SCREEN PLAY by Dudley Nichols based on Oliver H. J. Garrett's adaptation of the Charles Nordhoff–James Norman Hall novel. Score, Alfred Newman. Photography, Bert Glennon. Editor, Lloyd Nosler. Song, "Moon of Manakoora," by Frank Loesser and Newman. Hurricane staged by James Basevi. Directed by John Ford. Co-director, Stuart Heisler. Produced by Samuel Goldwyn. Associate producer, Merritt Hulburd. Released by United Artists. Running time, 110 minutes.

Marama	DOROTHY LAMOUR
Terangi	JON HALL
Madame De Laage	MARY ASTOR
Father Paul	C. AUBREY SMITH
Dr. Kersaint	THOMAS MITCHELL
Governor De Laage	RAYMOND MASSEY
Jailer	JOHN CARRADINE
Captain Nagle	JEROME COWAN
Chief Mehevi	AL KIKUME
Tita	KUULEI DE CLERCQ
Mako	LAYNE TOM, JR.
Hitia	MAMO CLARK
Arai	MOVITA CASTANEDA
Reri	RERI
Tavi	FRANCIS KAI
Mata	PAULINE STEELE
Mama Rua	FLORA HAYES
Marunga	MARY SHAW
Warden	SPENCER CHARTERS
Captain of Guards	ROGER DRAKE
Girl on ship	INEZ COURTNEY

(The movie won an Oscar for best sound recording. It was presented to Thomas T. Moulton, sound director of the Goldwyn Studio Sound Department.)

Hold tight! Here it comes!!

With the fury of a hundred rocket engines, a howling wind roars out of the Pacific, whipping giant waves across the beaches of tiny Manakoora Island. The wild storm tears apart coral reefs, splinters piers, pulls stately palm trees up by their roots.

It pushes huge waves over the land, sweeping men and women along with it. Their mouths are wide open as they scream in horror. But so loud is the wind, their cries go unheard.

Nothing can stop the rushing waves. They smash huts, strip corrugated iron roofs from houses, swallow a stone church crowded with islanders. Like a giant hand crushing a matchbox, the raging storm levels everything on the defenseless Polynesian island. When at last the killer winds die down, you find yourself gripping the arms of your seat, stunned and drained of all emotion.

Such is the movie magic of James Basevi, Hollywood's super special effects man. He was the creator of the earthquake in *San Francisco* and the locust plague in *The Good Earth*. But the storm he brewed for Samuel Goldwyn's *The Hurricane* is considered the pinnacle of cinema miracles.

Nowhere is illusion the high art that it is in the movies. In the 1930s, the major studios needed whole warehouses just to house the equipment of their special effects departments. Ropes, airplane motors, cables and explosives were tools of the trade. There were miniature cities built to stage make-believe air raids and huge tanks where sea disasters took place far from the ocean.

Yet most of the efforts of these technicians went into small bits of business because real things often do not look real in films.

• Real rain, for example, photographs like scratches across the film. So movie rain comes from overhead sprinklers. The water is sometimes mixed with milk so it photographs clearly.

• Snow has to be made to order. Special effects men at first used chopped chicken feathers. There were some near fatalities when feathers became lodged in actors' nostrils. So they later substituted parched cornflakes, crushed potato chips, and eventually plastic snowflakes which sprinkle to the set from revolving drums.

• White soap or mashed potatoes usually substitute for ice cream because the real thing melts under the hot lights. On the other hand, when Stan Laurel appears to bite into a cake of soap, don't pity him. He's really eating cheese. And he loves cheese.

• For bursting shrapnel, a paper bag is filled with black cardboard chips and flashlight powder, then tossed into the air and exploded by a time fuse. The chips look like steel scraps flying through the air. When bullets seem to kick up dust near running soldiers, tiny powder charges are buried, then exploded by underground wires. When arrows seem to have pierced cowboys, they have really been sewn into their costumes.

Basevi, one of Hollywood's most inventive creators of ersatz catastrophes, was usually reluctant to disclose the secrets of his work. The studios felt the less moviegoers knew about film magic the more they would marvel at the spectacle.

But one picture Basevi did discuss freely was *The Hurricane* because its storm scene, which lasts twenty minutes (and took nearly four months to design, produce and film), is regarded as *the* classic movie spectacle. Basevi, an Englishman schooled as an architect, got a $400,000 budget to do the hurricane. He spent $150,000 to build a native village. The other $250,000 went to destroy it.

The movie, which had two South Sea islanders as the major characters, proved to be a difficult one to cast. When stripped to their essentials, most stars look like candidates for a Charles Atlas course. So director John Ford launched an extensive search. He finally found Jon Hall, twenty-four, an unknown actor with a magnificent physique, and Dorothy Lamour, twenty-two, a former Miss New Orleans, who one year before had been a $75-a-week stock player. She had originated her sarong roles in *The Jungle Princess* (1936) and seemed ideal for the part of a Polynesian beauty. A few years later her sarongs would make her one of World War II's most popular pinups.

The picture opens as an ocean liner passes a desolate South Sea isle. Dr. Kersaint (Thomas Mitchell), who had once lived there, blows a kiss to it and a lady passenger (Inez Courtney) asks the reason. He says it is the island of Manakoora, once the most beautiful of all the Polynesian isles. "What happened to it?" the lady asks. "It made the mistake of being born in the heart of the hurricane zone," the doctor says. And so begins the story.

Terangi (Hall), a strapping Polynesian who is first mate on a trading schooner, marries Marama (Miss Lamour), daughter of Manakoora's native chief. All the island's natives celebrate the wedding at a massive feast. But the couple's happiness is short-lived. On a voyage to Tahiti, Terangi gets into a fight with a white bully and breaks his jaw.

The bully turns out to be a man of influence and a Tahitian official sentences Terangi to six months in jail. Terangi's friends ask for mercy. But De Laage (Raymond Massey), the French governor of Manakoora, who has the power to have Terangi sent to his home island and then pardon him, is a stickler for the letter of the law. Even De Laage's wife (Mary Astor) appeals for Terangi when she learns his wife is pregnant. Still De Laage won't be swayed. "He's broken the law," the governor says adamantly.

Unable to stand the confinement and determined to see Marama, Terangi makes one escape attempt after another. Each time he is flogged and each time his term is increased. Finally, faced with sixteen years' imprisonment, Terangi makes one more dash for freedom. He gets out but hits a guard so hard he kills him.

In a small outrigger Terangi makes an epic 600-mile voyage to Manakoora to rejoin Marama and his little daughter, born in his absence. De Laage hears that Terangi has returned and sets out to hunt him down. But the barometer suddenly drops and "the wind that overturns the land" begins to lash the island.

Now Basevi steps into the spotlight. He built a huge set more than 600 feet long showing the forefront of the island. It had wharves, huts, a church and trees. The beach ran into a limpid lagoon— really a 200-yard-long tank. Across the lagoon, Basevi put up whirring airplane propellers, mounted on towers, to create the fierce winds.

Water from twelve fire hoses streamed in front of the propeller blades to send clouds of spray pouring over the set and actors. Wave machines —steel rollers that revolved and slid up and down like pistons—churned the peaceful lagoon into an angry maelstrom. To simulate a tidal wave, Basevi let loose 2,000 gallons of water down chutes topped by big tanks.

The only shots for which a so-called miniature set was used were those showing the devastation of houses and the church. Even this was really no miniature because it was actually sixty by forty feet. All the other hurricane scenes were real. Actors really buffeted the winds. The women were lashed into trees as the massive waves crashed over them. But the men had to hang on. That unforgettable shot of the wind lifting away an entire tree with its clinging human occupants was done by wires. As a giant wave smashed over the tree, wires hoisted it into the air.

In another memorable sequence, Terangi lashes his wife and child to a tree and plunges back into the floodwaters to try to reach the church and De Laage's wife. Director John Ford, master-minding the action with an electrical control board, pushed a button signaling the start of the storm devices. The wind machines roared and spray swept over the figures in the tree. Hall, who used no double, slid into the water.

Ford pressed another button, signaling the release of the first tidal flood tank. The waves rolled across the lagoon, engulfed Hall and swept him under. He came up fighting and plunged on. Another wave rushed up and covered him. And another and another. Finally he reached the church,

secured the rope he carried on his waist to its door and pulled De Laage's wife to the safety of the treetops.

A little-known fact is that all the accompanying dramatic sounds—the wind's howl and the waves' thunder—were recorded separately. The engineers' main problem was to avoid monotony because the sounds of high wind, rising and falling, have an odd musical effect. And so they improvised—shaking marbles in a revolving box or rubbing sandpaper on steel wire—to simulate, ingeniously, on the sound track the roars and moans and sighs of the storm. It was done so well that the sound department won an Academy Award.

When the wind has finally spewed out all its anger, it has stripped the island of all life—except for a few islanders, Terangi, his family and Madame De Laage (whose coiffure miraculously came through untouched). Gone are the houses, trees, the soil itself. De Laage's schooner is sighted and Terangi builds a signal fire. But Madame De Laage urges him to escape and so he puts out to sea in a canoe with his wife and child.

De Laage spots them with his binoculars. He knows, however, that Terangi has saved his wife. "It's only a floating log," she tells him, hoping her hidebound husband will show compassion. There is a moment of suspenseful silence as De Laage embraces her. "Yes," De Laage says finally, "it's only a floating log." And he turns his back on the little canoe.

Terangi begins serving his sentence for slugging a white bully on Tahiti. Captain Nagle and the jailer (John Carradine), at right, look on.

Captain Nagle joins Father Paul, Dr. Kersaint and Madame De Laage in pleading for a pardon for Terangi. But Governor De Laage turns them down.

As the storm rages, Dr. Kersaint (Thomas Mitchell) leaves to deliver a baby. Madame De Laage (Mary Astor) and Father Paul (C. Aubrey Smith) caution him about the danger of going into the hurricane.

In a more peaceful time, Father Paul gives thanks for the safe arrival of the trading schooner on which Terangi is first mate. At left, in white, is Captain Nagle (Jerome Cowan). Governor De Laage (Raymond Massey), in white, stands in crowd with his wife.

Native girls cover Madame De Laage with blossoms.

IV

FUNNY MEN

Special bank guard Egbert Sousé (W. C. Fields) keeps a sharp lookout as he makes his rounds. *(Photo by Screen Gems, copyright © 1969)*

Sousé conjures up visions of grandeur and wealth to persuade Og Oggilby (Grady Sutton) to "borrow" money from the bank for a stock purchase.

W. C. FIELDS • THE BANK DICK
THE MARX BROTHERS • A NIGHT AT THE OPERA
LAUREL AND HARDY • WAY OUT WEST
CHARLIE CHAPLIN • CITY LIGHTS

(Photos by Universal, courtesy United Artists Corp.)

W. C. Fields

The Bank Dick

(Released November 29, 1940)

ORIGINAL STORY AND SCREEN PLAY by Mahatma Kane Jeeves (W. C. Fields). Musical direction by Charles Previn. Art direction by Jack Otterson. Editor, Arthur Hilton. Photographed by Milton Krasner. Directed by Edward Cline. Produced and distributed by Universal. Running time, 74 minutes.

Egbert Sousé	W. C. FIELDS
Agatha Sousé	CORA WITHERSPOON
Myrtle Sousé	UNA MERKEL
Elsie Mae Adele Brunch Sousé	EVELYN DEL RIO
Mrs. Hermisillo Brunch	JESSIE RALPH
J. Pinkerton Snoopington	FRANKLIN PANGBORN
Joe Guelpe	SHEMP HOWARD
Mackley Q. Greene	RICHARD PURCELL
Og Oggilby	GRADY SUTTON
J. Frothingham Waterbury	RUSSELL HICKS
Mr. Skinner	PIERRE WATKIN
Repulsive Rogan	AL HILL
Loudmouth McNasty	GEORGE MORAN
Otis	BILL WOLFE
A. Pismo Clam	JACK NORTON
Assistant Director	PAT WEST
François	REED HADLEY
Miss Plupp	HEATHER WILDE
Dr. Stall	HARLAN BRIGGS
Mr. Cheek	BILL ALSTON
Colored Depositor	BILLY MITCHELL
Cop	PAT O'MALLEY
Woman in Bank	JAN DUGGAN
Boy in Bank	BOBBY LARSON
Bank Employee	RUSSEL COLE

He had a cure for insomnia. ("Get plenty of sleep.")

He had his own philosophy of life. ("If at first you don't succeed, try, try again. Then quit. No use being a damn fool about it.")

And he gave advice freely, although it was not for anyone who aspired to live the pious life. ("Never give a sucker an even break.")

W. C. Fields. Swindler, con man, pool hustler, pitchman, card shark, petty chiseler, snake-oil salesman, bunko artist. He played them all in over forty movies with consummate artistry, concealing his fraudulent ends with remarkable versatility.

In *Poppy* (1936), he sells a "talking" dog whom he has made speak through ventriloquism. What will happen now—when Fields leaves? As Fields counts his money, the dog says, "Just for that [selling me], I'm not going to talk any more." Whereupon Fields beats a hasty exit.

Later in the same movie, when he gets a hot dog at a carnival, Fields tells the vendor he'll pay for it when the carnival engagement ends. The vendor becomes enraged. Fields shoves back his half-eaten hot dog. "How," says the vendor, "do you expect me to sell a half-eaten hot dog?" "First, you insult me," says Fields pompously. "Then you ask my advice regarding salesmanship. You, sir, are a dunce. D-U-N-C-E. Dunce."

The bulbous-nosed, raspy-voiced comic is, of course, a transparent windbag. And in the end he is usually exposed for the spineless phony he is. In *Mississippi* (1935), try as he may, he can't shed a fifth ace he has planted in a poker game. Finally his opponent puts a pistol on the table and calls. "Just a little ole pair," sputters Fields, folding his five aces quickly. "I was only bluffing."

But Fields struck the most responsive chord with his audiences when he played the underdog. He was the long-suffering husband, bullied by his frumpy wife, second-guessed by his carping mother-in-law, chased by dogs, put upon even by babies.

Of them all, Fields was perhaps least fond of children. One of them was Baby LeRoy, an infant actor whom Fields looked on as a scene-stealer. A story goes that Fields got his revenge one day when he spiked the toddler's orange juice with gin. As the staff tried to get the baby going, Fields kibitzed from the sidelines: "Walk him around, walk him around." It was to no avail. Baby LeRoy was irrevocably looped. "The kid's no trouper," Fields grumped. "Send him home." Whether or not the story is apocryphal, it is true that youngsters were the butt of many Fieldsian jokes. His most quoted thought on the subject was: "Any man who hates children can't be all bad."

Fields—his real name was William Claude Dukenfield (sometimes spelled Dukinfield)—was born in Philadelphia around 1879. Nobody has ever been able to pin down the precise year. Before he was in long pants, he had had heated arguments with his father, a fruit and vegetable peddler. When his dad clobbered him over the head with a shovel handle, he ran away from home.

Fields was only eleven. But he learned to live by his wits, selling papers, marking cards, pilfering food. Before he was twenty-one, he knew the inside of jails. In fact, he got his famous balloon nose not from drinking—although he was better than a two-quarts-a-day man in his later years—but from fighting in a brawl.

It was as a juggler that he started his acting career. He practiced sixteen hours a day until he mastered the art. At thirteen he was playing in circuses and carnivals. As he grew up he added a comedy patter, became a vaudevillian, and toured Europe, where he played before King Edward VII of England. In 1914, Florenz Ziegfeld put him in his Follies. Fields was an instant hit. Over the next decade he became a top-drawer comedian in many Broadway shows.

Still, the most quoted story of his early years comes from his touring days. Fields was so afraid his luck would run out, he opened bank accounts in every town on the circuit. That way, he figured wherever he might be stranded, he wouldn't be broke. When he died, he reportedly had hundreds of bank accounts all over the country. A few may to this day be gathering interest under one of the many fictional names Fields became famous for —Ouliotta Hemoglobin, A. Pismo Clam, Otis Criblecoblis, and Mahatma Kane Jeeves.

During his early years Fields married Harriet Hughes, a dancer. She apparently did not share his idea of humor. One of her complaints was that he always ate with a bottle balanced on his head. They separated shortly after having a child—W. C. Fields, Jr. (who became a corporation lawyer)—but never divorced because his wife was Catholic. Fields later lived with a succession of lady friends, one of them a striking Ziegfeld beauty.

He made his first picture, *Pool Sharks* (1915), when he was thirty-six, and went on to do more than thirty-three features and many short films. Fields often put in his own routine and gags, frequently ad-libbed, and later wrote his own scripts.

Some of his most popular pictures were: *If I Had a Million* (1932), *It's a Gift* (1934), *The Man on the Flying Trapeze* (1935), *David Copperfield* (1935) (he played Micawber and stuck to the script here), *My Little Chickadee* (1940), with Mae West. Of them all, *The Bank Dick*, which he made late in his career (1940), shows him at his wittiest.

Fields plays Egbert Sousé (Soo-say, careful to accent the final *e*), who has done little more than bend an elbow at the Black Pussy Cat Café after winning a bank night prize. His whiskey ways, of course, draw the wrath of his shrewish wife Agatha (Cora Witherspoon) and his scowling mother-in-law (Jessie Ralph). Even when he's out of the house, Egbert can't escape being henpecked. He temporarily takes over direction of a movie on location in his town, only to have his brat of a child (Evelyn Del Rio) bust in and insist on being put in the picture.

But then his fortunes change. Egbert is resting his elegant girth on a bench when two fleeing bank robbers pause to squabble over their loot. They fight and one of them is knocked out. The other, dashing off just ahead of the police, throws his gun at Egbert. Startled, he tips over backward. When the cops show up, Egbert is sitting on the holdup man (George Moran).

Mr. Skinner (Pierre Watkin), the grateful bank

president, rewards Egbert with a bank calendar. He also appoints him the bank's special guard. When Egbert comes home with the evening paper's account of his "heroics," his wife casually tosses it in the fire and goes on with her card game.

Before the bank opens the next morning Egbert stops at the Pussy Cat Café for a "depth bomb," his favorite pick-me-up drink. There he runs into con man J. Frothingham Waterbury (Russell Hicks), who is selling shares in the Beefsteak Mine. Waterbury convinces Fields that the shares will enable him to loll in splendor at a country estate with fleets of armored cars rolling up, hauling strongboxes stuffed with money. His only job would be to sign receipts. "I'll have a fountain pen by that time," says Fields gleefully. To raise cash, he prevails on Og Oggilby (Grady Sutton), his sappy prospective son-in-law and a bank teller, to "borrow" the money from the bank.

His first day on the job, Fields jumps a kid in a cowboy suit waving a toy pistol. "Is that gun loaded?" Sousé asks. "Certainly not," snaps his mother, pulling the boy away. "But I think you are." As she marches indignantly out of the bank, the kid asks why the man has a funny nose. "You'd like to have a nose like that full of nickels, wouldn't you?" she replies.

Later that morning, incorruptible J. Pinkerton Snoopington (Franklin Pangborn), the bank examiner, shows up. Sousé delays the prissy auditor by treating him to a "Michael Finn." Then he steers him into his hotel, where the tipsy Snoopington promptly reels out a second-story window. Fields retrieves him on the first bounce and tucks him in bed.

Still the iron-willed Snoopington manages to show up at the bank the next morning. In the meantime the mine has struck a bonanza.

But before Og and Egbert can cash in their stock, the second holdup man (Al Hill) returns to the bank and fills his satchel with cash and the Beefsteak Mine stock. He yanks Sousé along as a shield, forcing him to drive the getaway car. Fields careens through the streets, across ditches with ditchdiggers ducking in the nick of time. He screeches around curves, missing collisions by a hair's breadth.

"Give me the wheel," the thug orders. "Here it is," Fields says, pulling it off the steering column. When the rear tires start falling off, Fields remarks matter-of-factly: "Going to be very dangerous." Finally an overhanging tree branch kayos the gunman and Fields screeches to a halt on the edge of a precipice.

Sousé, a hero again, gets a $5,000 reward for capturing the bandit and sells his story to a film company for another $10,000. His money problems are over. And off he goes to the pleasures of the Pussy Cat Café.

Fields, who was not unlike the character he played in many ways, went on to make some memorable radio shows with Charlie McCarthy. They had a running feud. Charlie called Fields "a two-legged martini. . . . You weren't born, you were squeezed out of a bar rag." Fields fired right back but particularly enjoyed ribbing the sponsor, Lucky Strike. He used to mention an imaginary son named "Chester." It didn't immediately occur to the cigarette firm that he was sneaking in a plug for a rival tobacco company.

A kidney ailment plagued Fields in his later years and he made only five more pictures after *The Bank Dick*, appearing mostly in minor roles. At the end, when he was sixty-seven, he had been in a sanitarium for more than a year. He died, of all days, on Christmas morning, 1946.

Fields left an estate of about $800,000, most of it earmarked to establish the "W. C. Fields College for Orphaned White Boys and Girls, Where No Religion of Any Sort Is To Be Preached." But his wife and son successfully contested the will and his request was never fulfilled.

Even though the orphanage never came into being as a monument to his memory, Fields will always be remembered as one of the unique comics of the golden age of movies. "There is always something funny . . . in the most depressing drudgeries . . . of everyday life," wrote film historian William K. Everson. "If there were not, and we were unable to see it, life would be hardly worthwhile. Fields made us see it. In laughing at him, we were laughing at life."

A bit overzealous his first day on the job, Sousé throttles cap-pistol-toting Bobby Larson, whom he mistakes for a holdup man. Mother Jan Duggan groans in outrage.

Franklin Pangborn, one of a host of distinguished character actors appearing in *The Bank Dick*.

There's something on the great man's mind. Russell Cole tries to clear the air.

Fields looks over the shoulder of an agitated depositor (Billy Mitchell) who wants to draw out all his funds. "Every time I come in here you is wearing a hat," the suspicious man says to the teller. "And it looks like you is getting ready to take off."

The end of the road for holdup man Repulsive Rogan (Al Hill). Looking on are Sutton, Richard Purcell, Pat O'Malley, Fields, and Pierre Watkin.

Gottlieb (Sig Rumann) the impresario is besieged by the Marx brothers as he tries to make a phone call in his office. From center, left, Harpo, Chico, Groucho. That's Allan Jones with cigar.

Rosa (Kitty Carlisle) consoles Harpo, who has been discharged as a valet.

(Photos by MGM)
(© 1935 Metro-Goldwyn-Mayer Corp.; © renewed 1962 Metro-Goldwyn-Mayer Inc. as successor in interest to Metro-Goldwyn-Mayer Corp.)

The Marx Brothers

A Night at the Opera

(Released November 15, 1935)

A SCREEN MUSICAL COMEDY adapted by George S. Kaufman and Morrie Ryskind from a story by James Kevin McGuinness. Songs: "Alone" by Nacio Herb Brown and Arthur Freed; "Cosi-Cosa" by Bronislau Kaper, Walter Jurmann and Ned Washington. Dances by Chester Hale. Scored by Herbert Stothart. Editor, William Le Vanway. Cameraman, Merritt B. Gerstad. Directed by Sam Wood. Produced by Irving Thalberg. Presented by Metro-Goldwyn-Mayer. Running time, 93 minutes

Otis B. Driftwood	GROUCHO MARX
Fiorello	CHICO MARX
Tomasso	HARPO MARX
Rosa	KITTY CARLISLE
Ricardo	ALLAN JONES
Lassparri	WALTER KING
Gottlieb	SIG RUMANN
Mrs. Claypool	MARGARET DUMONT
Captain	EDWARD KEANE
Henderson	ROBERT EMMET O'CONNOR
Steward	GINO CORRADO
Mayor	PURNELL PRATT
Engineer	FRANK YACONELLI
Engineer's Assistant	BILLY GILBERT
Dancers	RITA AND RUBEN

GROUCHO (*stepping up to the bar with Chico*)—Two beers, bartender.

CHICO—I'll take two beers, too.

GROUCHO—Have you any stewed prunes?

STEWARD—Yes, sir.

GROUCHO—Well, give them some hot coffee. That'll sober them up.

GROUCHO (*on being presented with a dinner check*)—$9.40? This is outrageous. (*Hands it to woman dinner companion.*) If I were you, I wouldn't pay it.

That's a sampling of the wit of the Marx brothers at the peak of their career in what many critics regard as their best movie, *A Night at the Opera*.

Remember that zany trio? There was:

Groucho—with painted-on rectangular mustache, cigar, black eyebrows above eyes leering behind steel-rimmed glasses, frock coat, uncreased pin-stripe trousers and a stooped-over, sliding walk like he was passing under a low bridge.

Chico—with pointed velvet hat, short, tight-fitting jacket, and an improbable Italian accent.

Harpo—the golden-haired, pixieish, maniacal mute who talked in shrill whistles, beeps of an auto horn and semaphore hand signals, and wore a bulging raincoat out of which came rubber tires, a barber's pole, a block of ice, canned goods and a dozen settings of silver cutlery.

It was only after a long show-business apprenticeship that the brothers came to Hollywood. There were two other brothers in the act when the trio started—Gummo and Zeppo—but they dropped out later to become theatrical agents.

Minnie, their immigrant mother, had taken them out of the slums of Manhattan's East Side and molded them into a touring vaudeville act. They were essentially a musical team but their talent for aggressive comedy was discovered one day in Nacogdoches, Texas. Half the audience deserted the act when an accident involving a mule took place outside the theatre. Groucho was so incensed he ignored his lines and insulted the audience as they returned. Instead of bridling at his tongue-lashing, they took the insults for comedy and laughed uproariously. The brothers quickly realized the potential of this form of comedy. Their act was made.

From vaudeville, they went to Broadway, where they scored a success in the 1925 show *The Coconuts* by George S. Kaufman and Morrie Ryskind (who would become script writers for *A Night at the Opera*). In four years they were in the movies. Starting with a film version of their Broadway hit, they turned out one free-wheeling picture a year through 1933.*

The heart of the Marxes' slapstick humor was their ability to turn the world upside down. They poked fun at respectability. They ridiculed the upper classes. They unloosed sheer anarchy at formal banquets, grand opera performances and city hall receptions. Their wild shenanigans unhinged the movie from all logical thought and action.

At first they were a huge success. But after a while their formula began to grow old. By 1934, box office receipts for *Duck Soup*, their latest picture, were so disappointing, Paramount decided not to renew their five-year contract.

But MGM Producer Irving Thalberg picked it up. He felt the trouble with their humor was that they were too detached from reality. Unlike other comedians, who were underdogs, the Marx brothers were always on the offensive, always attacking. The audience never had a chance to see them reduced to despair, and so could never share their comeback and triumph.

To add human appeal and make them more sympathetic, Thalberg put them on the defensive, made them come close to defeat. They even forgot themselves long enough to help young lovers. In place of wild formless romps, Thalberg added plot,

lavish sets, and separated music from comedy so that straight scenes contrasted with funny ones.

Finally, Thalberg got the idea of trying out their material before shooting in the studio. The brothers got up a fifty-minute vaudeville act based on scenes from their upcoming film, *A Night at the Opera*. They toured for twenty-five days. Writers sat in the audience and watched the reaction, throwing out lines or altering them according to the laughs they got. The Thalberg prescription proved to be just the right tonic.

As Otis B. Driftwood, a seedy entrepreneur and swindler, Groucho advises millionairess Mrs. Claypool (Margaret Dumont) to sponsor an opera company. He convinces her this will assure her a lofty place in high society. Mrs. Claypool gives $200,000 to the company's director (Sig Rumann) who signs up the renowned Rodolfo Lassparri (Walter King) and a lovely soprano, Rosa Castaldi (Kitty Carlisle). Meanwhile, Groucho has erroneously signed a little-known singer in the chorus, Ricardo Baroni (Allan Jones), who is Rosa's sweetheart. When the opera company sails from Milan to New York, Riccardo, his friend Chico, and Harpo, discharged valet of Lassparri, stow away in Groucho's trunk.

Some of the funniest scenes of all the Marx brothers movies follow.

1) *The cabin scene:* Groucho finds himself and his steamer trunk in a telephone-booth-size stateroom. Out of the trunk pop the three stowaways. One of them, Harpo, is asleep. In come two chambermaids, who start making up the bed with Harpo still snoozing, floating on their shoulders. Then an engineer squeezes in to turn off the heat, followed by a manicurist. "Do you want your nails long or short?" she asks Groucho. "Better make 'em short," he says. "It's getting crowded in here."

The engineer's assistant arrives and shoehorns himself into the tangle of bodies that seem like a subway train at rush hour. Then comes a girl asking if her aunt Minnie is in the cabin. "If she isn't," says Groucho, "you can probably find somebody just as good."

"Can I use your phone?" the girl asks. "Use the phone?" says Groucho. "I'll lay you even money you can't get in the room."

A cleaning woman announces she's come to mop up. "You'll have to start on the ceiling," says Groucho. "It's the only place that isn't being occupied."

A steward pushes in with dinner. Finally, Mrs.

---

* Zeppo was in their first five movies, leaving before *A Night at the Opera*. Gummo made no pictures.

Claypool, the grande dame, shows up in her finest regalia. She opens the door, letting loose a human avalanche that cascades into the corridor.

2) *The scene where Groucho and Chico negotiate a singer's contract:*

CHICO—Hey, wait. Wait. What does this say here?

GROUCHO—Oh, that? . . . That's in every contract. That just says if any of the parties is shown not to be in their right mind, the entire agreement is automatically nullified. . . . That's what they call a sanity clause.

CHICO (*laughs*)—You can't fool me. There ain't no Sanity Claus.

GROUCHO—Now pay particular attention to this first clause because it's most important. It says the —ah—party of the first part shall be known in this contract as the party of the first part. How do you like that? That's pretty neat, eh?

CHICO—No, that's no good.

GROUCHO—What's the matter with it?

CHICO—I don't know. Let's hear it again.

GROUCHO—It says the party of the first part to be known in this contract as the party of the first part.

CHICO—It sounds a little better this time.

GROUCHO—Well, it grows on you. Would you like to hear it once more?

CHICO—Ah, yeah . . .

GROUCHO (*finally*)—Look, why should we quarrel about a thing like this? We'll take it right out. (*They each rip off the top of their contracts. Chico doesn't like the second part any better. They tear this off. They continue tearing until the contracts dwindle to the size of an envelope. Now the eighth and ninth parts go and they are left with contracts the size of a postage stamp.*)

GROUCHO—Now I've got something you're bound to like.

CHICO—No, I don't like it.

GROUCHO—Don't like what?

CHICO—Whatever it is, I don't like it.

Rip!

3) *The City Hall scene:* The stowaways cut the beards from three sleeping foreign generals, glue them on, and get a public welcome at City Hall. But they are exposed as impostors when Harpo, called on for a speech, stalls by drinking water and unwittingly washes off his beard. They flee with Groucho warning, "This means war."

4) *The opera finale:* At the company's premiere of *Il Trovatore,* the brothers run mad, breaking up Lassparri's performance to get the lead for Riccardo. Harpo and Chico slip "Take Me Out to the Ball Game" into the orchestra music and Groucho sails down the aisles hawking peanuts and popcorn. Then Harpo swings up into the flies and disrupts Lassparri's aria by sending down a series of wrong backdrops behind the singer. Finally, Chico and Harpo kidnap the tenor and substitute Allan Jones. He is an immediate success. Mrs. Claypool is delighted. The lovers are reunited. And we leave Groucho and Chico renegotiating Jones's contract. "The party of the tenth part . . ."

In a Hollywood career that spanned three decades, the brothers made 14 movies. Chico died in 1961 and Harpo in 1964. Both were seventy. In 1969, Zeppo and Gummo were retired, living in Palm Springs, California, getting in a round of golf now and again.

Groucho lives in Beverly Hills and is just as sharp and witty in his seventy-third year as he was in his heyday. Asked his opinion of nudity in the theatre, he said in a newspaper interview: "When I heard about *Hair,* I was kind of curious about the six naked primates on stage. So I called up the box office and they said tickets were $11 apiece. That's an awful price to pay. I went into my bathroom at home and took off all my clothes and looked at the mirror for five minutes. And I said, 'This isn't worth $11.'"

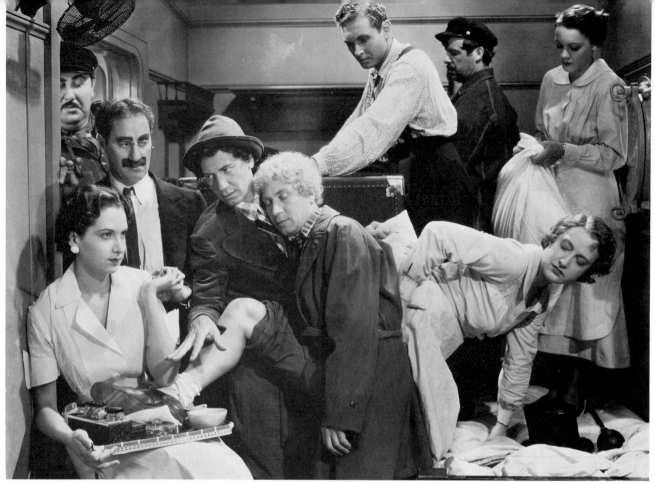

The hilarious cabin scene. It gets so crowded, Groucho tells a cleaning woman to do the ceiling because it's the only space unoccupied.

Stowaways Harpo, Chico and Jones, disguised as Italian aviators to slip by immigration officials, get a heroes' welcome. Groucho, of course, goes along with the deception. Robert Emmet O'Connor, center, playing a detective, looks on skeptically.

Harpo contributes some nonsense in the opera orchestra pit.

Chico and Groucho kidnapping tenor Lassparri (Walter King) to get Allan Jones on stage in his place.

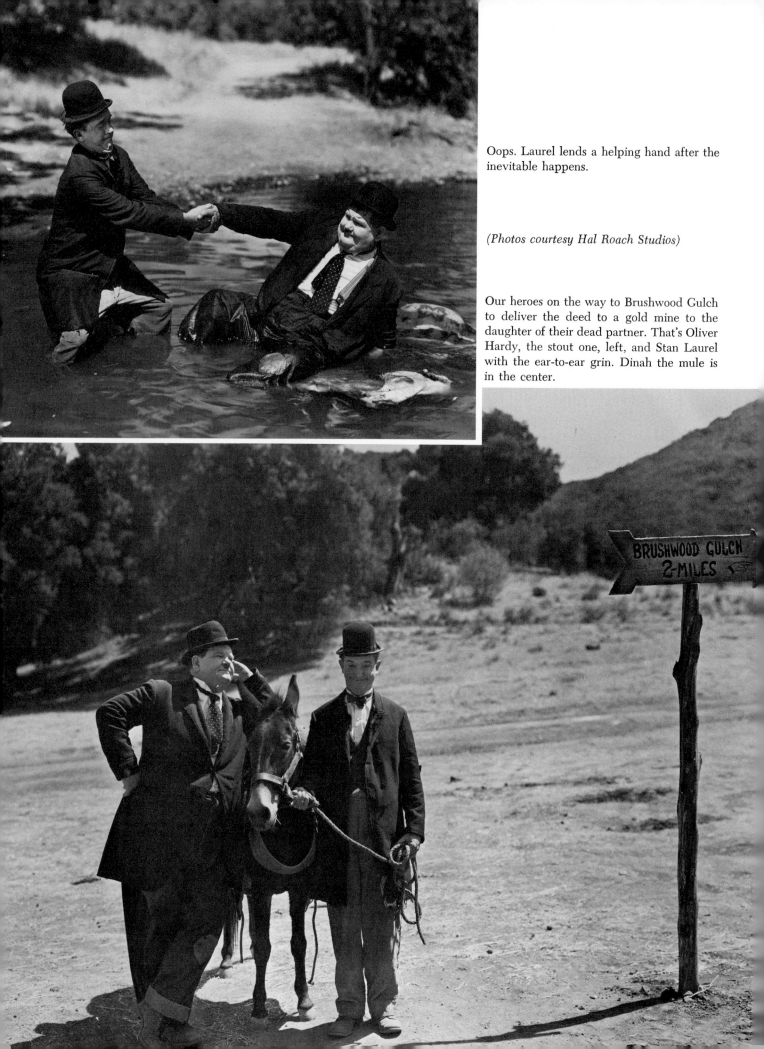

Oops. Laurel lends a helping hand after the inevitable happens.

(Photos courtesy Hal Roach Studios)

Our heroes on the way to Brushwood Gulch to deliver the deed to a gold mine to the daughter of their dead partner. That's Oliver Hardy, the stout one, left, and Stan Laurel with the ear-to-ear grin. Dinah the mule is in the center.

BRUSHWOOD GULCH
2-MILES

Laurel and Hardy

Way Out West

(Released April 16, 1937)

SCREEN PLAY by Charles Rogers, Felix Adler and James Parrott from a story by Rogers and Jack Jevne. Photographed by Art Lloyd and Walter Lundin. Editor, Bert Jordan. Directed by James W. Horne. Stan Laurel Productions for Hal Roach —MGM. Running time, 65 minutes.

Stanley	STAN LAUREL
Ollie	OLIVER HARDY
Lola Marcel	SHARON LYNNE
Mickey Finn	JAMES FINLAYSON
Mary Roberts	ROSINA LAWRENCE
Sheriff	STANLEY FIELDS
Sheriff's Wife	VIVIEN OAKLAND
Quartet	THE AVALON BOYS (including CHILL WILLS)
Dinah the mule	HERSELF

Stan Laurel. Thin. Frail. Sad-faced. A meek, soft-voiced scarecrow. He played the grinning, eye-blinking simpleton, well intentioned but hopelessly incompetent.

Oliver Hardy. Fat. Pompous. Perpetually exasperated. A master of the long-suffering look, the slow burn, the withering gaze. Babe, as his friends called him, played the dunderhead to end all dunderheads, the prize ignoramus who thinks he knows it all.

For a quarter of a century, many moviegoers considered Laurel and Hardy America's top comedy team. Between 1926 and 1951, they made over sixty comedy shorts and twenty-seven full-length films, moving with ease from silent films to talkies.

Highbrow critics never considered them first rate, partly because of the slow pace of their humor and partly because they were overshadowed by Keaton, Chaplin and then the Marx brothers. But audiences the world over howled long and loud at their antics. Their comedy was low comedy, relying on physical action rather than clever lines. And so their appeal was universal.

For example, in *Putting Pants on Philip*, their first official "Laurel and Hardy" short, Laurel is a Scotsman just off the boat. Every time he passes a ventilation grating, his kilt flies up, exposing his natty undershorts. Hardy plays his mortified uncle, embarrassed to have to escort this kilted dodo through town. Laurel stops to take some snuff and sneezes off his undershorts. Unaware, he starts off without them. When he walks over the next grating, his kilt starts billowing and the camera quickly cuts to a curious crowd. The horrified women are dropping like flies, fainting all over the street.

However, in a more typical vein, Laurel usually blunders into some outrageously impractical piece of business. And Hardy, steaming mad, moves in to show him how it should be done. Hardy winds up ruining everything and taking the consequences.

Hardy, who weighed nearly three hundred pounds, once summed up the essence of the team to their biographer, John McCabe, like this: Laurel was "the dumb, dumb guy who never has anything bad happen to him." Hardy was "the smart, smart guy who's dumber than the dumb guy only he doesn't know it. . . . One of the reasons people like us, I guess, is that they feel so superior to us."

Laurel, idea man of the partnership, was born Arthur Stanley Jefferson in 1890 in the little English

129

town of Ulverson. His father was an actor and theatre manager and the younger Laurel made his debut at the age of sixteen wearing his father's cut-down trousers. He toured in musicals, circuses and vaudeville as a comic and pantomimist, then came to America in the same troupe as Chaplin. He was, in fact, Chaplin's understudy.

Hardy, whose full name was Oliver Norvell Hardy,* was born in 1892 in Harlem, Georgia, the son of a lawyer. He studied law at the University of Georgia for a while. But he had sung in a minstrel show as a kid and the show business bug had bitten him. So Hardy began acting in films, eventually joining the Roach company. In contrast to Laurel, who had starring roles, Hardy played subordinate parts.

Laurel eventually settled in Hollywood and joined Hal Roach's Studio, where he made comedy shorts. Later, however, he concentrated on writing, producing and directing comedies. In 1926 he began his lifetime partnership with Hardy—Laurel was thirty-six then, and Hardy was thirty-four—a relationship that began quite by accident.

One day, while Hardy was preparing to act in Get 'Em Young, he scalded his arm in a home accident. Laurel, who was directing the film, pinch-hit for Hardy and took his role. "When the picture was finished," Laurel recalled, "Roach liked it and he asked me to write myself into the next one. By then, Hardy was ready . . . and I appeared with him in it."

Roach thought they made perfect foils. And so he began featuring them in a series called the Laurel and Hardy comedies. Laurel reluctantly agreed to return to acting. But while he was with Roach he never gave up having a hand in the writing, direction and editing of his own pictures.

The team began turning out a flurry of two-reelers —as many as a dozen in a single year. They were an immediate hit. As the years passed, their popularity increased and their sight gags tickled the funnybone of city dwellers in America as well as back-country peasants in Asia and South America. Their more famous fans included Churchill, Stalin and Tito. In fact, the Yugoslav President had his own library of Laurel and Hardy films. In their heyday there were over two million members of Laurel and Hardy fan clubs in Europe alone. One U.S. club that still exists today, the Sons of the

* Some versions have a second "e" in his middle name— "Norvelle."

Desert, has regular meetings and an annual banquet at which the duo's films are screened.

Among their outstanding shorts were: Two Tars (1928), You're Darn Tootin' (1928), Brats (1930), and Towed in a Hole (1933). Perhaps their best was The Music Box, a story of the trials and tribulations of a pair of harried piano movers. It won an Academy Award as the best short subject of 1932. (Laurel also got a special Oscar in 1960 for "creative pioneering" in cinema comedy.)

Their feature-length movies began in 1931 with Pardon Us and went on to include such top vehicles as Fra Diavolo (The Devil's Brother) (1933), Sons of the Desert (1933), Babes in Toyland (1934), Blockheads (1938), Swiss Miss (1938) and A Chump at Oxford (1940). But for sheer uninterrupted slapstick, with no time out for subplots or romantic diversion, many consider their best movie Way Out West (1937).

With their faithful mule Dinah, the two are bound for Brushwood Gulch to deliver the deed of a gold mine to Mary Roberts, the orphan daughter of their dead partner. Laurel flags down a stagecoach by baring his leg, à la Claudette Colbert. Once aboard, Hardy tries to impress the only lady passenger (Vivien Oakland). But the best he can do is bathe her in rather uninspired small talk. "A lot of weather we've been having lately," he tells her.

Outside the Mickey Finn Palace Saloon, the boys take time out for a charming soft-shoe routine. (Later, they sing a duet, "In the Blue Ridge Mountains of Virginia.") Although their mission is supposed to be kept secret, Laurel instantly blurts out the reason for their visit to saloonkeeper Mickey Finn (James Finlayson). The girl the boys are seeking is Finn's kitchen slavey. But since they have never seen her, the scheming Finn passes off his wife, blonde showgirl Lola Marcel (Sharon Lynne), as the heiress.

When Lola asks if it is true that her dear Daddy is dead, Laurel says, "Well, I hope he is. They buried him." The boys hand over the deed. But on the way out they run into the real Mary Roberts (Rosina Lawrence). "We handed the deed to the wrong person," Laurel exclaims. "That's the first mistake we made since that guy sold us the Brooklyn Bridge."

They storm back. But Finn and his wife refuse to return the deed. The boys snatch it away and the feathers start flying. Finn regains it and the boys yank it away again. It goes back and forth like a hot potato until Lola chases Stan into her bedroom and he pops the deed down his shirt. In a hilarious scene, she chases him under, then onto the bed, as Stan slithers and squirms. Finally she tickles him into hysteria and recovers the deed.

Finn and Lola lock it away in a safe. But, undaunted, the boys steal back at midnight. In the longest slapstick scene, the two devise a pulley system rigged to the mule to get Hardy to an upstairs window. With one of his famous looks, Hardy glances at the camera and crosses his fingers, letting the audience in on his misgivings. Predictably, Stan lets go to spit on his fingers and lets Hardy down with a bang. Finn comes racing out in nightshirt and rifle. A hide-and-seek scene follows which ends when the boys find refuge in a piano. When Finn starts playing it, they crash through the bottom, covered in an avalanche of wires and wood.

The duo, however, manage to wrest Finn's gun away, force him to open the safe, and leave him trussed in a chandelier. Then, with the real Mary Roberts joining them, they scoot out of town, off and running to their gold mine.

In 1941 the two went to work for 20th Century-Fox and MGM. But they had no direct say in the making of the films, and their pictures declined in quality. Laurel called them "garbage."

Nevertheless, through all their years together, the two never had any quarrels that made the newspapers. "We had different hobbies," Laurel explained. "He liked horses and golf. You know my hobby—and I married them all."

Laurel was married eight times, to four women, and was sued by a fifth who claimed to have been his common-law wife. Virginia Ruth Rogers, his second, third and seventh bride, once said, "He's a good boy, really. But he has a marrying complex." (Hardy was no slouch in the marrying business, either. He was married three times.) Hardy had no children. Laurel had one daughter.

Ironically, their off-screen personalities were nearly the opposite of their character roles. Hardy was quiet and retiring and exceedingly courteous, a throwback to his Southern upbringing. Laurel was assertive, bright, quick-witted.

When they were making their last movies, television began showing their old comedies. They received thousands of fan letters. But they had kept no property rights to these vintage films so neither shared in the profit of the showings. Laurel did not enjoy seeing them on TV because he felt they were ruined by commercials and time cuts.

Despite their long association, they did not become close personal friends until their movie career ended and they began touring together. They were particularly touched to see that their popularity had not waned in Europe. When they steamed to Ireland, thousands crowded the pier at Cobh cheering. "All the church bells in Cobh started to ring out our theme song ['The Cuckoo Song']," Laurel said. "Babe looked at me and we cried. . . . I'll never forget that day. Never."

Hardy died in 1957 at the age of sixty-five. He lingered for a year after suffering a paralytic stroke that left him helpless. Laurel, too, had a stroke in 1955. He partially recovered but declined to appear on stage after Hardy's death. He spent his last years with his fourth and eighth wife, Ida, in their Santa Monica, California, home, on a bluff overlooking the Pacific Ocean.

He became a diabetic and suffered a heart attack in 1965. But he always kept his sense of humor. One day as he lay in bed he told his nurse, "I'd much rather be skiing than doing this."

"Oh, Mr. Laurel, do you ski?" the nurse asked.

"No," he said, "but I'd much sooner be skiing than doing what I'm doing."

He died a few minutes later. He was seventy-four.

Time out for a soft-shoe routine with the Avalon Boys quartet in the background.

Stan blabs the reason for their secret mission to saloon boss Mickey Finn (James Finlayson) while Ollie looks on with exasperation.

132

After delivering the deed to the wrong girl, the boys stumble across the right one, Mary Roberts (Rosina Lawrence).

Back at midnight, the boys devise a pulley system to get to the saloon's safe on the second floor. You know the outcome.

In a side-splitting scene, the boys try to regain the deed which they have erroneously given to show girl Lola Marcel (Sharon Lynne). That's Lola on top of the pile-up.

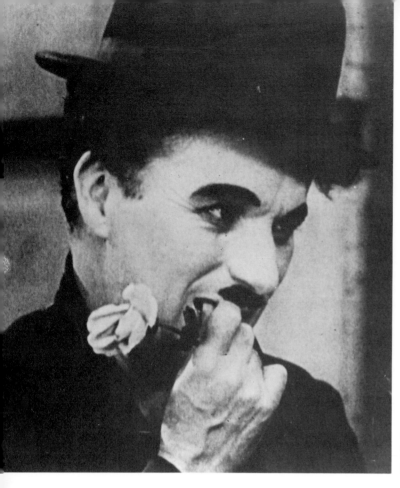

Two views of the haunting sad smile of the little tramp when the blind girl sees him at the end.

(Photos by United Artists)

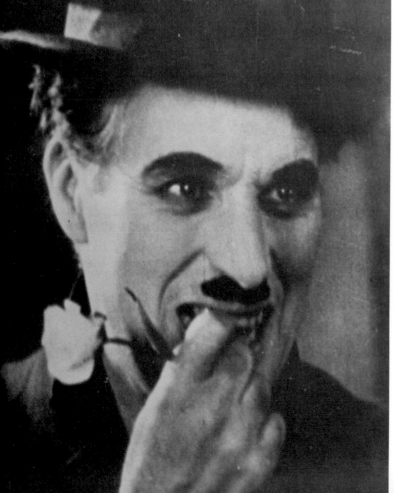

134

Charlie Chaplin

City Lights

(Released February 6, 1931)

WRITTEN, DIRECTED AND PRODUCED by Charles Chaplin. Directors: Harry Crocker, Henry Bergman, Albert Austin. Photography by Rollie Totheroh, Gordon Pollock and Mark Marklatt. Settings by Charles D. Hall. Music composed by Chaplin.* Musical arrangements by Arthur Johnston. Musical direction by Alfred Newman. General manager, Alfred Reeves. Released by United Artists. Running time, 87 minutes.

A Tramp	CHARLIE CHAPLIN
A Blind Girl	VIRGINIA CHERRILL
Her Grandmother	FLORENCE LEE
An Eccentric Millionaire	HARRY MYERS
His Butler	ALLAN GARCIA
A Prize Fighter	HANK MANN
Janitor and Official	HARRY BERGMAN
Streetcleaner and Crook	ALBERT AUSTIN
Distinguished Man in Café	STANHOPE WHEATCROFT
Old Tramp	JOHN RAND
Foreman	JAMES DONNELLY
Referee	EDDIE BAKER
Newsboy	ROBERT PARRISH
Extra in Night Club Scene	JEAN HARLOW

A little tramp is scurrying along the street trying to elude a gang of boys who are teasing him. Through a flower-store window, a lovely former blind girl watches, amused. The tramp turns and sees her. The girl notices him staring and giggles to a friend. "I've made a conquest."

She goes out to give the pathetic figure in rags a white rose and a coin. At first the tramp backs

---

* Although he credited himself for the score, Chaplin, in fact, did not write all the music. "La Violetera" ("Who'll Buy My Violets"), a song popularized by Raquel Meller, was the theme for the blind flower girl.

away shyly. But the girl calls after him and he lets her press the flower and coin into his hand.

"You?" the girl says, stunned. By touch, she remembers the hand as the familiar one which so many times had put money into her own. It was he who paid for her eye operation. It was this forlorn and comic man whom she had dreamed of as young and handsome and rich, her Prince Charming.

"You can see now?" the tramp asks.

"Yes," the girl replies uncertainly. "I can see now."

They stand and look at each other, the camera playing from face to face. The tramp absently puts his hand—still holding the rose—into his mouth. He smiles. It is a heartbreaking expression, a painful look blending shame and joy and fear. Joy because the great deed of his life has at last been recognized. Shame because of who he is and what he must look like to her. Fear because he knows that recognition means his feeble hope of love is forever over.

This is the end of *City Lights*, perhaps the most poignant closing scene ever filmed. The movie is certainly Chaplin's masterpiece, which is saying a lot for an actor hailed as a genius and a legendary, if controversial, figure in his lifetime. His little vagabond—the awkward fellow with dog-eared shoes, baggy pants, bamboo cane, toothbrush mustache and incongruous derby—became the symbol of the bumbling underdog out of place in the modern, rush-a-day world.

The tramp's antics provided belly laughs for millions. But as much as the public adored Chaplin on the screen, it could not accept his off-screen unorthodox moral standards and unpopular political views. Chaplin, a British subject, was barred from the United States in 1952. He has not been back since. His movies are only rarely shown in this country today. And a whole generation of Americans have grown up who know of the great clown only from books.

Born in London in 1889, Chaplin was the son of struggling variety actors. His mother, a music hall soubrette, lost her voice and then her mind. Like a Dickens waif, Chaplin spent his early life in the workhouse, a home for orphans and destitute children, and on the streets of London where he begged or danced for pennies. He later became a juvenile actor. At twenty-one he came to the United States with a traveling music hall troupe and joined the infant movie industry. It was here that he found himself.

In *My Autobiography*, Chaplin recalls how he devised the famous tramp character strictly by chance. One day Keystone's Mack Sennett called to him on the set of a hotel lobby. "We need some gags here," Sennett said. "Put on a comedy make-up." Chaplin had no idea what to do. But on the way to the wardrobe he worked it out in his mind. "I wanted everything a contradiction," Chaplin recalled. "The pants baggy, the coat tight, the hat small, the shoes large." To make himself look older, he added a small mustache.

Once costumed, he knew exactly who he was. "A tramp, a gentleman, a poet, a dreamer, always hopeful of romance and adventure . . . [but] not above picking up cigarette butts." Sennett told him to get on the set and see what he could do. Under Sennett, comedy was spontaneously worked out. "I entered [the lobby] and stumbled over the foot of a lady," Chaplin said. "I turned and raised my hat apologetically. Then turned and stumbled over a cuspidor. Then turned and raised my hat to the cuspidor. Behind the camera, they began to laugh." So was born a character and a career.

In 1914, his first year in Hollywood, Chaplin made thirty-six films, writing and directing many of them (two-reelers) himself. His popularity was immediate. Audiences welcomed his originality and fresh comic inventiveness in a medium that had produced only the broadest slapstick. Within two years he was earning over $600,000.

In 1919, Chaplin joined with Mary Pickford, Douglas Fairbanks and director D. W. Griffith to form the United Artists Corporation. Thus he won independence by becoming a producer as well. After writing *The Kid* (1921), a successful six-reeler he played in with Jackie Coogan, Chaplin created, directed and starred in such full-length United Artists classics as *The Gold Rush* (1925) and *The Circus* (1928).

What was to be the greatest challenge of his career came after the arrival of sound. All the studios frantically began converting to talking pictures. But Chaplin insisted that the tramp, a pantomime character, would never talk. He would add sound effects and music, but that was all.

City Lights became the test of his instincts. Chaplin began by searching for an actress who could play a sightless girl without detracting from her beauty. He was about to despair when he saw a film company rehearsing on a Santa Monica beach. One of the girls in a bathing suit waved. She was Virginia Cherrill, a lovely blonde with little acting experience. Even before her screen test, Chaplin knew he had found his leading lady.

The plot of *City Lights* brings Chaplin and Miss Cherrill together just after the movie opens. Trying to avoid a traffic cop, the Little Tramp steps through a parked limousine. The blind flower girl, hearing the door close, thinks a rich man has gotten out and tries to sell him a flower. When the tramp realizes she is blind, he gives her his last dime. Then, enchanted by her beauty and flattered because she has mistaken him for a wealthy man, he sits nearby and watches her. By and by she lifts a bucket of water and, unwittingly, empties it on Charlie. Unwilling to embarrass her, he sits still as a stone, drenched but wordless.

That night, Charlie stops a drunken millionaire (Harry Myers) from jumping into the river and drowning himself. In doing so, Charlie gets dunked. And in a hilarious episode, the tramp and the millionaire take turns rescuing each other.

Charlie drives the wealthy man to his home in the morning and passes the flower girl going to her stand. The rich man gives him money to buy some flowers and Charlie drives her home. But when he returns to the millionaire's home, Charlie finds the rich man is now sober and doesn't remember him. And so it goes. When the rich man is in his cups, he treats Charlie like a long-lost friend. But when he is sober he has his butler throw Charlie out.

Meanwhile, the tramp undergoes a series of side-splitting adventures.

• As a street cleaner, he shies away from a horse parade only to come upon an elephant lumbering down a street.

• At an elegant garden party, he accidentally swallows a whistle and disrupts the guests as his tooting hiccups interrupt a pompous singer and summon dogs and taxis.

• In a nightclub, he confuses a string of confetti with spaghetti and chivalrously comes to the aid of an abused Apache dancer.

To get money to restore the flower girl's sight, he tries his hand at boxing. But he only turns the prize fight into a comic ballet as he dances behind the referee to avoid his fierce opponent.

Finally, in desperation, Charlie turns to the millionaire, who is again drunk. The rich man takes him home, where two burglars have just broken in. As the millionaire gives him the money, the crooks come out and knock out the rich man. Then the police arrive. When the millionaire comes to, he fails to recognize Charlie and the tramp snatches the money and runs. Charlie goes to the blind girl's home, gives her the money and tells her he has to go away for a while. But promises to return. As police hustle him to jail, he disposes of his cigarette with a backward kick. Down but not out.

Then comes the recognition scene, the haunting finale when years later the girl discovers her benefactor's true identity. It is a scene that rarely fails to bring tears. Simple. Moving. Eloquent. In real life, we know the tramp would never win the girl. Therefore, we think that in a comedy he will. So the denouement is doubly painful because our own illusions are shattered along with Charlie's. James Agee has summed up the response of many critics to that last moment: "It is enough to shrivel the heart to see, and it is the greatest piece of acting and the highest moment in movies."

City Lights netted a handsome profit of $5,000,-000. Two years after the demise of the silent screen, Chaplin had made a non-talking movie into a financial and critical success.

Like many of Chaplin's leading ladies, Miss Cherrill quickly faded from the spotlight. After a few minor films, she gave up movies in favor of matrimony. She had a succession of husbands, including Cary Grant, finally moving to England in 1937, where she became the Countess of Jersey.

Chaplin went on to do *Modern Times* (1936), his last role as the tramp, and *The Great Dictator* (1940), his first talking picture. But then his career started turning sour, largely due to his off-screen life. Sentiment against Chaplin grew after he made speeches that some people thought were pro-Communist and when he lost a 1943 paternity suit to red-haired Joan Barry, a former protégée. Despite blood tests that indicated he could not have fathered her child, a jury found him guilty

after a first jury had been unable to agree on a verdict. By that time Chaplin had married and divorced three times. His wives were two sixteen-year-olds, Mildred Harris in 1918 and Lita Grey in 1924, and actress Paulette Goddard in 1936.

Chaplin kept making movies—*Monsieur Verdoux* (1947) and *Limelight* (1952)—but while they got good notices in Europe, they got only mixed reviews in the United States. Then, in 1952, he went abroad with his fourth wife, playwright Eugene O'Neill's daughter Oona, whom Chaplin had married when he was fifty-four and she eighteen. While he was at sea, U. S. Attorney General James P. McGranery rescinded Chaplin's entry permit. He said Chaplin would have to answer to charges of moral turpitude and Communist sympathies.

Rather than face a hearing, Chaplin gave up his permit. His wife later renounced her U.S. citizenship and became a British subject. However, in 1958, Chaplin surprised U.S. officials when he settled all American tax claims against him for $425,000.

The Chaplins moved to a magnificent twenty-room, $350,000 villa on thirty-seven acres above the lakeside resort of Vevey, Switzerland. There, most of Oona's and Chaplin's eight children were born. After his exile, Chaplin made two movies—the anti-American *A King in New York* (1957), never shown in America, and *A Countess from Hong Kong* (1967) starring Marlon Brando and Sophia Loren. Neither was successful.

And so he has lived on his kingdom in the Swiss highlands for two decades. In 1969 he was eighty and his hair was all white. But he could sit on his terrace at sunset and look back on life philosophically. "I believe that fortune and ill fortune drift upon one haphazardly as clouds," Chaplin said in his autobiography. "Knowing this, I am never too shocked at the bad things that happen and am agreeably surprised at the good."

Despite his still unreconciled dispute with the Justice Department, Chaplin remains in the eyes of the American public the ageless and enduring clown who made the world laugh. In 1950 and again in 1964, revivals of his movies packed New York theatres. "It seems unlikely that any dancer or actor can ever have excelled him in eloquence, variety or poignancy of motion . . ." wrote critic Agee. "The finest pantomime, the deepest emotion, the richest and most poignant poetry are in Chaplin's work."

Charlie, in his famous little tramp getup, admonishing a couple of newsboys who are teasing him. *(Copyright 1950 United Artists Corp.)*

Dressed to the teeth, Charlie buys a basket of flowers from the blind girl (Virginia Cherrill) with whom he has fallen in love.

That look of fright in the street cleaner's (Chaplin) face comes from what he sees heading his way—a horse parade. *(Copyright 1950 United Artists Corp.)*

In the ring with Hank Mann.
(Copyright 1950 United Artists Corp.)

139

V

LIFE STYLES

GONE WITH THE WIND
HOW GREEN WAS MY VALLEY
THE GOOD EARTH
MAYERLING
GOODBYE, MR. CHIPS

Clark Gable as the dashing, opportunistic Rhett Butler.

The lovely Vivien Leigh in her most famous role, Scarlett O'Hara.

(Photos by MGM)
(© Selznick International Pictures, Inc.; © renewed 1967 Metro-Goldwyn-Mayer Inc.)

Gone With the Wind *

(Released December 15, 1939)

IN TECHNICOLOR. Produced by David O. Selznick.* Directed by Victor Fleming.* Screen play by Sidney Howard.* Based on Margaret Mitchell's novel. Musical score by Max Steiner. Photographed by Ernest Haller * and Ray Rennahan.* Costumes designed by Walter Plunkett. Film editors, Hal C. Kern * and James Newcom.* Production designed by William Cameron Menzies.* Art direction by Lyle Wheeler.* A Selznick International Picture released by Metro-Goldwyn-Mayer. Running time, 3 hours, 39 minutes.

Scarlett O'Hara	VIVIEN LEIGH *
Rhett Butler	CLARK GABLE
Ashley Wilkes	LESLIE HOWARD
Melanie Hamilton	OLIVIA DE HAVILLAND
Mammy	HATTIE MC DANIEL *
Gerald O'Hara	THOMAS MITCHELL
Ellen O'Hara	BARBARA O'NEIL
Jonas Wilkerson	VICTOR JORY
Suellen O'Hara	EVELYN KEYES
Careen O'Hara	ANN RUTHERFORD
Prissy	BUTTERFLY MC QUEEN
Aunt "Pittypat" Hamilton	LAURA HOPE CREWS
Dr. Meade	HARRY DAVENPORT
Mrs. Merriwether	JANE DARWELL
Reminiscent Soldier	CLIFF EDWARDS
Belle Watling	ONA MUNSON
A Yankee Deserter	PAUL HURST
Brent Tarleton	FRED CRANE
Stuart Tarleton	GEORGE REEVES
Charles Hamilton	RAND BROOKS
Frank Kennedy	CARROLL NYE
Tom, a Yankee Captain	WARD BOND
Bonnie Blue Butler	CAMMIE KING

"I know it will be the leading line on my obituary," said David O. Selznick. And so it was. Even though he made movies for twenty-six more years

---

* Academy Award winner.

before he died in 1965, *Gone With the Wind* was his supreme triumph.

No other picture of its day received as much advance publicity (three years) or ran as long on the screen (3 hours, 39 minutes). Except for the 1959 *Ben Hur* (11), none won more Oscars (10.).

It played before the largest movie audience in history (over 300,000,000 people), made more money (a domestic and Canadian gross of over $75,000,000) than any other film except *The Sound of Music* (over $80,000,000 from U.S. and Canadian outlets).

And yet, the film initially owed its phenomenal success to the happy outcome of a blunder. In 1936, Kay Brown, Eastern story editor for Selznick, had read an advance copy of the book and found it enthralling. Excited by its movie possibilities, she air-mailed it and a synopsis to her boss. "I beg, urge, coax and plead with you to read this at once," she said in a telegram. "Drop everything and buy it."

Selznick read only the synopsis, felt the story was too long to film. So he passed up the movie rights. But when John Hay (Jock) Whitney, Selznick International board chairman, offered to buy the novel on his own, Selznick quickly thought again. "I'll be damned if you do," he said and quickly closed the deal. The price: $50,000, a figure that today represents .0007 per cent of the movie's gross.

The 1,037-page novel had come from the pen of a frail Atlanta beauty who stood an inch under five feet and weighed scarcely a hundred pounds. Margaret Mitchell, whose Pulitzer Prize-winning book was discovered by a Macmillan editor on a scouting trip, had originally titled her first novel, *Tomorrow Is Another Day* (the book's last line). But Macmillan felt too many authors had recently used the word "tomorrow" in naming their works and asked her to change it. After giving it deep thought, she found her inspired title in the thirteenth line of the English writer Ernest Dowson's poem,

"Cynara." It reads: "I have forgot much, Cynara! Gone with the wind."

Selznick was undecided whether to film the book immediately or wait until the story was not quite as fresh in the public's mind. He sailed for a Honolulu vacation. On returning, he found that the book had become a sensational best seller. That settled it. He announced immediate plans to make a movie.

The public's fan mail clamored for Clark Gable to play Rhett Butler. But finding the actress to portray the fiery, willful Scarlett O'Hara was more of a problem. Selznick launched a nationwide search. His aides scoured the country, interviewing 1,400 girls, reaping acres of publicity. They tested 90, including such stars as Lana Turner, Paulette Goddard, Joan Bennett, Jean Arthur, Susan Hayward and Frances Dee. But no Scarlett was found and production was starting.

Then, one December day in 1938, Selznick's brother, agent Myron Selznick, brought Vivien Leigh to the lot. Miss Leigh, a talented but little-known performer, was then twenty-five years old. Filming was under way on the first take, the burning of Atlanta. "Dave," Myron said to Selznick, "I want you to meet Scarlett O'Hara." By the fading light of the dying flames, David O. Selznick saw the raven-haired, wasp-waisted British actress for the first time. The search for Scarlett was over.

The choice of an English girl to play the heroine of the Confederacy whipped up a storm of resentment. The Ocala, Florida, chapter of the United Daughters of the Confederacy protested. But Mrs. Walter D. Lamar, President-General of the UDC, smoothed ruffled feelings by pointing out that the better families of the Old South were only a generation or two removed from England. And, she added, there was a resemblance in the language of the two societies. Actually, most Southerners were relieved the part at least didn't go to a damn Yankee.

Selznick's headaches, however, were just starting. Three directors, one after another, had to be called in to pilot the film. The first was George Cukor, who had made a reputation as a "woman's director." But after several weeks Selznick thought he worked too slowly and lacked the "big feel" of the story. So Victor Fleming, who later admitted he never read the book, replaced Cukor, vowing to put back the "guts" he thought Cukor had taken out of Scarlett.

However, Miss Leigh didn't take too kindly to his interpretation. Violent quarrels raged between Fleming and Miss Leigh, often over trifles. Precious time was wasted because the script, still incomplete, sometimes had to be written on the set. Fleming told a friend he was so frustrated he once considered driving his car over a cliff. In fact, one day he did collapse and Sam Wood took over. But Fleming was back in a week and eventually the most talked-about movie in Hollywood history was finished.

Metro-Goldwyn-Mayer picked Atlanta for the world premiere and set the date for December 15, 1939. A gala spirit immediately swept Georgia. Governor Eurith D. Rivers proclaimed a public holiday. Atlanta Mayor William B. Hartsfield outdid him, proclaiming a three-day festival.

Confederate flags snapped in the breeze next to the Stars and Stripes. Women donned hoopskirts. Men wore beavers and tight trousers, sprouted goatees, sounded Rebel yells. When the film stars arrived, half of the city's 300,000 people turned out to greet the motorcade that carried the movie folk down historic Peachtree Street.

Highlight of the hi-jinks was the gala charity ball at the City Auditorium. Paying $10 a ticket, some 5,200 attended, including the cast in their most colorful costumes. The town's leading executives were there and so were governors of five Southern states. They were: Rivers of Georgia, Prentice Cooper of Tennessee, Frank M. Dixon of Alabama, Burnet Rhett Maybank of South Carolina and Fred Cone of Florida.

Gable escorted the mayor's daughter, Mildred Hartsfield. The mayor reciprocated by escorting Carole Lombard, Gable's wife. At the ball, Miss Margaret Palmer, chosen from the unmarried Junior Leaguers as "Atlanta's Scarlett," led the grand march. One notable absentee was Miss Mitchell (Mrs. John Marsh). She said her father's illness kept her away. But she came to the premiere the next evening.

It was a night to remember. Loew's Grand reproduced across its entrance the stately white pillars of Tara, the O'Haras' plantation house. Inside the theatre, a select audience of 2,000 alternately cheered, whistled, laughed and wept. Selznick, they found much to their satisfaction, had been faithful to the book.

The story has practically become an American legend. Scarlett O'Hara of Tara plantation, a Georgia belle, loves scholarly Ashley Wilkes (Leslie Howard) of nearby Twelve Oaks. At a party at the Wilkes plantation, Ashley announces his engagement to Melanie Hamilton (Olivia de Havilland). Scarlett begs him to forget Melanie and marry her, but Ashley refuses. Rhett Butler, a visiting Charlestonian, overhears the conversation and teases Scarlett. But she has no time for Butler. Realizing that Ashley is going through with the marriage, Scarlett spitefully accepts the impetuous proposal of Melanie's brother Charles (Rand Brooks). Both Ashley and Charles leave for the army immediately after marrying, and Charles dies shortly afterward.

Scarlett, a bored widow now, goes to Atlanta to visit Aunt "Pittypat" Hamilton (Laura Hope Crews). She immediately creates a scandal by dancing with Rhett while still in mourning. But as the romantic illusion of the war turns to grim reality, Scarlett passes the time helping at the hospital. However, Atlanta is a doomed city. Sherman begins his devastating March to the Sea and it's only a matter of time before Atlanta must fall. With panic in the street, Scarlett keeps a promise to Ashley and stays on to take care of the ailing Melanie, now in her last days of pregnancy. Finally, after delivering the baby without medical assistance, Scarlett persuades Rhett to help them escape. He takes them out of an Atlanta of burning houses and buildings and they head home.

But Tara has changed almost beyond recognition. Scarlett's strong and competent mother (Barbara O'Neil) lies dead of typhoid. Her father (Thomas Mitchell) has sunk into drunken fantasies. Union raiders and deserters have taken everything of value. Foraging through the scorched earth for a single turnip, Scarlett vows: "As God is my witness, I'm going to live through this. And when it is over, I'll never be hungry again."

Scarlett becomes the head of the house, the one to whom everyone turns. Her real strength emerges as she begins the long ordeal of getting Tara back on its feet. She, her sisters, and her ever loyal, ever scolding Mammy (Hattie McDaniel) work side by side in the fields. Scarlett shoots down a Yankee deserter (Paul Hurst) who comes to take what little is left, and uses the money she finds on him to keep them from starving.

Ashley returns from the war, his legacy of Twelve Oaks a ruin. Scarlett begs him to run off with her, but he turns her down. He, the educated, noble idealist, is useless as a practical help in running Tara. Finally, in desperation, Scarlett dresses herself in a gown made from her mother's velvet portieres, and goes to Atlanta determined to find the money for taxes.

She meets her sister Suellen's beau, Frank Kennedy (Carroll Nye), now beginning to prosper in Reconstruction Atlanta. Scarlett seizes the opportunity and tricks him into marrying her by telling him Suellen has recently married someone else. She persuades him to let her open a sawmill, employing cheap convict labor, and drags an unwilling Ashley in as a partner. But it is Scarlett's hardheaded management that makes the venture a success. While driving to the mill alone one day, she is attacked in Shantytown. Frank is killed in a reciprocal raid, and Scarlett is once more a widow.

Almost at once, Scarlett marries Rhett. After all the years of skimping and conniving, she is finally able to luxuriate in nouveau riche grandeur. They live in an ostentatious mansion with their daughter Bonnie Blue. But Scarlett continues to throw herself shamelessly at Ashley, until a double tragedy strikes. Bonnie Blue dies in a horseback-riding accident. Shortly afterward, Melanie dies. As Scarlett watches the grief-stricken Ashley, she realizes at last that he has always loved Melanie and that all her advances have been in vain. She tries to turn to Rhett. But Rhett, tired of her constant rejection and selfishness, walks out.

"Oh, my darling," Scarlett calls after him, "if you leave me, what shall I do?" Gable turns in the doorway. "Frankly, my dear," he says, "I don't give a damn." Many moviegoers remember that as the last line. But it is actually Scarlett who has the curtain line. "I'll think of it all tomorrow at Tara," she tells herself. "I can stand it then. Tomorrow, I'll think of some way to get him back. After all, tomorrow is another day."

The movie won the Oscar for the best film of 1939 over such strong entries as *Goodbye, Mr. Chips, The Wizard of Oz, Wuthering Heights, Stagecoach, Ninotchka* and *Mr. Smith Goes to Washington.* Other *Gone With the Wind* winners included Vivien Leigh (Best Actress), Hattie McDaniel, the first Negro to win an Academy Award (Best Supporting Actress), Victor Fleming (Director) and Sidney Howard (Best Screen Play).

The Old South in all its antebellum splendor. From left, Leslie Howard, Olivia de Havilland, Thomas Mitchell, Barbara O'Neil, Miss Leigh and Rand Brooks.

The famous Atlanta charity ball scene. Scarlett, wearing her widow's black, dances with Rhett Butler while other dancers look on scandalized.

Scarlett amid the wounded and dying at the Atlanta railroad station.

Mammy (Hattie McDaniel) and Melanie Hamilton (Miss de Havilland) and Scarlett as they work to rebuild their devastated plantation home, Tara.

Rhett and Scarlett flee a burning Atlanta.

Returning from the coal pits, Welsh miners sing as they carry their lanterns and lunch pails.

(Photos by 20th Century-Fox)

How Green Was My Valley *

(Released December 26, 1941)

BASED ON A NOVEL by Richard Llewellyn. Screen play by Philip Dunne. Music by Alfred Newman. Camera, Arthur Miller.* Art direction, Richard Day and Nathan Duran.* Interior decoration, Thomas Little.* Film editor, James B. Clark. Costumes, Gwen Wakeling. Produced by Darryl F. Zanuck. Directed by John Ford.* Presented by 20th Century Fox. Running time, 120 minutes.

Mr. Gruffydd	WALTER PIDGEON
Angharad	MAUREEN O'HARA
Mr. Morgan	DONALD CRISP *
Bronwen	ANNA LEE
Huw	RODDY MC DOWALL
Ianto	JOHN LODER
Mrs. Morgan	SARA ALLGOOD
Cyfartha	BARRY FITZGERALD
Ivor	PATRIC KNOWLES
Mr. Jonas	MORTON LOWRY
Mr. Parry	ARTHUR SHIELDS
Ceinwen	ANN TODD
Dr. Richards	FREDERIC WORLOCK
Davy	RICHARD FRASER
Gwilym	EVAN S. EVANS
Owen	JAMES MONKS
Dai Bando	RHYS WILLIAMS
Mervyn	CLIFFORD SEVERN
Evans	LIONEL PAPE
Mrs. Nicholas	ETHEL GRIFFIES
Motshell	DENNIS HOEY
Iestyn Evans	MARTEN LAMONT
Meillyn Lewis	EVE MARCH
Ensemble Singers	TUDOR WILLIAMS

AND THE CHORUS OF THE WELSH
PRESBYTERIAN CHURCH OF LOS ANGELES

---

* Academy Award winner.

To the east lies England. To the north and west, the Irish Sea. And to the south, the Bristol Channel.

This is Wales, a slice of the United Kingdom a little larger than New Jersey, a land of wild, rugged mountains, rushing streams and lush green valleys.

It is a country of heroic individuality, a land of 3,000,000 people who have resisted assimilation since the days of King Arthur. Cardiff (population: 260,000) is its capital and largest city and coal mining has been its most important industry.

The rich coal fields lie in the valleys of southern Wales, whose grass-covered slopes have turned black with slag. It is here that generations of coal miners have lived and died in small, terraced houses pressed one against another. In rows leading up the pitifully scarred hillsides, their windows look on the next tiny terraced house across the narrow way. Beyond that are more rows of similar cottages and then a dreary view of smoke, dust and the pit-heads. Out of sight are the green valleys beyond the hills.

The Welsh are plain, hard-working, religious people who for centuries have kept alive their own language, literature and traditions. They are proudest perhaps of their music. Welshmen are as quick to sing as other men are to swap stories, and nearly every village has its choral group. With pride, they sing stirring songs of Wales's ancient warriors who fought invaders long ago.

These are the people Richard Llewellyn, a native son, recalls nostalgically in his novel *How Green Was My Valley*. And they are the men and women who come to life in John Ford's moving film version.

The book was a collection of incidents etched deeply in Llewellyn's memory. And Ford, following the book's theme, created his appealing picture not by plot but by eloquence of mood and characterization. In fact, there is no plot. Nor are there starring roles. Instead, the action sweeps like scudding clouds from one spellbinding incident to another, scene after scene unfolding with the romantic, humorous, poignant and tragic events of one miner's family.

Other directors have tried this difficult technique only to see their attempts fail. But Ford, who has won more Oscars than any other director, successfully blended the episodes into a rich fabric that, while it does not pull all its ends together, spreads out a lovely gossamer pattern of reminiscence.

An immeasurable part of the film's success was due to the picture's remarkable set. Producer Darryl F. Zanuck wanted to shoot the movie in the Rhondda Valley, the great coal-mining district of South Wales. But the war canceled his plans. So he built an entire Welsh village and coal mine in the San Fernando Valley of California.

In a glen so inaccessible that it wasn't on some maps, 150 workmen put up a row of stone cottages, cobblestone streets, shops, a pub, a tobacconist, a market place and a workable colliery.

The most unique part of the eighty-acre community was the creation of a huge slag hill. The workmen stripped it of vegetation and blighted it with fifty carloads of slag rock and black paint. A studio painter stood by with a spray gun to keep the hill black when filming was taking place.

But, undeniably, the key to the film's warm, poetic quality was the acting. None of the incidents could have achieved their haunting, dreamlike effect without the artistry of its cast. Donald Crisp, the distinguished British screen actor (who once worked as an assistant to D. W. Griffith), won a best-supporting Academy Award for his strong performance as the head of the Morgan family. Sara Allgood played his wife with consummate skill.

There were also memorable performances by Maureen O'Hara, Walter Pidgeon and Anna Lee. But perhaps the most sensitive characterization was turned in by Roddy McDowall, who was the young boy Huw (pronounced Hugh). McDowall, twelve, had come over from England when war broke out. Although he had appeared in more than a dozen British films, he had only one previous, minor role in Hollywood.

Authentic local color was achieved by the use of the off-screen voice of Rhys Williams, a Welsh

actor, as the grown Huw reminiscing about the picture's episodes (Williams also plays the part of the town prize fighter), and the frequent hearty songs by an 80-member Welsh choir discovered in Los Angeles.

The film won the Oscar for best picture of the year and Ford received his third of four Academy Awards. The others are: *The Informer* (1935), *The Grapes of Wrath* (1940) and *The Quiet Man* (1952).

The story opens at the turn of the century in a little Welsh town where Gwillym (Gwil-um) Morgan (Crisp) and his five grown sons work in the coal mine. Their wages all go into a common fund that Mrs. Morgan (Allgood) keeps for the whole family. Then the mineowners announce a wage reduction and the Morgan boys talk of forming a union. Their old-fashioned father turns a deaf ear to the idea. He calls it "socialist nonsense." Their argument becomes so bitter, the sons leave home and move into a boardinghouse in the village. Only ten-year-old Huw, still in school, and Angharad (Ang-hah-rahd) (Maureen O'Hara), the sole daughter, stay with their parents.

The miners finally strike. Twenty-two weeks pass, and their mood grows increasingly bitter as winter comes. Some resent the elder Morgan's anti-union attitude. There is a night meeting in the woods, and Mrs. Morgan, believing they might harm her husband, goes to it to defend him.

On the way home in a gale, she slips into an icy pond. Huw leaps in and courageously keeps her afloat while shouting for help.

The Morgan boys return home to help their mother regain her strength. But with his legs frozen, Huw is bed-ridden for months. The village preacher, the Rev. Mr. Gruffydd (Griffith) (Pidgeon), keeps his spirits up and one day carries him to a hillside of daffodils. There, he urges him to take his first faltering steps. "You can walk, Huw, if you try," the preacher says. ". . . Come, lad." Huw does and falls into Pidgeon's arms.

Pidgeon has another interest in the Morgan family. There is unspoken love between him and Maureen O'Hara. But at last he tells her their love is hopeless. He will not let her suffer with him in his poverty. She eventually marries the mineowner's son, Iestyn (Yes-tin) Evans (Marten Lamont) and leaves for South Africa.

Huw gradually recovers the use of his legs. But on his first day in school he is hauled up before class for being late and ridiculed by Mr. Jonas (Morton Lowry), the strict schoolmaster. After school, the class bully gives Huw a bad beating. However, Dai Bando (Di Bahn-doh) (Williams), the village prize fighter, gives Huw boxing lessons. Huw returns to trounce the bully while his classmates cheer him on. When the sadistic teacher whips Huw after the fight, Dai Bando comes to school and gives the teacher a boxing lesson he doesn't soon forget.

Meanwhile the strike is settled. But the work force is cut and wages are still low. So four of the Morgan sons decide to leave the valley. Then disaster strikes. There is an accident in the mine and Ivor (Patric Knowles), who has married and stayed on, is killed the very day his child is born. Huw turns down a chance to go to college to work in the colliery and help provide for Ivor's wife and child.

Angharad returns from South Africa. The preacher sees her again and vicious rumors spread about their innocent relationship. Mr. Gruffydd denounces the gossip-mongers from the pulpit and then resigns.

As he is leaving, a shrill whistle at the mine signals another tragedy. There has been a cave-in. The elder Morgan is trapped below. Huw goes down, sloshing through the water to locate his father buried under tons of debris. The elder Morgan dies in the blackness in Huw's arms.

And so Huw has grown into manhood watching his family slowly disintegrate and a simple way of life change and disappear forever. As Huw packs to leave the valley, he looks back on it all. "Men like my father cannot die," he says. "They are with me still—real in memory as they were real in flesh —loving and beloved forever. How green was my valley, then."

The last sequence shows Morgan and Huw together in memory walking over the crest of a hill. The camera holds on them as a magnificent choir swells in mighty crescendo, singing one of the great Welsh songs.

Morgan (Donald Crisp), extreme right, and his sons. From left, John Loder, Roddy McDowall, Evan S. Evans, Richard Fraser, James Monk, and Patric Knowles.

Another photograph of the family with the two Morgan women—played by Sara Allgood, center, and Maureen O'Hara. In the background is a mine shaft. The men's faces are blackened after a day's work.

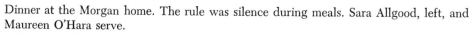

Dinner at the Morgan home. The rule was silence during meals. Sara Allgood, left, and Maureen O'Hara serve.

The Morgans' sons meet the eldest boy's fiancée (Anna Lee). Ivor (Patric Knowles) stands by her chair. Roddy McDowall, the youngest, is seated. Crisp, the father, is at left.

Dai Bando (Rhys Williams), left, the village prize fighter, gives Huw (McDowall) a boxing lesson after the class bully has licked him. Barry Fitzgerald, second from left, Bando's manager, Morgan and sons Davy (Fraser) and Ianto (Loder) all strike a fighting stance.

Roddy McDowall with Walter Pidgeon, playing the Rev. Mr. Gruffydd.

After their wedding feast, Wang Lung (Paul Muni) finds his wife, O-Lan (Luise Rainer),
planting a peach seed in their humble garden. It later grows into a sturdy tree.

The Good Earth

(Released August 6, 1937)

SCREEN PLAY by Talbot Jennings, Tess Schlesinger and Claudine West. Based on the novel by Pearl S. Buck. Adapted for the stage by Owen Davis and Donald Davis. Music score, Herbert Stothart. Art director, Cedric Gibbons. Associates: Harry Oliver, Arnold Gillespie and Edwin B. Willis. Wardrobe, Dolly Tree. Photographed by Karl Freund.* Film editor, Basil Wrangell. Montage by Slavko Vorkapich. Directed by Sidney Franklin. Produced by Irving Thalberg for Metro-Goldwyn-Mayer. Associate producer, Albert Lewin. Running time, 130 minutes.

Wang Lung	PAUL MUNI
O-Lan	LUISE RAINER *
Uncle	WALTER CONNOLLY
Lotus	TILLY LOSCH
Old Father	CHARLEY GRAPEWIN
Cuckoo	JESSIE RALPH
Aunt	SOO YONG
Elder Son	KEYE LUKE
Younger Son	ROLAND LUI
Ching	CHINGWAH LEE
Cousin	HAROLD HUBER
Liu, Grain Merchant	OLAF HYTTEN
Gateman	WILLIAM LAW
Little Bride	MARY WONG

Wang Lung (Paul Muni), an old Chinese farmer, cradles his dying wife, O-Lan (Luise Rainer), in his arms. Once a kitchen slave, O-Lan has borne him sons to help maintain the crops. Through feast and famine she has selflessly devoted her life to her husband and the land.

"O-Lan, you must not leave me," Muni says. "I say you must not. . . . I'll sell all my land if I could heal you."

"No, I would not allow that," she says. "For I must die sometime. But the land is there after me."

---

* Academy Award winner.

Her eyes close. Wang says: "I command you. I beg you. Stay with me."

"I cannot." She slowly lifts her eyes to his. "Forgive me," she says as her body goes limp.

Wang carries her to her bed and gently lowers her. Then he walks outside and stands next to a peach tree. Years ago on the day he took her as his bride, she had planted it from a seed he threw away. Now it is tall and stately. He looks into its branches heavy with rain. He places his gnarled hands against its trunk and rubs his cheek against the bark.

"O-Lan. You are the earth."

Such is the poignant ending of *The Good Earth,* a film translation of Pearl Buck's 1931 Pulitzer Prize-winning novel of famine, revolution and plague. Asian scholars have said it did more than anything else to acquaint the Western world with the China of the 1930s.

So popular was this second published book by the daughter of a missionary that it led the U.S. best-seller list for twenty-one months. So universal was its appeal that it was translated into more than thirty languages. So durable was its story that in 1939, when Pocket Books published the first modern American paperback, it chose *The Good Earth.*

Yet, had it been left to Louis B. Mayer, head of Metro-Goldwyn-Mayer, the book might never have reached the screen. Mayer's brilliant young associate, Irving Thalberg, had purchased the movie rights. But Mayer discouraged the project. "Irving, the public won't buy pictures about American farmers," Mayer said. "And you want to give them Chinese farmers?"

The Good Earth wasn't a farm story, Thalberg explained, but a saga of a man who marries a woman he has never seen and their lifelong loyalty to each other. The public, Thalberg thought, would be moved by such loyalty.

Mayer finally relented and Thalberg began arduous production preparations which were to take two years. To achieve authenticity, he sent a movie expedition to China. The crew filmed nearly two million feet of the Chinese countryside. They returned with eighteen tons of properties, including entire thatched-roof farmhouses, dismantled and shipped complete with water buffalo, rudimentary tools and threshing equipment.

All was reassembled on what studio publicists called the world's largest set. In California, MGM transformed a 500-acre tract in the San Fernando Valley into a complex of Chinese farms. Agricultural experts planted typical Asian crops of leek, cabbage and bamboo and built a Chinese irrigation system for rice fields.

While they worked, talent scouts scoured the West Coast recruiting English-speaking Chinese for sixty-eight parts. (The movie had no non-Oriental roles and used only one Western implement—an alarm clock.) Eventually, about 1,400 actors appeared in the picture. In one crowd scene, actors stretched as far as three-quarters of a mile from the camera.

But the key challenge was the casting of the leads. Thalberg picked Muni, who had already established his ability as a character actor par excellence. The surprise was his choice of Miss Rainer, a twenty-four-year-old Austrian actress.

A native of Vienna, Miss Rainer (pronounced Rhine-er), was virtually a born actress. At sixteen, she gave a sensational audition and became a leading lady in Max Reinhardt's company. She quickly rose to become one of the stars of the European stage. At twenty-two, a Hollywood scout saw her touring Europe in *Six Characters in Search of an Author.* MGM signed her and she won an Oscar for her second movie, a 1936 performance as Anna Held in *The Great Ziegfeld.*

But the dark-haired, five-foot-three-inch beauty puzzled Hollywood. She was a kind of female Marlon Brando. She told reporters she hated movies. She ran around in slacks and wore no make-up off screen.

When the Oscar banquet was held, she said she wouldn't attend unless she got assurances she would get an award. None came and she didn't show up. Studio aides rushed to her house and found her in slippers and negligee. At their insistence, she slipped into an evening gown and appeared hours late at the banquet. She won her golden statue with her hair in disarray.

But no one faulted her acting. And in *The Good Earth,* she faced the enormous task of playing a woman of another race and culture, a character foreign to everything European. Moreover, nearly all O-Lan's moments of suffering, courage, joy and pain had to be projected by pantomime because the part had less than a dozen lines.

To perfect her role, she haunted Chinatown in Los Angeles, visited the Chinese settlement in San Fransico and talked incessantly with Chinese players in the production. "Not to learn to imitate them," she said later. "But to know them so that I could imagine the character. I cannot imitate. I have to understand."

Although there was no name for it then, Rainer was probably the movies' first method player. She once contrasted her approach and Muni's like this:

"He knew what he wanted to do in each scene. By what door he would enter, how he would make an exit, where each piece of furniture must be. When something was changed that was difficult for him. He had to change his idea of the scene. But as for me, I didn't care. I never knew how I was going to walk on or off the set, or just what I would do when I got there. . . . I wait until we make the scene, then I do it. I throw myself into the part—well, as though I were living it. . . . I do it all with my feelings."

When the movie was finished, critics hailed her performance, rating it over Muni's. She never laughed, rarely spoke, only occasionally smiled. But her eyes told everything about this stoic woman. "She pierces to the heart of Miss Buck's saga . . . ," Howard Barnes wrote in the New York *Herald Tribune.* "Rainer takes you inside the very being of O-Lan."

Ironically, Thalberg never saw a scene on film. He died in 1936 of pneumonia at the age of thirty-seven. Albert Lewin, an associate, took over.

The drama opens with dawn breaking at a farm where Wang Lung awakens on his wedding day. He goes to the Great House of the village for his bride, O-Lan, and finds the slave girl huddled near a stove. The plain and humble O-Lan trots behind him to the farm. When he tosses a peach seed into a rice field, she picks it up. After the wedding feast he finds her planting the seed outside their humble home.

As the months pass, Wang and O-Lan tend their field, tilling the soil, carrying water, hoeing. When harvest time comes, a storm approaches, menacing the ripened wheat. Heavy with child, she joins the men in the fields to rescue the crop. When she faints from exhaustion, Wang carries her home. He is about to leave for a midwife, but she sends him back to the wheat. Silent and alone, she delivers her own son. Wang celebrates by going to the Great House and buying a rice field to add to his little grain patch.

In time Wang's fields grow to six and his family to three children—two sons and a daughter. But when they see refugees fleeing from the north, they know that famine is upon the land. The earth dries. Crops shrivel. Wang's uncle (Walter Connolly) implores him to sell his land. "Before I sell it," Wang says, "I'll feed it to my children." Starving villagers break in on Wang and find O-Lan cooking—earth.

In the end they decide to follow the refugees and return to their land when the famine is over. Life is not much easier in the city, and O-Lan has to teach her children to beg. When revolution comes, O-Lan is swept along with a mob storming the palace. She is knocked unconscious in the crush. But when she comes to, she finds a bag of priceless gems that have been lost in the scuffle. Captured as a looter, she is saved from a firing squad when the soldiers are suddenly summoned elsewhere.

With money from the jewels—O-Lan keeps only two pearls—Wang returns and buys the magnificent Great House with all its rich lands. The new prosperity allows Wang to go to the city for business. Here he is fascinated by the teahouse dancer, Lotus (Tilly Losch), and he takes her as a second wife. To her he gives O-Lan's pearls. O-Lan accepts his second mate without complaint.

But Lotus brings discord. She seduces his eldest son (Keye Luke), and Wang finds them together. As Wang beats him, workers from the fields report an army of locusts blackening the sky. Wang will be wiped out if he loses his crops. However, his young son, who has gone to an agricultural college, tells him the plague can be fought. His strategy is to limit the area the swarming locusts can devastate until the winds change. O-Lan joins Wang and his workers as they set up fire lanes and ditches. When the pests keep coming, the men use shovels, gongs and their hands and feet to fight them off until the wind shifts and carries them off. The crops have been saved.

This is the movie's most stirring scene. The expedition that went to China filmed the whirring horizon of insects during their travels. Later, studio cameramen shot the close-up advance of the locusts on a specially constructed miniature movie stage.

That night O-Lan's son marries and there is a gala wedding feast. But O-Lan is too sick to take part. Wang knows she is dying and comes to her in her last moments, pleading with her to live on. He places in her hands her treasured pearls. And so she dies knowing that, after all, she is wanted. Wang sadly realizes that all his joys and hopes and successes have been realized through her because she and the good earth have been as one.

Critics acclaimd the movie. "A real cinema epic," said *Time* magazine. ". . . Sure to rank as one of the great pictures of all time." Said *Variety:* "It is picture-making at its finest. . . . It would be understood among any folk without words, so elemental and penetrating is its appeal." Frank Nugent, the New York *Times* reviewer, called the movie "one of the finest things Hollywood has done this season or any other."

The film cost $2,800,000—as much as any MGM picture since the lavish 1926 Ben Hur production—but it grossed $3,500,000 for a handsome profit. Although the movie missed winning an Academy Award—it was nominated but lost out to *The Life of Emile Zola*—Oscars went to cameraman Karl Freund and to Miss Rainer. She was the first performer to win two Academy Awards and the only actress to achieve this honor in two consecutive years until Katharine Hepburn did it in 1967 and 1968.*

Yet, only two years later, her Hollywood career was over. At the age of twenty-seven, she was considered washed up in films. Trying to cash in on her double Oscar victory, MGM cast her in a quick series of bad films. Her box office appeal waned and she quit the movies, influenced by her husband, playwright Clifford Odets, who had no great love for the film colony.

Eventually her marriage also broke up. She appeared on the Broadway stage and returned to Hollywood in 1943 for one last movie, *Hostages*, a war film that flopped. Later, she married publisher Robert Knittel, had a daughter and returned to her native Vienna.

Miss Rainer left no great body of work behind in Hollywood. To today's generation of movie buffs, she remains unknown. But to those who saw *The Good Earth*, nothing will ever erase the memory of the depth of feeling she projected on the screen as the peasant wife who, to millions of moviegoers, was the soul of China.

---

* Miss Hepburn, who won her first Oscar in 1933 for *Morning Glory*, got her second for *Guess Who's Coming to Dinner* (1967) and shared her third with Barbra Streisand (*Funny Girl*) in 1968 for *The Lion in Winter*.

Wang Lung and O-Lan at work in their fields.

After the great famine, O-Lan begs alms with a bowl.

Wang Lung, now rich, visits the teahouse dancer Lotus (Tillie Losch), who becomes his second wife.

O-Lan and younger son (Roland Lui).

Locusts have darkened the sky. Wang Lung, O-Lan and their helpers fire a field of ripe grain to try to hold the insect horde back until the wind shifts.

Charles Boyer as the ill-fated Archduke Rudolph, heir to the throne of the Austro-Hungarian Empire.

Mayerling

(U.S. release, September 13, 1937) *

BASED ON THE NOVEL *Idyl's End* by Claude Anet. Screen play by Joseph Kessel and J. V. Cube. Music by Arthur Honegger. Camera by Thirard. Directed by Anatole Litvak. A Pax Film release of Nero Film production made in France. Running time, 91 minutes.

Archduke Rudolph	CHARLES BOYER
Baroness Marie Vetsera	DANIELLE DARRIEUX
Countess Larisch	SUZY PRIM
Emperor Franz Joseph	JEAN DAX
Empress Elizabeth	GABRIELLE DORZIAT
Count Taafe	JEAN DEBUCOURT
Baroness Vetsera (Hélène)	MARTHE REGNIER
Chief of Police	VLADIMIR SOKOLOFF
Loschek	ANDRÉ DUBOSC

Snow falls softly in January in Vienna, blanketing the lovely Austrian capital with a white, fairy-tale-like mantle. Outside the romantic city, beyond the echoes of the bittersweet waltzes, the swirling flakes sweep silently down on the verdant Vienna Woods and on the famous royal hunting lodge called Mayerling.

It was here on a bleak winter morning in 1889 that a tragedy occurred, a bizarre scandal that rocked the great Austro-Hungarian Empire. Dashing Crown Prince Rudolph, thirty-one-year-old heir to the throne of the Hapsburg dynasty, and his beautiful seventeen-year-old mistress, Marie Vetsera, were found dead together. The slaying has baffled historians for nearly a century.

After the bodies were discovered, the royal family made immediate but clumsy attempts to try to cover up the double death and illicit affair. Emperor Franz Joseph, Rudolph's father, at first issued a court communiqué saying his son died of apo-

plexy. The next day Rudolph's death was attributed to heart failure while hunting. Finally the Austrian court admitted it was suicide, which it attributed to the Prince's deranged mental condition. Thus the Roman Catholic Church permitted Rudolph's burial among his ancestors in the imperial tomb, the Kaisergruft.

Still, there was no word about Marie Vetsera. Her body was removed from Mayerling. It was said that a sword was fastened to her back to make her appear erect. Then, propped between two soldiers—some versions had it that the escorts were her uncles—the dead girl was driven by carriage to the Abbey of Heiligenkreuz (Holy Cross). There, in a small local cemetery not far from Mayerling, her body was secretly buried.

Despite the frantic efforts to hush up the evidence, the story of Marie Vetsera's death leaked out. But no details were released about how she died. Over the years, so many court documents about the tragedy have been destroyed that the deaths of Rudolph and Marie have become one of the nineteenth century's true-life romantic mysteries.

Was there a suicide pact? Did Marie kill Rudolph and then herself? Or was the slaying a political crime?

Some believe that Marie poisoned her lover or blew out his brains in a jealous fit. Others think that Franz Joseph had his own son assassinated because he feared Rudolph's liberal ideas would have brought about social upheaval. Still others say that Rudolph, who had led a dissolute life, was a sick, frustrated man who had long been morbidly concerned with death. He had reportedly asked others to join him in a double suicide before Marie allegedly accepted, thrilled at the thought of being found in bed with the heir to the throne. And so, according to this theory, Mayerling was merely the last act in a sick psychopathic melodrama.

---

* Paris premiere, February 1936.

Most historians feel that Rudolph, an unstable neurotic, lonely in life, did not want to be alone in death. He didn't get along with his father. And his court-arranged marriage to Belgian King Leopold's daughter Stephanie, a homely woman of little charm, had made him despondent. During Rudolph's last few weeks, he reportedly asked the Pope to dissolve the marriage. Instead, the Pontiff is said to have informed Franz Joseph, who told his son he, as Emperor, would never permit the divorce. So, according to the best evidence, Rudolph drove with Marie to the lodge at Mayerling where they spent a last blissful night together. The lovers decided in favor of death by a bullet rather than by poison. Marie lay down on the bed, weeping slightly but resigned to her fate.

One report said that Rudolph's valet heard two shots close together. Another said the prince lost his nerve after shooting Marie and spent the night next to his dead sweetheart before his resolve returned. Whichever is true, the most widely believed account has it that Rudolph drank a glass of brandy and placed flowers in the dead girl's hands. He sat next to her on the bed, looked into a hand mirror, lifted a pistol and fired. The bullet shattered his head terribly. Death was so quick, his finger still gripped the trigger when he was found.

If the mystery of Mayerling proved an irritant to historians, it became an inspiration to writers. The event gave dramatists a free hand. The story is history. And yet it is not history. Here are the final moments of a tragedy whose earlier events have never been clarified. Mayerling is the last scene of a nineteenth-century tale of Romeo and Juliet that challenges writers to tell us how they came into the tomb.

Dramatists took up the challenge three times during the 1920s and 1930s. First came Zoë Akins' 1926 play, an adaptation of Ernst Vajda's *The Crown Prince*. Next, in 1935, came Maxwell Anderson's tragedy, *The Masque of Kings*. The following year, the French movie (with English subtitles) *Mayerling* appeared with Charles Boyer and Danielle Darrieux (Dan-yel Darry-ou).

The movie version has none of the political or philosophical overtones of the plays. It is a simple, romantic tale of star-crossed lovers. In tender human terms, it solves the mystery of the hunting lodge by creating a suicide pact. History leans to this account as much as any other.

Director Anatole Litvak sought an actress who could combine charm, innocence and youth. He found her in Miss Darrieux, a petite, soulful-eyed beauty who was already a film veteran at twenty-one. Opposite her, Litvak cast Charles Boyer, who had established himself as a French stage actor of the first magnitude but then had floundered in Hollywood because of language difficulties. In *Mayerling*, working in his native tongue renewed his assurance. Together, Darrieux and Boyer gave a poetic and poignant charm to the story.

The movie opens in Vienna where Rudolph is picked up by police as he joins a student rebellion protesting the despotic rule of his father, Emperor Franz Joseph (Jean Dax). The iron-willed Emperor forces him to abandon his liberal activities and then to enter into a loveless marriage. A staff of unsympathetic people surround Rudolph, spying on him and gossiping about his every move.

Struggling to free himself from this oppressive court atmosphere, he goes incognito to a fair. There he meets lovely, seventeen-year-old Marie Vetsera. They see a puppet show, toss rings over a swan's neck. And so begins a romance.

The next night Marie goes to the opera and is startled to see Rudolph in the royal box beside the Emperor and Archduchess Stephanie. In the months that follow, Rudolph and Marie see each other frequently. She comes to the Hofburg, the royal court, at night, or they meet elsewhere secretly. Rudolph finds an escape from his despair in her youth and serenity.

Count Taafe (Debucourt), Rudolph's enemy, and his spies will tolerate the prince's affairs but not a great love. Taafe writes to Marie's mother, who immediately takes her daughter to Trieste for six weeks "to cure her of this madness."

While she is gone, Rudolph falls into a depression again, partying and drinking every night. Marie returns in the midst of one of his revelries and he rages at her. "Haven't you ever seen a man drunk before? I'll love all the women in Vienna if I want. And you can do nothing. Nothing." A lesser woman would have turned on her heels. But Marie only looks straight into his eyes.

"Well," he shouts, "why don't you say something?"

In a gentle voice, she says, "*Ah, mon amour, comme tu souffres* [Oh, my love, how you suffer]." The scene is the turning point of their romance. In this moment Rudolph realizes that he loves not just a pretty though naïve girl, but a sensitive mature woman.

Now he decides that nothing matters to him

except Marie. He secretly writes the Pope, asking him to annul his marriage, and then gives Marie a wedding ring inscribed, "United in Love unto Death." When he puts it on her finger, he asks her to make a wish. What has she asked for? he asks curiously. "To die before you," she replies.

Rudolph's happiness is short-lived. The Emperor gets the Pope's answer—a refusal. Franz Joseph commands Rudolph to forget Marie. A prince belongs first to his country and his people. "I'll give you twenty-four hours to end the affair," the old man says.

That evening, the night of the season's most brilliant palace ball, Rudolph waltzes with Marie to open the dancing. The gossiping is at fever pitch throughout the court. When the Archduchess leaves, Marie refuses to bow and the two exchange icy stares.

The lovers flee to Rudolph's hunting estate at Mayerling. There they spend a joyous day and then make a death pact. Marie asks only that she not know when the last moment has come.

She goes to bed and Rudolph sits by the fire. When dawn comes, he picks up his pistol. As Marie sleeps, he fires it with steady hand. His old servant (André Dubosc) comes to the door. But Rudolph sends him away, saying it was a hunter's shot in the woods.

Now we see blood trickling from Marie's forehead to her face, tranquil in death. Rudolph sits on the bed and looks at her for the last time. There is a second shot, off camera, and we see his hand struggling to find hers, reaching it and clasping it.

The reviews were as glowing for *Mayerling* as they were for Darrieux and Boyer. "The picture triumphs where the stage has so far failed," said John Mason Brown. A "great photoplay," said Frank S. Nugent in the New York *Times*, "superbly produced, poetically written . . . and faultlessly played." Howard Barnes of the New York *Herald Tribune* called Boyer's acting "nearly perfect." Eileen Creelman of the now defunct New York *Sun* said Darrieux's Marie was an endearing, tender young girl glowing in the joy of her first and last love. "Hollywood stardom should not be far off for her."

It wasn't. Miss Darrieux, who off stage was a temperamental and fiery Parisienne, swept into Hollywood with a five-year contract and a salary three times bigger than President Roosevelt's. MGM hailed her as "the world's greatest actress."

She did only one film—*The Rage of Paris* (1938). Then she returned to France, saying she was unhappy in America. Thereafter, she made movies in Europe, returning to this country after World War II for occasional films. Her many pictures include *La Ronde* (1950), *Five Fingers* (1952) and *Lady Chatterley's Lover* (1955).

Boyer, of course, returned to America to launch a celebrated movie career as one of the screen's great lovers. His pictures include *Algiers* (1938), in which he played Pepe Le Moko, *All This, and Heaven, Too* (1940), *Flesh and Fantasy* (1943) and *Arch of Triumph* (1948), among many others.

There was no Academy Award nomination for foreign films then but *Mayerling* received the prize of the New York film critics for the year's best foreign picture. MGM did another version in 1968 with Omar Sharif and Catherine Deneuve. However, it was a cold and passionless film that failed to stir much interest.

And what of the real-life lovers?

Today, Rudolph's ashes lie near his royal predecessors under the little church of the Capuchin Friars in Vienna. A few miles away, the grave of Marie Vetsera has been restored. Surrounded by a black wrought-iron fence, it has become something of a tourist attraction. Sentimental European women make pilgrimages to put flowers next to the upright headstone that bears the name, "Marie Freiin v. Vetsera." ("Freiin" means baroness.) Below there is a German inscription, a quotation from Job: "He cometh forth like a flower, and is cut down."

Mayerling has become a convent where Carmelite nuns, who are never seen, pray for Rudolph's soul. Parts of the two-story building are open to the public and nuns guide tourists through a church near which the double slayings took place. It has been suggested that, had Rudolph lived, the course of history might have been changed. Poor Franz Ferdinand became his successor. It was his assassination at Sarajevo in 1914 that set off the chain of events leading to World War I.

Rudolph, frustrated politically by his father, lives a carefree life of wine and women.

Rudolph's cousin (Suzy Prim) secretly tells young Baroness Marie Vetsera (Danielle Darrieux) that Rudolph wants to see her. Marie is at the piano.

Rudolph relaxes after a long night of drinking.

Rudolph gives Marie a wedding ring. It is inscribed, "United in Love unto Death."

Marie talks to her maid as she gets ready for a rendezvous with Rudolph.

163

Dr. Wetherby (Lyn Harding), standing on dais with hands on jacket, addresses his pupils in the Brookfield School dining hall. Pupils from Britain's Repton School gave up part of their vacation to appear in the film, which was made in England.

Goodbye, Mr. Chips

(Released July 28, 1939)

A SCREEN DRAMA by R. C. Sherriff, Claudine West and Eric Maschwitz from the novel by James Hilton. Editor, Charles Frend. Photography, F. A. Young. Directed by Sam Wood. Produced in England by MGM. Running time, 110 minutes.

Mr. Chips	ROBERT DONAT *
Katherine	GREER GARSON
John Colley	
Peter Colley I	
Peter Colley II	TERRY KILBURN
Peter Colley III	
Peter Colley as a young man	JOHN MILLS
Staefel PAUL VON HERNREID (later PAUL HENREID)	
Flora	JUDITH FURSE
Wetherby	LYN HARDING
Chatteris	MILTON ROSMER
Marsham	FREDERICK LIESTER
Mrs. Wickett	LOUISE HAMPTON
Ralston	AUSTIN TREVOR
Jackson	DAVID TREE
Colonel Morgan	EDMOND BREON
Helen Colley	JILL FURSE
Sir John Colley	SCOTT SUNDERLAND

(A musical version of *Chips* was done in 1969 with Peter O'Toole as the gentle old schoolmaster and Petula Clark as his wife.)

In 1934 a British magazine asked novelist James Hilton to write a story for its Christmas issue. Because the deadline was drawing near, the editor could give Hilton only two weeks' time.

He spent the first week searching for an idea.

---

* Academy Award winner.

When he found it he put it on paper in only four days. It was a long nostalgic character sketch of a professor in an English boys' school. As Hilton recalled later, the story—really a novelette because it ran 20,000 words—practically wrote itself.

"I wrote 'Mr. Chips' . . . working from morning till night and with so few alterations that my original typescript might almost have been given to the printers," Hilton said. "I don't think I have ever written so quickly, easily and with so much certitude that I needn't think twice about a word, a sentence or a movement in the narrative."

Because Hilton's father was an elderly schoolmaster, English critics suggested that he had been the model for Mr. Chips. But Hilton denied this vigorously and often. At any rate, his novelette was put between hard covers and shipped to America. At first it had little impact. Then one day renowned critic Alexander Woollcott praised it highly on the radio. To Hilton's surprise, it became a best-seller and Irving Thalberg bought it for MGM.

The book had the virtue of honesty and simplicity. In sparse, understated yet moving prose, it told of a shy young master whose strict adherence to the rules made him an unpopular and lonely figure. But he married a beautiful and intelligent young woman whose love and vivaciousness transformed him into a warm and understanding figure. When she died in childbirth, he devoted himself to the school and became an institution, revered by generations of his pupils.

But the book had one major shortcoming. Hilton made almost all his points directly. We know young Chips is shy only because Hilton says he is. We know his wife is dynamic and engaging, again because Hilton says so. The weakness of the novel is that there are only a handful of anecdotes that let the reader discover for himself the qualities of the shabby professor and the others.

And yet this is the very strength of the movie. The screen adapters—R. C. Sherriff (whose previous credits include *The Invisible Man*), Claudine West (*Smilin' Through*) and Eric Maschwitz (*Balalaika*) —took Hilton's bare-bones framework, expanded it, and fleshed it out with heart-warming incidents.

For instance, Chips's character change, which Hilton merely alludes to, comes to life when we see him catching pupils having a snack after hours in their dorm. Instead of punishing them, which they fully expect, Chips overlooks their boyish fun. He shuts the door and backs out of the room, muttering something about a cat making the noises. The boys, of course, are stunned.

Those same pupils, whom Hilton merely sketched, we see vividly before us in the film—reciting Latin, bustling and cheering on the football fields, silent with stiff backs in the dining hall. The result is a movie that transcends its prototype.

MGM decided to make the picture at its studio in Denham, England. To add authenticity, it filmed many scenes on location at Repton. The school, then three hundred and eighty-two years old, co-operated handsomely. Two hundred boys gave up a week of their holiday to be extras. The headmaster even played a linesman in one of the football scenes.

The question now was—who would play Chips? The problem was that even Hilton had no idea what he looked like. He hadn't bothered to describe Chips physically because he was more interested in depicting his character. This omission had given illustrators of his book and magazine articles free rein.

"We will have a complete gallery of Mr. Chips of all sizes and shapes by the time the illustrators are through," Hilton said. "And they're all rather right. My feeling is that the main thing is to concentrate upon an actor who has the feeling of the character. I would rather have an American who can feel what it ought to be than an Englishman who is selected just because he has the English accent. Now Wallace Beery has the warmth for it. Some people would think that an extraordinary casting. So many people think of Chips as a little wispy man."

Charles Laughton was among those first considered. But the part went to Robert Donat following his successful appearance as the English doctor in *The Citadel*. The role called for him to appear at several stages of the doctor's career. In *Chips*, he would have to portray the teacher at twenty-four, forty, sixty-four and finally, eighty-three.

Born in 1905 into a poor Manchester family, Donat went to grammar school on a kind of installment plan. "Each morning," said Donat, "the master would rap his desk and declaim loudly, 'School fees, please.' Whereupon each schoolboy was expected to hand over threepence, the price of one week's education. No threepence, no lesson."

Later his mother sent him to study elocution with James Bernard to eliminate a stutter and regional dialect. He liked his lessons so much, he quit school to become an actor.

Donat played with stock companies for twelve years until 1933 when he began making movies. He scored a success as Culpeper in *The Private Life of Henry VIII* (1933), which starred Charles Laughton. He went on to achieve wide recognition in *The Count of Monte Cristo* (1934), *The 39 Steps* (1935), *The Ghost Goes West* (1936) and *The Citadel* (1938).

But Donat became best known for his moving and sensitive portrayal of the aged teacher in *Goodbye, Mr. Chips*. It won him the Oscar for best actor of 1939.* Making her screen debut in the picture was the Irish-born Greer Garson, who received rave reviews for her brief but eloquent performance as Chips's wife.

The film opens as boys flood across old Brookfield School's quadrangle, chattering excitedly on the first day of the new term. All wear straw hats and pass, single file, through the huge doorway of the main building, observing the time-honored "Call-Over" tradition. A master stands with a list of pupils. And as each boy goes by, he calls out his name: "Cobb, Corn, Cosgrave, Cotter, Currie Major, Currie Minor, Danvers . . ."

Then, in flashback, we see Mr. Chipping—or Chips as the boys come to call him—arriving in bowler hat at Brookfield in 1870 to teach Latin. When pupils rag the young instructor, the timid, dignified Chips is at a loss. In a lower school study hall, the boys playfully tip off his cap, disarrange his gown and start a minor riot. Dr. Wetherby

---

* In 1958, Donat, who had long suffered from asthma, died at the relatively youthful age of 53. Because of frequent illness, he made only 19 films in his quarter-century screen career.

(Lyn Harding), the headmaster, arrives to quiet things and later gives Chips a dressing down.

Thereafter, Chips becomes a strict disciplinarian. He punishes a star athlete by keeping him out of an important match. The boys and even other masters grow cool toward him and he, too, becomes distant, settling into a dull, lonely life. When promotions come, Chips is passed over.

Then, at forty, Chips goes on a walking tour in Austria and meets Katherine (Miss Garson), a gay, chipper English girl. They fall deeply in love and marry. When they return, she immediately charms everyone, particularly the boys. She shows Chips how to win their confidence by coping with them in a kind, human way. Under her guidance, Chips emerges as a warm, lovable if crotchety character.

Then a tragedy occurs. Katherine and her baby die in childbirth. But Chips goes on, remembering all that Katherine taught him. He keeps up her gracious custom of inviting all the new boys to tea and cake and so he comes to know intimately the second and third generation of Brookfield boys.

One day Ralston (Austin Trevor), a new, no-nonsense headmaster, urges Chips to retire. He says Chips's methods are too old-fashioned.

"I know the world's changing," Chips replies. "I've seen the old traditions dying one by one . . . grace and dignity and feeling for the past. . . . You're trying to run the school like a factory for turning out money-mad, machine-made snobs. . . . Modern methods! Poppycock! Give a boy a sense of

humor and a sense of proportion and he'll stand up to anything!"

In the end, the school and the alumni rally to support Chips and he stays on. Eventually Chips does retire. But he lives next to the campus and continues to have the new boys in to tea, to tell them how he caned their fathers and grandfathers and to send them away with a chuckle from one of his academic jokes. By now, Chips is a living legend. All the boys savor his stories and repeat them to classmates. Finally, when the headmaster goes into the army in World War I, Chips is called back to run the school.

In the tearful last scene Chips, now in his eighties, lies on his deathbed and overhears a master and the doctor talking about him. Poor old chap, they say. Must have had a lonely life. Pity he had no children.

"You're wrong," Chips says. "I have—thousands of them, thousands of them—and all boys."

Chips smiles and the camera shows a superimposed shot of boys in the school yard. In Chips's vision, they advance at Call-Over, repeating their names as their proud school song swells in the background. Sampson, Scott, Martin, Bullock, Forrester. . . .

Boys of all ages, sizes and shapes come forward. And as the procession gets down to the last few lads, little Peter Colley (Terry Kilburn), Chips's favorite, who comes from four generations of Brookfield pupils, steps up. Looking straight into the camera, he says in his youthful treble, "Goodbye, Mr. Chips—goodbye."

Chips (Robert Donat) meets Katherine (Greer Garson), his future wife. Chatting with them is Staefel (Paul Henreid), at right, a German instructor at Chips's school. The movie was Miss Garson's screen debut.

Chips introduces his bride to his boys, who are surprised to find her so beautiful and charming.

Opposite, top:
Now retired, Chips lives at Mrs. Wickett's just across the road from the school. Holding his cap and gown is Mrs. Wickett (Louise Hampton).

Opposite, bottom:
Chips's grown-up pupils honor him with a toast.

VI

MONSTERS

After stealing away with Ann, Kong places her gently in a tree while he takes care of the business of the moment—battling jungle monsters.

Frustrating his pursuers, Kong lifts a log bridge and all but first mate Driscoll (Bruce Cabot) and Denham, extreme left of center group, go hurtling to their deaths in a ravine below.

**KING KONG
DRACULA
FRANKENSTEIN**

(Photos by RKO)

King Kong

(Released April 7, 1933)

SCREEN PLAY by James Creelman and Ruth Rose from an original story by Merian C. Cooper and Edgar Wallace. Directed by Ernest B. Schoedsack and Mr. Cooper. Technical director, Willis O'Brien. Chief photographer, Edward Linden. Editor, Ted Cheeseman. Musical director, Max Steiner. Executive producer, David O. Selznick. Produced by RKO Radio Pictures. Running time, 100 minutes.

Ann Darrow	FAY WRAY
Carl Denham	ROBERT ARMSTRONG
Jack Driscoll	BRUCE CABOT
Captain Englehorn	FRANK REICHER
Weston	SAM HARDY
Native Chief	NOBLE JOHNSON
Witch King	STEVE CLEMENTO
Second Mate	JAMES FLAVIN
Charlie, the cook	VICTOR WONG
Grocer	PAUL PORCASI

He stands high above the alien city, perched on the very top of the Empire State Building. He has carried with him a girl whose blonde beauty has touched his savage heart. He thumps his chest and roars defiance at a squadron of single-engine biplanes circling just outside his massive paws.

He is King Kong. And he is trapped far from the primeval forest on Skull Island. There, he was a god to a tribe of savages, the ruler of a prehistoric world. But he is in man's domain now. And civilization has summoned the airplane to conquer him.

His paw lashes out at one of the planes. Down it spins, trailing a white plume of smoke. But his brute strength is no match for man's technology, and machine gun bullets rip into his body, piercing it again and again like needles in a pincushion. Once, twice, he sways. For an instant he looks at the willowy girl who has unwittingly lured him from his jungle kingdom. Then he gently puts her down, loosens his hold, and plunges a hundred and two stories into the asphalt canyons of New York City.

To a generation who grew up before television, the spectacular death of Kong remains one of the most thrilling movie episodes ever seen. One can only guess at the number of youngsters who looked up wide-eyed at the silver screen when the gorilla five times the size of a man hurtled into space. I know I was one of them. One rainy afternoon in the 1930s, I plunked down a dime at the third-run Lakeland Theatre (nicknamed "the Dump") in Brooklyn. I can still remember crouching low in my seat when the massive Kong made his first frightening appearance, beating a tattoo on his chest.

King Kong is, of course, best remembered for its special effects. RKO created its movie magic with tiny animated models of animals that had movable arms, legs, eyes and mouths. Kong, who towered so menacingly on the screen, was an eighteen-inch miniature. Studio cameramen photographed these animated models against plain backgrounds. Technicians later superimposed the shots on film of live human action and jungle sets to achieve what Hollywood calls a "composite."

In the three decades since it was made, no film has yet surpassed *King Kong* in camera technique. Few have proved so durable. *Kong* opened in 1933, the only movie to play both Radio City Music Hall and the Roxy at the same time. RKO revived it many times over the next three decades and it became one of the most widely seen pictures in history. There is even one story, probably apocryphal, that in a theatre in South Africa the movie has played for over twenty years. On New Year's Day,

1969, when *Kong* appeared on a late TV film show, the New York *Times* television section gave it feature play over five football bowl games. Later the same year the newspaper ran two long feature stories—one a reminiscence piece by Fay Wray, the other a light, make-believe interview with Kong—in its theatre section.

Just why *Kong* continues to draw interest is not clear. On the surface, it is just an offbeat adventure story of a beast destroyed by his strange infatuation for a beautiful girl.* The film would seem to have its biggest impact among adolescents. Yet, curiously, many adults never tire of it, seeing it every time it is reissued. (In her *Times* article, Miss Wray said she has gotten letters from film aficionados claiming to have seen *Kong* forty to fifty times. Rod Steiger, she added, said he has seen it twenty-two times.)

Some critics say its underlying theme is really one of unfulfilled sex with the Empire State Building providing the world's biggest phallic symbol. Others see suggestions of racial overtones running through its plot. Kong, who is black, is subdued by whites in the jungle and exploited by whites in civilization. In *The New Statesman*, Paul Johnson called Kong "a prehistoric *Lear*." Others find the great ape representative of Man, or, since *Kong* was made in the Depression, symbolic of the oppressed worker breaking his chains.

But to many of today's sophisticated moviegoers, the film is merely low camp, a simple-minded story so awkward in its attempt to create a love motif between a superbeast and a girl as to be laughable. "If the love that Kong felt for the heroine was sacred," wrote critic William Troy with tongue firmly in cheek in *The Nation*, "it suggests a weakness that hardly fits in with his other actions. If it was, after all, merely profane, it proposes problems to the imagination that are no less real for being crude."

If there is no unanimity on *Kong*'s ultimate meaning, it is nonetheless clear that Miss Wray screamed her way to film immortality. ("When I am in New York," she says, "I look at the Empire State Building and feel as though it belongs to me.") A twenty-six-year-old Canadian-born actress, she played the

girl of Kong's dreams, donning a blonde wig for the part. When she signed the movie contract, director Merian C. Cooper told her she would have "the tallest, darkest leading man in Hollywood."

(Over the years, Miss Wray has come up with her own thoughts on the movie. She feels that *Kong* should be classed as an adventure fantasy, not as a horror film. "If Kong were purely a horrifying and horrible fellow," she said, "the sympathy he evokes when, finally, he is struck down wouldn't exist. There is no doubt about such sympathy. Even I, seeing the film a year or so ago, felt a great lump in my throat on behalf of Kong.")

James Creelman and Ruth Rose wrote the screen play from an original story by Cooper and Edgar Wallace. The movie opens as Carl Denham (Robert Armstrong), a flamboyant motion picture adventurer, leads a film expedition on a mysterious voyage. Just before they embark, Denham goes ashore searching for a heroine for his movie.

He finds Ann Darrow (Miss Wray), a beautiful but penniless and hungry girl, on the streets of New York. And he persuades her to go along. He tells her he's going to make a movie of something that's never been seen before. "It's money and adventure and fame," Denham says. "It's the thrill of a lifetime."

After weeks of sailing, Denham finally tells the crew they're headed for Skull Island. It's an uncharted isle west of Sumatra, Denham says, where a monstrous beast is said to live. The natives of the island, named for its mountain shaped like a skull, have built a great wall to keep the monster out. "And you expect to photograph it?" the captain asks. "If it's there, you bet I'll photograph it," says Denham. Suppose it doesn't like having its picture taken? Denham is asked. "Now you know why I brought along those cases of gas bombs," he says.

Skull Island is first seen through a mist, a harbinger of the strange world awaiting them beyond the wall. No one is in sight when they land, but they can hear distant drums. A strange tribal ceremony is going on. As they approach, they see huge native dancers cloaked in furry gorilla skins circling a flower-draped maiden. Hundreds are chanting, "Kong, Kong." Suddenly, all sound and motion stop. The natives have spotted Denham and his crew. He comes as a friend, Denham says. But when the tribal chief sees Ann, he calls her "golden woman" and demands that she become the tribal offering to Kong. Denham refuses. But that

---

* Those who contend this was the screen writers' one and only theme point out that the movie opens with an Arabian proverb: "And the beast looked upon the face of beauty, and lo, his hand was stayed from killing. And from that day forward, he was as one dead."

night natives steal aboard Denham's ship, kidnap Ann and tie her to a stone stake.

Then, from the black, concealing wilderness comes Kong, his massive body illuminated by a hundred torchlights. He looks at Ann curiously, then tears off her fetters and carries her back to the jungle. Miss Wray, queen of the early thrillers, does her thing and fills the sound track with earsplitting screams. She undoubtedly rates the all-time Oscar for loudest and most convincing shrieking in a feature-length movie. ("I screamed up and down the scale with a wide variety of inflections," she recalled. "The studio chose the one that produced the most ice up and down the spine.")

Denham and his men go to the rescue. But they are no match for Kong's steamy, primitive world teeming with beasts from another age. They manage to bring down a dinosaur with a gas bomb. But a water monster rises from a bog and upsets their raft. Then a brontosaurus chases the survivors to a log bridge where Kong confronts them. With a mighty roar, he shakes the log, sending all but Denham and mate Jack Driscoll (Bruce Cabot) to their deaths in a ravine far below.

In his book, An Illustrated History of the Horror Film, Carlos Clarens describes in detail how RKO accomplished its remarkable animation of Kong and the prehistoric monsters. "The models were built of rubber and sponge. . . . An articulated metal frame allowed movements of the limbs, mouth, and eyes. . . . After each almost imperceptible movement, the model was photographed, the camera stopped, and the model reset. When run on the screen, these individual stages gave the illusion of life. Each of Kong's steps would require a dozen separate exposures, and 25 feet of film flashing on the screen for half a minute was the maximum result of a day's work." For close-ups, the actors stood before a giant-sized bust and hand of Kong. One of the picture's major achievements is that it did not let its technical wizardry get in the way of its gripping story.

The prehistoric battles royal are coming thick and fast now. Kong hears Ann scream and lumbers over in time to take on a huge lizard. It's nip and tuck until Kong snaps the lizard's jaws. Then Kong lugs Ann to his cave. But while a giant winged creature diverts Kong, Driscoll reaches Ann and they escape.

This sets the stage for the resourceful Denham's greatest ploy. When Kong follows Ann and Driscoll to the beach, Denham hurls a gas bomb that kayos the beast. "The whole world will pay to see this," Denham cries. ". . . We're millionaires, boys, I'll share it with all of you."

The scene shifts to a crowded Broadway theatre. Up in lights, a sign says, "King Kong. The Eighth Wonder of the World." Inside, the curtain rises and the audience gasps in astonishment to see the mammoth gorilla bound in chrome steel chains and ringbolts. "Look at Kong," Denham says. "He was king and a god in the world he knew. But he comes to civilization merely a captive, a show to gratify your curiosity."

Ann is standing nearby and Denham says, "And now I want to introduce Ann Darrow, bravest girl I have ever known. . . . There the Beast. And here the Beauty." Driscoll and Ann pose together beneath Kong for photographers. But the sight of Ann and the exploding lights enrage Kong. "He thinks we're attacking the girl," someone cries. Kong rips off his chains and bounds off into the streets.

Within minutes, Kong has sent a subway train and its terrified riders crashing from its elevated tracks. (Episodes showing him chewing up city dwellers and tossing a woman to the streets—considered too violent—were later cut from reissues.) The city is in a panic. Police cars race after him, sirens screaming.

Now comes the film's most celebrated scene. Kong finds Ann, plucks her out of her hotel room and climbs the Empire State Building. Used to the safety of mountains, he takes her to the very top. "There's one thing we haven't thought of—airplanes," says Driscoll. "If he should put Ann down, they could fly close enough to pick him off." And so, in a few moments, fighter planes are swirling around Kong. And they are pouring lead into his massive body.

Strangely, at this moment, as the pathetic beast totters above the civilization that is destroying him, all our fear of him vanishes. Instead of the terrorizer, Kong has become the terrorized. Some in every audience laugh. Some pity him. But some of us are moved to feel even more. Perhaps the adults who are compelled to watch this movie again and again —in their twenties, their thirties and their forties— perhaps they are sharing their frustration and defeat.

Kong is everyone who has in some degree been overwhelmed by the modern world and its machines. Everyone who has searched in vain for a lost love. Everyone who has known utter loneliness. We, too, are swaying in the dark wind, bellowing unheard challenges, beating our breasts before our adversaries. But we are doing this in fantasy and so, like Kong, we are doomed. And when he is falling, we are falling, tumbling along the steel shaft of man's highest monument, hurtling through the empty void of night and dreams to become a wreck at the feet of our conqueror.

And so it is Denham who has the last word as he pushes past the street crowd to see the body of Kong.

"Well, the airplanes got 'im," says a cop.

"No, it wasn't the airplanes," Denham replies. And in a sentence he sums up the weird tale that has just unfolded before our startled eyes. "It was Beauty killed the Beast."

Fay Wray, the Canadian-born actress who became immortalized as King Kong's girl friend.

Movie entrepreneur Carl Denham (Robert Armstrong) rehearses Ann Darrow (Miss Wray), his new leading lady, while sailing to remote Skull Island.

174

Top, left:
Kong tears the wings of a prehistoric winged creature that has attacked Ann in the giant ape's cliff home. *(Courtesy WOR-TV)*

Top, right:
Driscoll and Ann escape from Kong down a vine. Kong pulls it up but they drop safely into a lake at the base of the cliff.

The Eighth Wonder of the World in captivity—for a while. On stage, from left, Driscoll, Ann and Denham.

Kong has finally met his match. He clutches one plane in his paw after he climbs to the top of the Empire State Building. But the squadron's machine guns prove too much for him.

"I bid you welcome." Count Dracula (Bela Lugosi) smiles as he greets a visitor to musty Castle Dracula.

Renfield (Dwight Frye) has cut his finger and the count looks greedily at the trickle of blood.

(Photos by Universal Pictures)

Dracula

(Released February 14, 1931)

FROM THE NOVEL by Bram Stoker and the play by Hamilton Deane and John Balderston. Scenario by Garrett Fort. Photography by Karl Freund. Art director, Charles D. Hall. Editors, Milton Carruth and Maurice Pivar. Sound by C. Roy Hunter. Producer, Carl Laemmle, Jr. Associate producer, E. M. Asher. Directed by Tod Browning. Released by Universal. Running time, 84 minutes.

Count Dracula	BELA LUGOSI
Mina Seward	HELEN CHANDLER
John Harker	DAVID MANNERS
Renfield	DWIGHT FRYE
Professor Van Helsing	EDWARD VAN SLOAN
Dr. Seward	HERBERT BUNSTON
Lucy Weston	FRANCES DADE
Martin, Sanitarium Guard	CHARLES GERRARD
Maid	JOAN STANDING
Briggs	MOON CARROLL
English Nurse	JOSEPHINE VELEZ
Innkeeper	MICHAEL VISAROFF
Coach Passenger	DAISY BELMORE

The dark figure with the piercing eyes stands holding a candle on the broad stone stairway of his musty, vaulted-ceiling castle. He is dressed formally —white tie, tails, black full-length cape. His voice is precise and languid with an East European accent and his pauses give emphasis to the word he wishes to stress in each sentence.

"I am—[*pause*]—Dracula. . . . I bid you welcome," he says and smiles. But it is not a friendly smile. There is something missing, something sinister there.

The black hair is combed straight back and the flesh is like alabaster and the lips are livid as if cold blood flowed through them.

Through the massive cobwebs, he leads the way upstairs. But when he passes, the webs remain unbroken. Outside, somewhere in the blackness of the Carpathian Mountains, a wolf howls. Another answers his forlorn cry: "Listen to them." He turns around slowly. "Children of the night. What mu-u-u-sic they make."

In the richly appointed, medieval guest room, a huge fire burns and a sumptuous meal is spread out. He opens a dusty bottle. "This is very old wine," he says, pouring it into a polished glass. Ah, but aren't you drinking too? he is asked. "I never drink—[*pause*]—wi-i-i-ne."

Dracula, a popular success as a late nineteenth-century novel, then as a play in the 1920s, was released as a movie on St. Valentine's Day, 1931. Universal had no idea how it would be received, and so distributed it without any mention of the picture's horror theme. Advertisements said only, "The story of the strangest passion the world has ever known." Lines soon formed at the Roxy Theatre in New York. The film was an immediate hit—making more money for Universal than any other picture that year—and touched off a series of sequels that still thrill audiences today, nearly forty years later.

Why are we fascinated by Dracula, this creature that feeds on human blood, this prince of the undead who rises from the grave when the sun has set?

It is, I think, because, unlike other Hollywood monsters, Dracula is a man who walks among us. And he is more than that. He is an aristocrat, a titled nobleman with a great Hungarian castle. He dresses impeccably and has the cultured manners and good taste to play the gracious host to his victims.

Where other monsters—like Frankenstein's crea-

177

tion, the wolfman, the zombies, and the Egyptian mummy Karis—were subhuman or bestial, Dracula is a man of intellect. Where other Hollywood monsters killed aimlessly, Dracula's slayings were premeditated because his victims would join him after death in the vampire world.

Where they used brute force to kill, Dracula was more subtle. He went stealthily to his victim's bedroom, sometimes in the form of a bat, and took his sleeping prey with a tender bite that was almost a caress. In fact, an irresistible allure pervades his entire being. Where other monsters repelled their prey, Dracula's suave, gallant air, his intense, burning eyes, exerted a hypnotic charm. Often, his female victims awaited their fate with eager anticipation.

Dracula was written in 1897 by Bram (short for Abraham) Stoker, a retiring British professor and later the business manager of the great actor Sir Henry Irving. The book was widely recognized as a magnificent tale of horror, particularly the first section that deals with the strange happenings at Castle Dracula.

The story first appeared on the stage in 1925 in England where Hamilton Deane, son of one of Stoker's childhood friends, adapted it. Raymond Huntley played the count. The drama was not a critical success but audiences packed the theatre nightly. During its five-year London run, the management posted a nurse in the lobby in case fright overcame anyone. The play had a long run in the provinces, where it was performed until 1941.

Dracula opened in New York in 1927 and repeated its English success. In the title role was a Hungarian actor—Bela Lugosi—who only a few years earlier had known no English and so, at first, had learned his stage lines phonetically. His vampire portrayal was to lead to lifelong fame in the part.

Tod Browning, who directed the film, sought Lon Chaney, the master of silent screen horror, for the role.* Although he did one sound movie, Chaney was hesitant about making the transition to talkies and died in 1930 before deciding to play Dracula. Lugosi was Browning's next choice. It was a wise one, indeed. The movie made Hollywood history—

---

* F. W. Murnau had done the first film version, a silent movie, in Germany in 1922. But he called it *Nosferatu the Vampire* because he had failed to secure permission to use Stoker's title.

due in no small sense to Lugosi's masterful portrayal.

Some critics feel the picture has not held up over the years, particularly in contrast to *Frankenstein*, which Universal released ten months later. But at a screening in 1969 the movie, at least to me, was still absorbing. It is true too much of the horror occurs off camera. But it is also true that Lugosi is fascinating to watch.

The movie is also particularly chilling because Universal used no music on its sound tracks then. So the scenes of terror—Lugosi rising from his coffin, for example—occur in dead silence. Also adding to the stark tension is the black and white photography, which helps create an eerie grayish world of nightmare.

The story opens as Renfield (Dwight Frye), an English real estate agent, makes his way by carriage to Castle Dracula in Transylvania. The sun is setting and shadows deepen in the rugged, alien countryside.

The carriage stops at an inn. When the innkeeper (Michael Visaroff) learns of Renfield's destination, he crosses himself and pleads with him to wait until morning. "We people of the mountains believe vampires live there who drink the blood of their victims by night." But Renfield says he is not superstitious. He must go on to meet a carriage at Borgo Pass at midnight.

Now we watch darkness steal over the landscape and, in the dank cellar of the castle, Dracula and his three wives rise from their coffins. Our first sight of Dracula shows him rising in a cloud of dust, fixing us with his cold, steely gaze. Over five centuries of life in death, he has exhausted the supply of victims near his castle and he has decided to move to England to find new blood. Thus, the reason for Renfield's visit.

At Borgo Pass, Renfield enters a second coach. As soon as it is on its way, the driver disappears and his place is taken by a bat that flaps overhead, leading the galloping horses through the dense fog to Castle Dracula.

There, in a magnificently chilling scene, Renfield meets Count Dracula. Once Dracula gets deed to his property in England and learns that Renfield has followed his instructions and told nobody of his trip to Castle Dracula, the Englishman's fate is sealed. His food is drugged and the count feasts on his blood.

Dracula's lust is so insatiable, he cannot wait to

get to England before he has another meal. Aboard ship, he comes out of his coffin at dusk and slaughters the entire crew. When the vessel arrives, it is literally a ghost ship—except for Renfield, who has become a maniac, catching flies and spiders for their blood.

In England, Dracula takes title to a ruined abbey near the estate of Dr. Seward (Herbert Bunston) who runs a sanitarium. Dracula's first victim is a flower girl on a London street. Then he meets Mina Seward (Helen Chandler) and her friend Lucy Weston (Frances Dade). He goes after them, slowly draining their blood until they become more and more lethargic, drifting into the world of the undead.

But Dracula has not counted on Professor Van Helsing (Edward Van Sloan), the great vampire fighter. When Dracula calls at Dr. Seward's home inquiring about Mina's health, Van Helsing notices that Dracula casts no reflection in a mirror. This, of course, is one of the classic tests of a vampire. When Van Helsing confronts Dracula with his discovery, Dracula smashes the glass. "For one who has not lived even a single lifetime," Dracula says, narrowing his eyes, "you are a wise man, Van Helsing." Later, Dracula returns and lunges at the vampire fighter. But the professor pulls out a cross. Dracula reels back, temporarily blinded by this symbol of goodness. He throws his cape across his face and flees.

In the predawn hours, Van Helsing and John Harker (David Manners), Mina's sweetheart, go to Dracula's abbey. They see him carrying Mina to the cellar. As the sun rises, Dracula slips into a coffin. But Van Helsing opens it, pounds a stake into Dracula's heart and we hear his agonized groan as he goes to eternal damnation.

With the box office success of Dracula, a host of vampire films followed. They included: *Dracula's Daughter* (1936), *Return of the Vampire* (1943), *Son of Dracula* (1943), *House of Dracula* (1945) and *The Return of Dracula* (1958). But the screen writers' imaginations failed to live up to Stoker's. Most of the films were second-rate.

Nevertheless, horror films had a revival in the 1950s and Hammer Studios in England began remaking the original American versions. Hammer's technicolor production of *Dracula*—called *Horror of Dracula* with Christopher Lee—has become a modern-day classic. In addition to Lee, others who played Dracula include Lon Chaney, Jr., John Carradine and Francis Lederer. But no one approached Lugosi's performance and total identification with the role.

Born in Lugos, Hungary, in 1884,* Lugosi studied at the Academy of Theatrical Art in Budapest and made his stage debut in *Romeo and Juliet* at twenty. He was a lieutenant in the Hungarian Army in World War I. In 1921, after the political revolution in Hungary, he came to the United States. In his early plays here, he continued doing romantic leads.

That all changed abruptly when he appeared in *Dracula* and then went to Hollywood to do the movie. Thereafter, he became typecast in horror roles. Some of the better ones were: *The Black Cat* (1934), *Mark of the Vampire* (1935), *The Raven* (1935), *The Invisible Ray* (1936) and *Son of Frankenstein* (1939). One non-horror role he did was as a Red commissar in *Ninotchka* (1939), starring Greta Garbo.

At the peak of his career he got as much fan mail as any of Hollywood's leading men, 97 per cent of it from women, according to Lugosi. However, his films became inferior as he grew older, degenerating finally into mere burlesque: *Abbott and Costello Meet Frankenstein* (1948), *Bela Lugosi Meets a Brooklyn Gorilla* (1952) and *Old Mother Riley Meets the Vampire* (1952).

In 1955, when he was seventy-one, he appealed to Los Angeles County authorities for help, saying he was a narcotics addict and wanted to be cured. Lugosi, who said he had made $500,000 playing horror roles but had spent it all, told authorities he had been taking drugs for twenty years. When he was released after three months, he told reporters he was convinced he was cured for good.

He died less than a year later, his funeral a crowning touch to his macabre screen career. According to his last instructions, he was buried with his Dracula cape.

---

* Some sources list 1882 as Lugosi's birth date.

Dracula has had his coffin moved to a ruined abbey in England where victim Renfield watches over it.

Dracula is about to take another victim, in this case Helen Chandler. *(Copyright Screen Gems Inc.)*

Miss Chandler has fallen under the vampire's spell and he leads her to his coffin.

Renfield has unwittingly led Dracula's pursuers to his abbey hideaway and for that he must die.

Professor Van Helsing (Edward Van Sloan), the famous vampire hunter, confronts the count. That's a cross Van Hesling is reaching for in his vest.

The monster (Boris Karloff) makes a friend. He meets a little girl (Marilyn Harris) and they toss flowers in a lake, watching them float. When the flowers are all picked, he throws her in and she drowns.

(Photos by Universal)

Frankenstein

(*Released November 21, 1931*)

BASED ON MARY SHELLEY's novel. Scenario and dialogue by Garrett Fort and Francis Edward Faragoh. Photography, Arthur Edeson. Editor, Clarence Kolster. Sound, C. Roy Hunter. Make-up, Jack Pierce. Directed by James Whale. Produced by Carl Laemmle. Released by Universal. Running time, 71 minutes.

Frankenstein	COLIN CLIVE
Elizabeth	MAE CLARKE
Victor	JOHN BOLES
The Monster	BORIS KARLOFF
Dr. Waldman	EDWARD VAN SLOAN
Fritz, the Dwarf	DWIGHT FRYE
The Baron	FREDERICK KERR
The Burgomaster	LIONEL BELMORE
Ludwig, Peasant Father	MICHAEL MARK
Maria, the child	MARILYN HARRIS
Bridesmaids	ARLETTA DUNCAN,
	PAULINE MOORE

He lumbers on the screen in a stiff-legged gait, this frightening soulless creature with sloping, double-domed forehead and hooded eyelids. Spikes jut from his neck. Surgical scars streak his face and wrists. He is a brute of a man, easily seven feet tall, with power enough in each of his loping arms to splinter a door.

This was the Frankenstein monster as created by Boris Karloff. He played the stitched-together giant in only three movies—the original *Frankenstein* (1931), *Bride of Frankenstein* (1935) and *Son of Frankenstein* (1939). But Karloff set the standard for Hollywood horror films to come. At the same time, he typecast himself for the rest of his career—something he said he never minded, even though he was in private life a gentle, cultured Englishman.

"The monster was the best friend I had," Karloff once said in an interview. "Certainly, I was typed.

But what is typing? It is a trademark, a means by which the public recognizes you. Actors work all their lives to achieve what I got with just one picture. It was a blessing."

Karloff was born William Henry Pratt in the London suburb of Dulwich in 1887, youngest of nine children. His father was a member of the British Indian civil service and Karloff's schooling and early training was pointed toward a career in the consular service. But at the age of ten young Karloff played the part of a demon in his parish's annual Christmas pantomime. From that day he was sold on an acting career.

Karloff attended the University of London before leaving for Canada in 1909. However, success didn't come easily. Failing to land a stage job, he worked as a farm hand and as a logger. He dug ditches, hoisted barrels, drove a truck. When there was no work he slept on a park bench. Finally he got a job with a touring stock company. He was hired for thirty dollars a week. But after his debut, his salary was cut to fifteen.

For his stage name, he took his mother's family name of Karloff and added Boris to keep the Slavic flavor. In 1919 he appeared in his first Hollywood movie as an extra, a swarthy Mexican soldier, in *His Majesty, the American*, starring Douglas Fairbanks. It took twelve more years before he achieved recognition in *Frankenstein*.

Karloff was lucky to get the role. It was reportedly offered to Bela Lugosi, who had just created a sensation in *Dracula*. But Lugosi said he turned it down because the make-up would obscure his features. Another version was that he made a bad test. At any rate, director James Whale, who had been impressed by Karloff as a gangster in the film *Graft*, asked him to test for the monster. Karloff wasn't exactly thrilled about the non-speaking part. But he never forgot what it meant to his career.

"Half a dozen actors made tests for the part," Karloff said. "But I was the lucky one. I say 'lucky' because any one of them probably would have played it just as well as I did—and would have reaped the benefits that came to me."

Nevertheless, playing the role was far from easy. He had to be at the studio at five-thirty every morning and spend nearly four hours with make-up specialist Jack Pierce. He became eighteen inches taller and sixty pounds heavier. "The make-up was quite painful," Karloff said, "particularly the putty used on my eyes." During the filming Karloff, a six-footer who weighed 175 pounds, lost twenty pounds.*

Ironically, Universal did not immediately appreciate Karloff's importance to the movie. The studio didn't even invite him to the West Coast premiere on December 6, 1931. Instead, it asked Colin Clive and Mae Clarke, the leading players. "But the public took to the monster," Karloff said. "He was so wicked, so unwieldy, they shuddered and felt sorry for him."

Frankenstein, a freely adapted version of Mary Shelley's classic nineteenth-century novel, which she wrote at twenty-one after conceiving the tale during a literary ghost-telling session with Percy Shelley, Lord Byron and other friends. In her book the monster is harmless, at first, but kills after the revulsion and fear of others provoke him. The movie twists the plot by making him a killer from the start because he is given a criminal's brain.

The stark, gloomy scene of gathering dusk in a graveyard sets the mood of the picture from the out-

---

* In a 1939 interview, Pierce told the New York *Times* how he created the monster make-up: "There are six ways a surgeon can cut the skull and I figured Dr. Frankenstein, who was not a practicing surgeon, would take the easiest. That is, he would cut the top of the skull off straight across like a pot lid, hinge it, pop the brain in, and clamp it tight. That's the reason I decided to make the monster's head square and flat like a box and dig that big scar across his forehead and have two metal clamps hold it together. The two metal studs that stick out the sides of his neck are inlets for electricity-plugs. Don't forget the monster is an electrical gadget and that lightning is his life force. . . .

"The lizard eyes were made of rubber, as was his false head. I made his arms look longer by shortening the sleeves of his coat. His legs were stiffened by steel struts and two pairs of pants. His large feet were the boots asphalt-spreaders wear. His fingernails were blackened with shoe polish. His face was coated with blue-green grease paint, which photographs gray."

set. Dr. Henry Frankenstein (Clive), a young scientist, and his hunchback assistant Fritz (Dwight Frye, who also appeared as Renfield in *Dracula*), are stealing a newly buried corpse for an experiment. In a stone mill tower near his family castle, Frankenstein has been putting together a human body in an attempt to create life. He has assembled it from the limbs and organs of corpses stolen from cemeteries, or executed criminals cut down from gallows. What he doesn't realize is that Fritz has unwittingly secured the brain of an abnormal psychopath.

Frankenstein's fiancée (Miss Clarke), his friend (John Boles), and his medical school professor (Edward Van Sloan) all try to discourage him. But nothing can stop him. In a raging storm accompanied by great bolts of lightning, Frankenstein raises his creation to the very top of the tower. There, while electricity crackles below in Frankenstein's laboratory labyrinth of transformers, dynamos and electrodes, the heavens are harnessed to give birth to this artificial man. When the monster is lowered, his hand quivers. "It's moving. It's alive," Frankenstein cries triumphantly.

But director Whale has still to give us his most shocking scene. When the monster has enough strength to walk, he is called into the laboratory. He lurches clumsily into the room and turns. In absolute silence, his gruesome features flash on the screen for the first time. We see those chilling, deep-set eyes, and we know this is the face of a depraved creature.

Frankenstein keeps his creation chained in a dungeon. There the hunchback cruelly tortures him by waving a torch in his face. One day he comes too close and the monster kills him. Eventually the brute escapes and roams the countryside.

There is a moving scene—cut from the original because it was thought too violent—when he meets a little girl (Marilyn Harris) playing by a lake. She is not repelled and invites him to play with her. They throw flowers into the water and watch them drift away. Finally the flowers are all gone and the monster tosses the girl in, then staggers away beginning to understand the terrible thing he has done. "Karloff's final departure, wringing his hands in an agony of dawning comprehension is as moving a moment as any on the screen," writes Ivan Butler in his book, *The Horror Film*.

It was this apparent spark of remorse that gave pathos and depth to the monster—a pathos made a great deal more of by Mary Shelley—and established him as one of the memorable screen characters. Karloff always received most of his fan mail from children and he found they were keenly aware of this softer trait he gave the monster's character. "If they say anything beyond asking for a photograph," Karloff said, "it's always to express great compassion for the monster."

When the dead body is discovered, the girl's father (Michael Mark) carries it into the village, where Dr. Frankenstein is celebrating his marriage with the townspeople. The merriment suddenly stops. The peasants take up torches and set out after the monster.

Frankenstein follows, becomes separated from them and stumbles into his creation on a bleak hilltop. The monster overcomes him and carries him off to an old windmill. But the searchers have heard Frankenstein's cries. They surround the mill and set it on fire. In the blazing tower, Frankenstein and the monster battle each other and the monster throws him from the top of the tower. An arm of the windmill breaks his fall. But the monster is trapped and perishes in the flames.

Frankenstein reportedly grossed about $12,000,-000 on a $250,000 investment and its success, along with that of *Dracula*, started a new film genre. Karloff began starring in a wide range of horror roles. He sent scores of fellow actors to macabre deaths. He was an ancient Egyptian brought back to life in *The Mummy* (1932), a diabolical oriental in *The Mask of Fu Manchu* (1932), an ax-wielding executioner in *Tower of London* (1939), a mad scientist in *The Man With Nine Lives* (1940), a grave robber in *The Body Snatcher* (1945) and a warped prison warden in *Bedlam* (1946). One of his few non-horror roles was as the mild-mannered Chinese detective in the *Mr. Wong* series. In all, he appeared in over 130 films.

His famous screen career obscured the fact that he was equally adept in other mediums. In 1941 he scored a personal triumph in his Broadway debut in *Arsenic and Old Lace*, appearing in the comedy 1,400 times. Later he played opposite Jean Arthur as Captain Hook in James M. Barrie's *Peter Pan* and made many television appearances as an actor and as the host for the "Thriller" series. But it is as a movie horror man that he will always be remembered.

Karloff was married three times—first to a dancer, then to a school librarian (with whom he had his only child, a daughter), finally to Evelyn Hope Helmore. She was a story editor and former production aide to David O. Selznick. They were wed in 1946 and were still married when Karloff died in 1969 at the age of eighty-one.

The monster, who has broken loose, confronts the horrified Elizabeth (Mae Clarke) on, of all times, her wedding day.

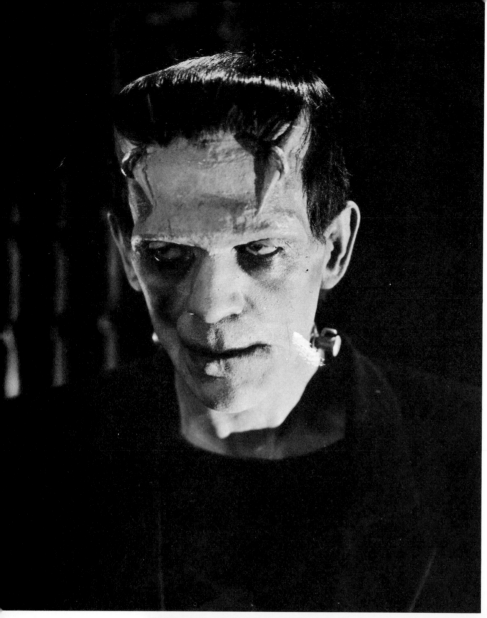

Karloff as the monster created by Dr. Henry Frankenstein.

Frankenstein (Colin Clive) works in his laboratory with his hunchback assistant (Dwight Frye) as the monster lies on the operating table.

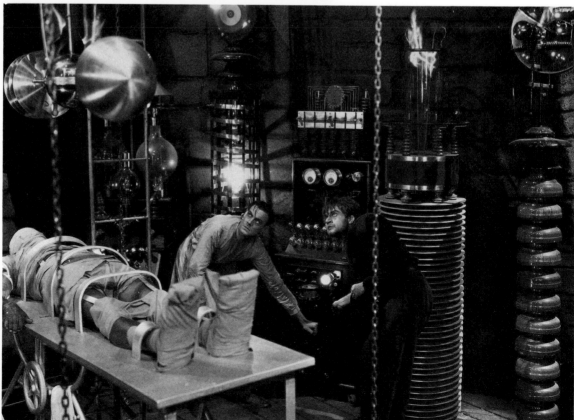

186

Frankenstein tracks down his creation on a hilltop (and now probably wishes he hadn't).

Crushed by a fallen beam in a mill tower, the monster meets his end in a raging fire.

Tom Joad (Fonda) in search of the Promised Land.

VII

WE THE PEOPLE

THE GRAPES OF WRATH
THE OX-BOW INCIDENT
ALL QUIET ON THE WESTERN FRONT
ALL THE KING'S MEN
I AM A FUGITIVE FROM A CHAIN GANG

(Photos by 20th Century-Fox)

The Grapes of Wrath

(*Released March 15, 1940*)

BASED ON JOHN STEINBECK'S novel. Screen play by Nunnally Johnson. Music by Alfred Newman. Photography by Gregg Toland. Art directors, Richard Day and Mark-Lee Kirk. Editor, Robert Simpson. Produced by Darryl F. Zanuck. Associate producer, Nunnally Johnson. Directed by John Ford.* Assistant director, Eddie O'Fearna. A 20th Century-Fox production. Running time, 128 minutes.

Tom Joad	HENRY FONDA
Ma Joad	JANE DARWELL *
Casy	JOHN CARRADINE
Grampa	CHARLEY GRAPEWIN
Granma	ZEFFIE TILBURY
Noah	FRANK SULLY
Rosasharn	DORRIS BOWDON
Pa Joad	RUSSELL SIMPSON
Al	O. Z. WHITEHEAD
Muley	JOHN QUALEN
Connie	EDDIE QUILLAN
Caretaker	GRANT MITCHELL
Davis	JOHN ARLEDGE
Uncle John	FRANK DARIEN
Winfield	DARRYL HICKMAN
Ruth	SHIRLEY MILLS
Policeman	WARD BOND
Floyd	PAUL GUILFOYLE
Bert	HARRY TYLER
Mae	KITTY MC HUGH
Driver	IRVING BACON
Thomas	ROGER IMHOFF
Wilkie	CHARLES D. BROWN
Leader	CHARLES MIDDLETON

Should movies be made for pure entertainment?

---

* Academy Award winner.

Or should they have a message? If any picture of the 1930s or 1940s is credited with bringing this simmering issue to a head in the movie industry, it must be *The Grapes of Wrath*. Even before 20th Century-Fox adapted John Steinbeck's Pulitzer Prize-winning saga of migrant sharecroppers from Oklahoma's Dust Bowl, the picture became a maelstrom of controversy. Darryl F. Zanuck bought the novel for $75,000, highest price for any book of the 1930s, including *Gone With the Wind*. He was immediately accused of planning to pigeonhole it under pressure from California and Oklahoma officials, business interests and agriculturists.

Next, when it became known that shooting had actually begun, he was accused of giving orders to pull punches, to blur the bitter portrait Steinbeck had etched of the mistreatment of the dispossessed Okies. Finally, when the film premiere in New York left no doubt that Zanuck had not compromised, had in fact been faithful to the entire tragic theme, the attack shifted to a basic issue.

Should movies be only showmanship? Or should they probe the issues of the day as well?

Martin Quigley, publisher of the important trade journal, *Motion Picture Herald*, led the attack against socially significant stories. In a signed editorial, Quigley said that movies are no place for such concepts. His argument was that the movies—because of their limitations and their need to treat problems theatrically—could not present true-to-life situations factually. Nor could they be dispassionate or analytical. What must happen, he said, is that such films inevitably break down into demagogic preachment and outright propaganda. And such was the result, he said, of *The Grapes of Wrath*.

The answer to Quigley's blast came from the nation's movie reviewers. The vast majority hailed the film as a masterpiece. Even the skeptical *Daily Worker* found no fault. "There are no caricatures or misrepresentations . . . ," said its critic, David Platt. "It fulfills every expectation."

Defending Zanuck, Ernest L. Mayer of the New York *Post* said Quigley's doctrine would leave room only for fairy tales, mysteries, thin men and the two Mickeys—Rooney and Mouse. Critic Archer Winsten added eloquently: "As long as motion pictures confine themselves to a pure amusement function, they remain a shining palace built on sand. When, as in *The Grapes of Wrath*, they join the battle of living issues, they anchor themselves to an enduring rock."

Boxoffice, a rival trade paper, ran a page of pictures from the film matched photo for photo with genuine shots of "Okies," taken by photographer Harold Bristol when he and Steinbeck toured Okie camps in 1938. *Life* later republished the photos. If anything, the pictures showed that Hollywood had underplayed the plight of the migrant workers.

But the most telling retort to Quigley came when students, housewives and job-seekers—a cross section of New Yorkers—jammed the Rivoli Theatre to see the world premiere. By 9:30 A.M., when the theatre opened, the line was two blocks long. When it was over, wrote Mark Murphy of the New York *Times*, the audience cheered. "They all seemed to think it a great movie, something strong—something about the common and poor people living and working together."

Unquestionably *The Grapes of Wrath* had done more than any prior Hollywood film to open the screen to honesty in movie making. Part of the reason was the careful way Nunnally Johnson condensed the 619-page book into a sparse, straight-line drama. He cleaned up the raw language, changed the ending from one of despair to one of hope. But he sacrificed nothing that was important to the biblical odyssey.

The movie opens with a magnificent shot of Tom Joad (Henry Fonda) walking along a lonely Oklahoma highway. Returning from prison after serving four years for killing a man in a dance-hall brawl, Tom finds that dust storms and new and more profitable farming methods (one caterpillar tractor can do the work of fourteen farmers) have forced his family off their land. But Pa (Russell Simpson) has seen a handbill saying thousands of workers are needed in California. There's good pay for 800 fruit pickers.

And so the Joad family of twelve packs its meager belongings aboard its old jalopy and, with its $150 savings, sets out for the Promised Land.

Everywhere, director John Ford's sure hand adds poignancy. As they are about to leave, the camera focuses on Ma (Jane Darwell), bewildered and heartbroken, burning her box of letters and keepsakes of a lifetime. She breaks the predawn silence with only two words: "I'm ready."

The rattling, patched-up, overloaded excuse for a pickup truck bumbles along U. S. Highway 66, its engines boiling like a teakettle. To the kids it's a joy ride. But the old people can't take it. Grampa (Charley Grapewin) is the first to die, and they bury him by night at roadside.

Casy (John Carradine), the renegade preacher, does not want to make a speech. But Tom knows authorities sometimes are more interested in a dead body than a live one. So Tom buries Grampa with his name and a note in a fruit jar. "This here is William James Joad, dyed of a stroke, old, old man. His fokes buried him because they got no money to pay for funerals. Nobody kilt him. Jus a stroke and he dyed."

Granma dies too. But Ma holds her in her arms, pretending she is sick, so agriculture inspectors won't stop them at the California border.

However, California turns out to be a far cry from the land of milk and honey. It is 1933, the depths of the Depression, and their destiny at the end of the rainbow is to be cheap labor. There are 800 jobs but 10,000 migrants. For the few jobs open, orchard growers can slash wages to starvation levels. At the camps there are hungry children begging for food and gunmen-guards to see no one gets out of line.

The Joads camp in an Okie settlement and a fight breaks out when a labor agent comes recruiting but won't tell how much he'll pay. In the melee, a deputy is clobbered. He accidentally shoots a woman and the police ride off with Casy. That night the camp is burned down.

The Joads finally stop at a decent government settlement where they get work picking peaches. One night Tom wanders out and runs into Casy, who has not been locked up, only run out of the camp. Now he's leading a strike to try to get wages up. He tells Tom police call him an "agitator."

Even as they are talking, vigilantes raid the strikers' camp. One of them crushes Casy's skull with a pick. Tom strikes back, killing Casy's assailant. But he is cut in the face before he can get away.

Police are after him, and because he is marked Tom knows he can no longer stay with the family. It is here that two of the movie's memorable scenes occur.

In his farewell to Ma, Tom tells her that Casy had made him understand life more clearly. "He was like a lantern," Tom says. "He helped me to see things, too." Tom says he has been thinking about his people living like pigs and good farmland lying fallow. One man owns a million acres while 100,000 farmers are starving. "I been wondering if all our folks got together and yelled."

"Oh, Tom," Ma says. "They'd cut you down just like they done to Casy." Still, Tom knows this must be his mission.

"But how will I know where you are?" Ma asks.

"Well, maybe it's like Casy says," Tom answers. "Fella ain't got a soul of his own. Just a little piece of a big soul. One big soul that belongs to everybody. . . . I'll be all round. . . . Wherever there's a fight so hungry people can eat. . . . Wherever there's a cop beating up a guy, I'll be there. . . . And when the people are eatin' the stuff they raise and livin' in the houses they build. I'll be there, too."

But the last words are left for Ma. The family is on the road without Tom, hopefully pushing on to something better. Despite all the hardship, despite their homelessness, despite hunger and even death, Ma carries them on with an unbroken, indomitable spirit.

"Rich fellers come up. They die. Their kids ain't no good. And they die out," Ma says. "But we keep a-comin'. We're the people that live. Can't wipe us out. Can't lick us. We'll go on forever. 'Cause we're the people."

The Joad family. From left, Charley Grapewin, Dorris Bowdon, Jane Darwell, Russell Simpson, Henry Fonda, Frank Sully (rear), Darryl Hickman (young boy), Shirley Mills, Frank Darien, O. Z. Whitehead, Eddie Quillan and John Carradine.

Forced off their land, the Joads load up their old jalopy and set out for California.

Just before they leave, Ma (Jane Darwell) burns her letters and keepsakes, making a complete break with the past.

Wherever they drive, there are police at the state lines telling them to move on. Tom is at the wheel with Ma and Rosasharn (Dorris Bowdon).

Casy (John Carradine), the renegade preacher, and Tom lie low in the weeds. With them is Muley (John Qualen), whose home was torn down by a wrecker.

As the family sleeps, Tom, in trouble with the law, says his farewell to Ma.

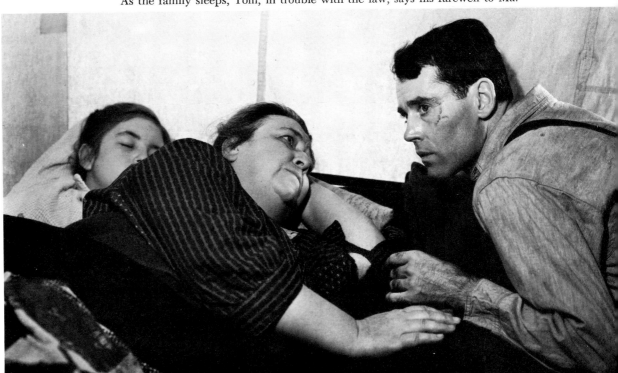

Gil Carter (Henry Fonda), left, and his sidekick Art Croft (Henry Morgan) have a
shot of whiskey after the long spring roundup.

Judge Tyler (Matt Briggs) tries to dissuade the townspeople from forming a lynch
party to go after the killers of a local rancher. At left is storekeeper Arthur Davies
(Harry Davenport). Carter and Croft look on.

The Ox-Bow Incident

(Released May 21, 1943)

PRODUCED AND WRITTEN for the screen by Lamar Trotti from the novel by Walter VanTilburg Clark. Photographed by Arthur Miller. Editor, Allen Mc-Neil. Music, Cyril J. Mockridge. Art directors, Richard Day and James Basevi. Directed by William A. Wellman. A 20th Century-Fox Production. Running time, 75 minutes.

Gil Carter	HENRY FONDA
Donald Martin	DANA ANDREWS
Rose Mapen	MARY BETH HUGHES
Mexican	ANTHONY QUINN
Gerald	WILLIAM EYTHE
Art Croft	HENRY MORGAN
Ma Grier	JANE DARWELL
Judge Daniel Tyler	MATT BRIGGS
Arthur Davies	HARRY DAVENPORT
Major Tetley	FRANK CONROY
Farnley	MARC LAWRENCE
Monty Smith	PAUL HURST
Darby	VICTOR KILIAN
Pancho	CHRIS-PIN MARTIN
Joyce	TED NORTH
Mr. Swanson	GEORGE MEEKER
Mrs. Swanson	ALMIRA SESSIONS
Mrs. Larch	MARGARET HAMILTON
Mapes	DICK RICH
Old Man	FRANCIS FORD
Bartlett	STANLEY ANDREWS
Greene	BILLY BENEDICT
Winder	PAUL E. BURNS
Sparks	LEIGH WHIPPER
Jimmy Carnes	GEORGE CHANDLER
Moore	GEORGE LLOYD
Sheriff	WILLARD ROBERTSON
Deputy	TOM LONDON

In 1942, in the midst of World War II, when battle films and escapist movies were the big box office attractions, 20th Century-Fox chose to make this stark drama of a lynching in the pioneer West. Just why the picture—which seemed to hold little prospect of financial success—came to be produced remains something of a mystery. Studio editors had decreed the powerful novel by Walter VanTilburg Clark too strong for the average moviegoer. Director William A. Wellman fought to do it. He eventually prevailed, but reportedly only by agreeing to direct any other two pictures the studio gave him.

The movie was not the first film on lynching— Hollywood had done *Fury* as late as 1936 and *They Won't Forget* in 1937. Nor was 1943 a crisis year for lynchings. There were only three that year. Statistically, the nation had come a long way since 1892, the year when lynchings reached their peak of 231.

But, as history would later show, it was still possible for a mob to abduct and murder a person in the South with almost certain assurance of escaping punishment. By 1943, nearly 2,000 persons had been reported lynched in America since Tuskegee (Alabama) Institute started keeping records in 1882. No state has been free of guilt. Death mobs have claimed black and white alike, women and even children.

So lynchings were deeply ingrained in the American mentality. And a film exploring the inner reasons that drive men to lawless killing was very much in order.

This is precisely what *The Ox-Bow Incident* does. It is not a wild, emotional shocker that displays mobs storming a jail, whipped up to a frenzy, killing in white-hot anger. Instead, quietly, inexorably, it

195

moves by small stages to a triple hanging in the lonely Ox-Bow Valley.

It takes us into each person's psyche, ever so briefly, suggesting that some have taken part in the "incident" not so much to punish men they believe are killers but to satisfy their own inner need. It is true that the mob leaders—Farnley (Marc Lawrence) and Major Tetley (Frank Conroy)—are in it to revenge a friend's slaying and because they have no confidence in the law's machinery. But most of the others have gotten mixed up for reasons that have nothing to do with justice or vengeance. Suddenly, they find it is too late to turn back.

What gives the movie even greater impact is the fact that it is presented in a simple Western format. There are the usual ranch hands and cattle and a saloon and a brawl. But imagine the surprise of a 1940s audience when it discovered that there was no hero, no one to bend the will of the mob, nothing to divert attention from the film's moving and tragic central event—the lynching itself.

The movie opens in Nevada in 1885. Two tired cowboys—Gil Carter (Henry Fonda) and Art Croft (Henry Morgan)—ride into the little half-empty town of Bridger's Wells. The only thing stirring is a little mutt that trots in front of the riders from between two wooden buildings and ambles across the dirt road. "It's deader than a cayute's grave," Carter says, summoning the image of death from the outset.

The two cowboys have just finished the spring roundup out on the range. They head for Darby's Saloon where the only drink is straight whiskey. That's all right with them. They're parched and dusty and haven't had good liquor in months.

Carter, whose disposition is cantankerous, picks a fight with Farnley, a local ranch hand, just to let off steam. Just as the brawl ends, a cowboy barrels into town with the news that cattle rustlers have shot and killed Larry Kinkaid, one of their neighboring ranchers. "Right through the head, I tell you," the cowboy says. Fired by Farnley, Kinkaid's best friend, the anger of the men in the saloon mounts quickly.

Cooler heads urge them not to go after the killers. White-haired storekeeper Arthur Davies (Harry Davenport) suggests waiting for the sheriff, who even now is at Kinkaid's ranch. "Don't let's go off half cocked and do something we'll be sorry for," Davies says. "If we hang these men ourselves . . . we'll be worse than murderers." But Davies is too

old and mild-mannered. Another moderate, Judge Tyler (Matt Briggs), is a pompous windbag who isn't forceful enough to command respect. "Of course, you can't flinch from what you believe to be your duty," Tyler says. "But certainly you don't want to act hastily."

In the end, they listen to Major Tetley, an ex-Confederate, and Farnley. "Whoever shot Larry Kinkaid ain't coming back for you to fuddle with your lawyer's tricks for six months, then be let off because Davies, or some other whiny old woman, claims he ain't bad at heart," Farnley tells the judge. "Kinkaid didn't have six months to decide if he wanted to die."

They form a posse and "Butch" Mapes (Dick Rich), the deputy sheriff, deputizes the men. Davies says it's illegal. Only the sheriff can deputize. But the men ride off anyway, led by Tetley, splendidly decked out in his old Rebel hat and tunic and mounted on a white horse.

Each has his own reason for joining the mob. Tetley is eager to show off his military prowess. It's also a chance to make his sensitive son prove he's a man. Farnley is hot-tempered, driven by a passion to see his friend's death avenged. Monty Smith (Paul Hurst), the bearded town bum, looks on the lynching as a spectacle to shake the boredom of the quiet frontier. Mapes is a sadistic bully who sees the lynching more as a means to power than as an act of justice.

Ma Grier (Jane Darwell), a hearty, massive woman who runs a boardinghouse, goes because she thinks she's doing her duty. Sparks (Leigh Whipper), the old Negro handy man who once saw his brother lynched, goes to pray for the men who will die. Carter and Croft don't believe in mob violence, but neither has the courage to prevent it. Besides, they are strangers from a nearby range and would be suspects themselves if they didn't go.

At first the posse finds no one. Then the night turns cold and someone says maybe they ought to turn back. "We'll be the laughingstock of the county if we turn back now," Ma fires back. And they go on.

A few hours later they come across three men sleeping by their campfire in Ox-Bow Valley. The men turn out to be Donald Martin (Dana Andrews), a young homesteader new to these parts, and two helpers—a Mexican (Anthony Quinn) and a senile old man (Francis Ford). The evidence is against them. They have fifty head of cattle with Kinkaid's brand and no bill of sale. (Martin says he bought them, paid cash and Kinkaid said he'd mail him a receipt.) The possemen recognize the Mexican as an outlaw wanted for murder and find he has Kinkaid's gun. (He doesn't deny he had run afoul of the law but he claims he only found Kinkaid's gun.)

Martin pleads for time to prove that the evidence is misleading. "Even in this godforsaken country, I've got a right to a trial," he says. But the riders' passions have gone too far. "You're getting a trial with twenty-eight of the only kind of judges murderers and rustlers get in what you call this godforsaken country," Tetley says. The major calls for a vote. Only seven of the twenty-eight possemen want to stop.

Martin says he has a wife and two children. He begs for time to write them a letter. The major gives him until dawn. When the sun rises, Martin gives his letter to Davies. But Martin refuses to let the old man read it aloud—even though Davies thinks that it might save his life.

Beneath a gnarled tree, the three men pray briefly and are lifted to their horses. Nooses are fixed around each of their necks. Then Mapes fires his pistol and the horses are whipped out from under them. When the major's son lacks the courage to hit one of the horses, the major strikes the boy with his pistol butt, dropping him. Tetley orders Farnley to finish the job with his gun. As the lynchers silently ride off, Sparks crouches by the bodies, singing a hymn.

On the way back to town the posse meets the sheriff, who is stunned to hear of the lynching. "Larry Kinkaid's not dead," the sheriff says. The sheriff tells them he left Kinkaid with a doctor, then arrested the rustlers who shot him. "The Lord better have mercy on you," the sheriff says. "You won't get it from me."

One of the men grumbles, "If you ask me, it's Tetley we ought to lynch." The major, more in a feeling of disgrace for his monumental mistake than in regret for the act of lynching itself, goes home

and shoots himself. The others gather in the saloon, raise $500 for Martin's widow, and hear Carter read Martin's letter. In the book, the letter is never read. But Martin's words in the film paraphrase a speech Davies had made in the novel in his vain attempt to stop the posse.

Martin's letter reads in part:

> A man just naturally can't take the law into his own hands and hang people without hurting everybody in the world, because then he's not just breaking one law but all laws. Law is a lot more than words you put on a book, or judges or lawyers or sheriffs you hire to carry it out. It's everything people have ever found out about justice and what's right and wrong. It's the very conscience of humanity.

> There can't be any such thing as civilization unless people have got a conscience, because if people touch God anywhere, where is it except through their conscience? And what is anybody's conscience except a little piece of the conscience of all men that ever lived?

Ironically, the letter, for all its noble thoughts, is a disappointment. It comes on too strong and weighty in this frontier wilderness. It doesn't seem to be appropriate for a condemned man to philosophize in his last private thoughts to his wife.

Nevertheless, the picture has made its point. No one can utter a sound after Carter reads the letter. They have taken the law into their own hands and committed a crime without solving any problems.

At the end, Carter and Croft ride off to deliver the letter to Martin's wife. They leave through the same part of town from which they came in at the start of the movie. It is almost a reverse mirror image. The little dog is there. He retraces his tracks across their path and through the same alleyway between the same two buildings. Life goes on.

Carter urges Major Tetley (Frank Conroy) to surrender the three suspected killers to the sheriff. But he doesn't press the point because he's a stranger himself and therefore suspect. Winder (Paul E. Burns) holds noose.

Donald Martin (Dana Andrews), who is to be one of the three lynch victims, writes a farewell letter to his wife. Next to him is one of his hired hands (Francis Ford), also named for death.

Major Tetley gives Martin a last chance to confess, but Martin insists he is innocent. The old man weeps on the lap of Sparks (Leigh Whipper), the town handy man. That's Anthony Quinn and Jane Darwell just above Whipper's hat.

The suspected killers are pushed onto their horses while members of the posse fit nooses around their necks. Quinn, on horse at left, plays a Mexican, the third lynch victim.

Paul Baumer (Lew Ayres) with his front-line mentor and pal, Sergeant Katczinsky (Louis Wolheim). *(Courtesy John R. Cooper)*

A close-up of Katczinsky's tough, granite-hard features.

(Photos by Universal)

All Quiet on the Western Front*

(Released August 24, 1930)

SCREEN PLAY by George Abbott from the novel by Erich Maria Remarque. Dialogue by Abbott and Maxwell Anderson. Cameraman, Arthur Edeson. Musical score by David Broekman. Editors, Edgar Adams and Milton Carruth. Assistant director, Nate Watt. Directed by Lewis Milestone.* Produced by Carl Laemmle, Jr., for Universal Pictures. Running time, 140 minutes.

Paul Baumer	LEW AYRES
Katczinsky	LOUIS WOLHEIM
Himmelstoss	JOHN WRAY
Tjaden	GEORGE (SLIM) SUMMERVILLE
Kantorek	ARNOLD LUCY
Muller	RUSSELL GLEASON
Gerard Duval	RAYMOND GRIFFITH
Kemmerick	BEN ALEXANDER
Peter	OWEN DAVIS, JR.
Mrs. Baumer	BERYL MERCER †
Albert	WILLIAM BAKEWELL
Poster Girl	JOAN MARSH
Leer	SCOTT KOLK
Suzanne	YOLA D'AVRIL
Behm	WALTER BROWNE ROGERS
French Girls	RENÉE DAMONDE
	and POUPÉE ANDRIOT

---

* Academy Award winner.

† In the original version and the European prints, ZaSu Pitts appeared as Paul's mother. The U.S. version was withdrawn after only one showing—to a preview audience. Miss Pitts had appeared in a comic role in a film just shown to the audience. When they next saw her in a dramatic scene with Ayres, they howled with laughter. Universal held up all prints and remade the movie with Beryl Mercer substituting in Miss Pitts's part.

As far back as the silent era, Hollywood portrayed war as a gory grand adventure. Combat was seen as the manifest destiny of kings, the supreme struggle between great powers, a gorgeous spectacle of scarlet tunics, gold braid and plumed helmets glinting in the sun.

This romantic celluloid image was shattered in sound movies in 1930, the year Universal released *All Quiet on the Western Front.* The film version of Erich Maria Remarque's World War I novel showed fighting from the stark viewpoint of the underling in the trenches, the dirty, frightened soldier who found no glory on the battlefield.

Moreover, it told about the war from the German side. With simple eloquence, it made the point that the German soldier suffered, bled, went hungry, laughed and loved too. When he was killed, there was no stirring martial music, no clash of cymbals. Just agony and terror. And the terrible sense of a young and unfulfilled life wasted.

Ironically, Germany, of all nations, reacted unfavorably to the movie. The protest originally came from a small minority. But it was militant, organized and vocal. When the picture opened in Berlin, Nazi goon squads picketed and let loose rats and snakes inside the theatre. Berlin's film censor eventually banned the picture, contending that it had a demoralizing effect on youth. Remarque, a German of French descent who had fought in the German Army in World War I and

---

* Actually, *The Big Parade* (1925) was the first major American film to show World War I as a dirty business. But it was a silent movie that succumbed to the traditional happy ending and is, overall, far inferior to *All Quiet on the Western Front* as an anti-war document.

was wounded five times, went into exile. Even after he left the country, the Nazis burned his book, seized his bank accounts, deprived him of his German citizenship. He came to the United States in 1939, where he wrote such filmed works as *Three Comrades* (1938) and *Arch of Triumph* (1948).

It was in this country that *All Quiet on the Western Front* had perhaps its sharpest impact. The New York *Daily News* gave the film four stars. "It is so magnificent, so powerful," its reviewer said, "that it hardly behooves mere words to tell of its heart-rending appeal, of its dramatic force, its breath-taking battle shots." The New York *American* hailed the picture as "the mightiest war drama ever screened in the ages of history." The New York *Times* called it a "notable achievement." The movie won the Academy Award for best picture of 1930 and its director, Lewis Milestone, won an award for best direction.

To make the film, Universal constructed a military camp on a sprawling ranch in southern California. Workmen converted twenty acres into a replica of the western front, and built a complete system of trenches. For the battle scenes, Universal recruited 2,000 ex-servicemen.

The actor best remembered from the movie is Lew Ayres, who played the lead role of Paul Baumer. Ayres was only twenty-one years old then, handsome and boyish-looking, the personification of clean-cut American youth. He had been playing in an orchestra at the Coconut Grove in Los Angeles, watching the great stars of the movie world dance before him every night. And so, one day, he too decided to be an actor. He got a bit part, which quickly led to a starring role opposite Greta Garbo in *The Kiss*. Then came *All Quiet on the Western Front*.

(Ayres went on to star in the Dr. Kildare series throughout the 1930s and early 1940s. During World War II he became a conscientious objector and lost public favor. But his reputation was restored when it was learned that he served with valor under fire as a non-combatant in the medical corps.)

The film tells the story of Paul Baumer, a German youth, and his friends who join the army at the onset of World War I. But it was more a series of sharply etched vignettes than a carefully plotted drama.

There is an opening scene showing Professor Kantorek (Arnold Lucy) exhorting Paul and his classmates to enlist. "My beloved gentlemen," says the prim schoolmaster, beginning quietly. ". . . It is not for me to suggest that any of you should stand with honor to defend his country. But I wonder if such a thing is going through your head." The students, tender, callow youths, are at their desks, listening intently as a military parade passes outside.

"I know that in one of the schools," Kantorek continues, "the boys have risen up in the classroom and enlisted as a man. . . . If such a thing should happen here, you would not blame me for a feeling of pride." His voice is rising now. "Your country calls. The field of honor calls. . . . Here is a glorious beginning for your lives. . . ." The boys are on their feet, cheering. And they leave to join up, expecting war to be a great lark.

The schoolmaster's myths begin to fade in training camp. Himmelstoss (John Wray), a meek postman who has become a cruel corporal, makes them fall on their faces and grovel in the mud. Their disillusion increases at the front where for days on end they sit hungry and disheveled in underground bunkers while shells burst all around them. But it is here that Paul meets Sergeant Katczinsky (played superbly by Louis Wolheim), a battered-nosed veteran, who teaches him to live amidst the horrors of war. And it is here that Paul learns that to the men in the trenches war is not beautiful and noble.

"How do they start a war?" asks one of the soldiers in a bull session.

"Well, one country offends another," someone answers.

"You mean there's a mountain over in Germany that gets mad at a field over in France?"

"Well, then, one people offend another."

"Oh, that's it. I shouldn't be here at all. I don't feel offended."

There's laughter and then Katczinsky says, "I tell you how it should all be done." All the soldiers grow silent. "Whenever there's a big war coming on, you should rope off a big field and sell tickets. And on the big day, you should take all the kings and cabinets and their generals. Put them in the center dressed in their underpants. And let them fight it out with clubs. The best country wins."

There are the first encounters with death. The French charge across the devastated no man's land, scores of them dropping under the withering machine gun fire. But enough of them get through to rout the Germans from their trench positions. Then the Germans launch a counterattack and send the French scurrying. At the end of the day the army's positions are the same as when they started. But the bodies of thousands litter the field of battle.

There is a glimpse into a crowded hospital at the front where Paul's wounded comrade Kemmerick (Ben Alexander) * is unaware he has had a leg amputated. Kemmerick complains of a pain in his toes. Then he remembers another soldier has complained of the same thing. With a startled cry, he realizes what has happened. There is the night rendezvous Paul and two buddies have with French farm girls, arriving naked after shedding their clothes to swim across a canal. The war is forgotten for one fleeting night.

Perhaps the most memorable scene is the one where Paul encounters a Frenchman (Raymond Griffith) in a shell hole and stabs him. Shells are bursting all around him and Paul must stay put. As life ebbs from the man, Paul is filled with remorse. He moistens the Frenchman's lips with water from the shell hole, pleading for forgiveness. "Oh, God, why do they do this to us?" he asks. "We only wanted to live, you and I. If they threw away these rifles and these uniforms, you could be my brother."

When the Frenchman dies, Paul pulls a picture of the man's wife and child from his pocket. "I'll write to her," Paul tells the corpse, whose eyes remain wide open. "I promise she'll not want for anything. And I'll help your parents, too. Only forgive me."

On home leave, Paul visits his schoolmaster and finds him making the same patriotic speech to a new crop of students. His professor is delighted to see him in uniform and insists that Paul tell the class what army life at the front is like.

"We live in the trenches," Paul says, restraining himself. "We fight. We try not to be killed. Sometimes we are. That's all." The professor, disappointed by this drab account, urges Paul to go on.

Unable now to hold back the bitter truth, Paul upbraids his teacher for filling his students' minds with jingoistic drivel. "You still think it's beautiful to die for your country. . . . The first bombardment taught us better. . . . When it comes to dying for your country, it's better not to die at all."

"Coward. Coward," the astonished students cry, trying to shout him down. But Paul can't stop. "There are millions out there dying for their country, and what good is it doing? . . . Every day is a year. Every night a century. Our bodies are earth. Our thoughts are clay. And we sleep and eat with death."

Back at the front, Paul's comrades are killed one by one until he and Sergeant Katczinsky are the only ones left. Then, Katczinsky's shin is hit by shrapnel. Paul carries him to a dressing station only to find that another tiny shell splinter has entered Katczinsky's skull and killed him.

Now Paul is alone in the trenches. In the famous next-to-last scene, he sees a butterfly, the only thing of beauty in this land of ugliness. His hand—actually, it is director Lewis Milestone's hand—goes out to it and, as it does, it attracts a French sniper. The camera alternates from the face of the rifleman to Paul, Paul to the rifleman. The hand comes closer to the butterfly, closer. Then a single shot rings out. His hand goes limp. And all is silence.

Ironically, the book tells us, Paul died on a day when there was a lull in the fighting. The army report summed up the action in the familiar phrase: "All quiet on the western front."

As the picture ends, we see a hillside covered with crosses. Paul and his dead comrades are marching away, their backs to us. As the ghostly procession passes, one by one they turn and stare accusingly at the audience. "You have done this to us. You have cut our lives short," their glaring eyes seem to say.

Even forty years after its first showing, the movie evokes telling moments of tenderness and poignancy and despair, draining the emotions because it leaves no hope. *All Quiet on the Western Front* stands as a milestone among anti-war pictures.

---

* The late Ben Alexander later achieved television fame as Officer Frank Smith on *Dragnet*.

Paul and the martinet Corporal Himmelstoss (John Wray).

Sloshing through the mud at camp before going to the front.

Paul comforts a dying German comrade (Ben Alexander) at a hospital at the front.

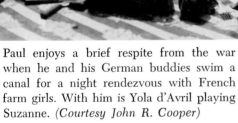

Paul enjoys a brief respite from the war when he and his German buddies swim a canal for a night rendezvous with French farm girls. With him is Yola d'Avril playing Suzanne. (*Courtesy John R. Cooper*)

Paul visits his sick mother (ZaSu Pitts) while on home leave. Neither knows they are meeting for the last time. (Miss Pitts played the role in the original version and the European print. But Beryl Mercer succeeded her and is usually credited for the part.)

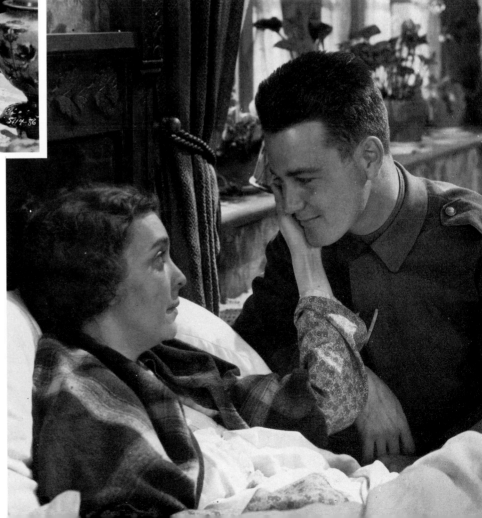

Huey Long, Kingfish of the bayous, boasted he bought legislators "like sacks of potatoes, shuffled 'em like a deck of cards." *(Photo by Associated Press)*

Willie Stark (Broderick Crawford) in a white linen suit, one of the favorite modes of attire of Huey Long, the Louisiana senator who inspired the book by Robert Penn Warren and the film by Columbia.

(Photos copyright Screen Gems, Inc.)

206

All the King's Men *

(New York Premiere, November 8, 1949)

SCREEN PLAY by Robert Rossen based on the Robert Penn Warren novel of the same name. Musical director, Morris Stoloff. Art director, Sturge Carne. Photographed by Burnett Guffey. Editor, Al Clark. Produced and directed by Rossen. Presented by Columbia Pictures. Running time, 109 minutes.

Willie Stark	BRODERICK CRAWFORD *
Anne Stanton	JOANNE DRU
Jack Burden	JOHN IRELAND
Tom Stark	JOHN DEREK
Sadie Burke	MERCEDES MC CAMBRIDGE *
Adam Stanton	SHEPPERD STRUDWICK
Tiny Duffy	RALPH DUMKE
Lucy Stark	ANNE SEYMOUR
Mrs. Burden	KATHARINE WARREN
Judge Stanton	RAYMOND GREENLEAF
Sugar Boy	WALTER BURKE
Dolph Pillsbury	WILL WRIGHT
Floyd McEvoy	GRANDON RHODES
Pa Stark	H. C. MILLER
Hale	RICHARD HALE
Commissioner	WILLIAM BRUCE
Sheriff	A. C. TILLMAN
Madison	HOUSELEY STEVENSON
Minister	TRUETT MYERS
Football Coach	PHIL TULLY
Helene Hale	HELENE STANLEY
Politician	JUDD HOLDREN
Man	PAUL FORD
Dance Caller	TED FRENCH

The remains of Huey Pierce Long lie under a heroic bronze statue of himself that stands before his splendid 34-story Capitol in Baton Rouge, Louisiana.

---

* Academy Award winner.

Shoulders back, double-breasted jacket pulled tight over his bulging stomach, the "Kingfish"—as he liked to call himself—rises among tall poplars and evergreens, rustling in a great sunken garden. If Huey could be brought back to life, the first thing he probably would do is get up on the stump and start thundering.

"I would describe a demagogue as a politician who don't keep his promises," he used to say. "On that basis, I'm the first man to have power in Loozyana who ain't a demagogue. I kept every promise I made to the people of Loozyana. None of these ex-es and bellyachers that have been fighting me down here ever kept promises when he was in office. It was an unheard-of thing in Loozyana until Huey P. Long got in."

This was the Louisiana governor (and later senator) whose career Robert Penn Warren fictionalized in his 1947 Pulitzer Prize-winning novel, *All The King's Men*. This was the same power-hungry politician Broderick Crawford so brilliantly brought to the screen two years later.

Warren, a professor of English at Louisiana State University when the forty-two-year-old Kingfish was killed in 1935, always claimed that he wasn't writing about Huey. But the career of his character, Willie Stark, so closely parallels Long's rise and fall that it is hard to see how Willie could be anyone else.

Like Long, Stark was a backwoods hick who started into politics as an idealist, made an unsuccessful bid for governor, then swept into office by rousing the masses with fiery, hip-shooting speeches. Like Huey, Willie soon became corrupted by the governorship, ran roughshod over people in his blind pursuit of power, offended a genteel judge and a young doctor, and died at the peak of his career when the doctor shot him in his skyscraper Capitol.*

When Columbia Pictures decided to make Warren's book into a movie, the studio's first task was to find an actor who could play the demanding role of the flamboyant Dixie dictator. Robert Rossen, the film's writer, director and producer, picked Broderick Crawford, a seasoned actor but one with virtually no box office draw. It was a big gamble for Rossen.

Crawford, who was then thirty-eight, was the only child of Helen Broderick and Lester Crawford, two celebrated comedians. Brawny (220 pounds) and crooked-nosed (the result of some football games and some fights), Crawford had scored a rousing stage success in 1937 as the dim-witted Lennie in *Of Mice and Men*. Then he went on to Hollywood. But his roles were generally limited to B-movie heavies—tough, hard-boiled villains. After twelve years he had compiled no record of distinction nor built any kind of following.

Nevertheless, Rossen felt Crawford's vague physical resemblance to Long, his machine-gun delivery and his blunt acting style made him the perfect man for the part. The film also marked the screen debut of Mercedes McCambridge, a thirty-one-year-old radio-trained actress who created a small sensation as Stark's vixenish, hard-nosed campaign manager.

Another inspiration was Rossen's decision to make the movie outside of Hollywood. By shooting most of the footage in Stockton (pop. 66,000) in northern California near the state capital of Sacramento, he added realism. Then, by casting townspeople—instead of professional extras—in all but the principal roles, he injected color and authenticity into the picture.

Finally, to make Stark a living figure in the consciousness of Stockton, Rossen launched a make-believe political campaign. Banners three and four stories high waved Stark's name across the face of Main Street buildings. Loudspeakers blared. School

---

* In real life, the doctor was Carl Austin Weiss, twenty-nine, a Baton Rouge specialist whose father was once president of the state medical society. But there remains a lingering dispute in Louisiana as to whether Weiss shot Long or a wild bullet from Huey's own bodyguards struck down the Kingfish. For a book probing the mystery, see *The Day Huey Long Was Shot*, also by David Zinman, former Associated Press newsman in New Orleans.

children wore Stark buttons. Cars carried his campaign slogan—"The Law of the People Is My Law" and "Win With Willie."

One evening Crawford, returning from a movie show with John Ireland and Joanne Dru, bet he could hurdle a trash can on a quiet corner. He missed by inches and the container careened noisily up the silent block. Two motorcycle cops screeched up. They picked Crawford up, started questioning him sharply. Suddenly one cop said, "Oh, it's Willie." They quickly released him, dusted him off and retrieved the trash can and its scattered contents. Rossen said he knew then the campaign had worked and that audiences would accept Crawford as Willie Stark.

The film is told through the eyes of Jack Burden (John Ireland), a newspaperman who becomes Stark's hatchet man. When we first see Stark he is a poor but honest lawyer in a dirt-road Southern town,* waging a crusade against a crooked political machine. His efforts are hopeless until several children are killed in the collapse of a school built by the machine. Then the townspeople, remembering Stark's warnings, rally to his cause.

State bosses astutely recognize Willie as a threat. So they immediately put him up for governor. There is method in their apparent madness. They are only using Willie to split the rival candidate's votes. And to be sure their scheme doesn't backfire, they encourage him to deliver dull, prepared speeches about tax programs.

He stumps the state—boring voters with statistic-crammed addresses—until Sadie Burke (Miss McCambridge) and Burden convince him he's being used as a stooge. Bitter and fighting mad, Stark crosses up the bosses by telling the people he was played for a "sucker."

Then, getting the feel of politics, he rolls up his sleeves, loosens his tie and talks to the people in their own language. It isn't long before Willie discovers the charisma of his oratory.

Four years later he launches his own campaign for governor. Sadie Burke is his manager and Burden his chief aide. Championing the cause of the Great Unwashed, he campaigns on a program of soaking the rich for the poor's benefit. He wins handily and gives the people new highways, schools, hospitals and bridges. But all of it is built on graft and the price comes high—political servitude. He

---

* The state is never mentioned in the film or the book.

builds a crack statewide machine and controls every political office down to dog catcher.

When the disenchanted Burden questions the means Willie uses to achieve his ends, Stark tells him that good comes only out of bad.

The whole fast-moving drama sweeps along in a kind of crackling, sparse newsreel style with brilliant staging of restless, milling mobs. They show up everywhere, howling in turbulent torchlight parades, political barbecues, football games, stump speeches.

Intoxicated with his ever widening power, Willie starts to get national ambitions. For a while it looks like nothing can stop him. His disillusioned foster son (John Derek) gets involved in a drunken driving accident. Willie's efforts to hush it up give his enemies ammunition to impeach him. But Willie beats them with his black book, threatening to expose their own indiscretions and shady deals. Yet his political victory has come only at heavy personal cost. Stark's frenzied drive to the top has warped his human values. He has lost all compassion. He has become totally ruthless. He drives venerable Judge Stanton (Raymond Greenleaf) to suicide by blackmailing him about a bribe the judge took in his younger days. Willie alienates his wife by having an affair with Sadie Burke, then tosses her over for Burden's pretty sweetheart, Anne Stanton (Joanne Dru).

But he has gone too far. Idealistic Dr. Adam Stanton (Shepperd Strudwick), Anne's brother, learns of Willie's affair with Anne. He hears, too, that Willie's tactics were responsible for pushing Judge Stanton, Adam's uncle, into an early grave. Tormented, the young doctor takes a gun to the Capitol and shoots Willie on the steps of the legislature. Stark's bodyguard guns down the doctor. But he moves in too late. Willie is dying at the very height of his career. Mortally wounded, he looks up at Burden and with his last sputtering breath, wonders how high he might have risen. "It could have been—whole world—Willie Stark . . ."

Reviewers hailed the movie as a work of crude eloquence and savage force. It won the Academy Award and brought Oscars to Crawford and Miss McCambridge. More significantly, its relevance has not faded over the years. Today, it remains one of Hollywood's most gripping and penetrating studies of the sordidness of political power and its intoxicating impact not only on the holder of high office but on all those gravitating around him.

Willie, a rustic lawyer with political ambitions, finds it hard to draw a crowd because his dull speeches are crammed with facts and figures. Jack Burden (John Ireland) stands behind Willie. His foster son (John Derek) holds handbills.

Coat and tie peeled, Willie learns to let loose with bombast and fire and talk the plain people's language. They put him in the governor's mansion. Sadie Burke (Mercedes McCambridge), his campaign manager, stands alongside.

A strategy meeting gets a little hot for politician Pillsbury (Will Wright) and he mops his collar. Willie relaxes with his feet on a table. Others are, from left, Tiny Duffy (Ralph Dumke), Burden, Miss Burke, and Sugar Boy (Walter Burke), Willie's bodyguard.

Burden leans on a bed while he holds a strained conversation with his sweetheart Anne Stanton (Joanne Dru), who has an affair with Stark.

Willie lies next to a pillar in the Capitol after an embittered young doctor has shot him.
It all might have been different, he mutters. Bending over him is Sugar Boy. Others are
Duffy with cigarette, Miss Burke, Burden and Pillsbury.

James Allen (Paul Muni), sentenced to ten years on a chain gang for a ten-dollar robbery in which he was forced to participate.

(Photos by Warner Bros.)
(Courtesy United Artists Corp.)

I Am a Fugitive from a Chain Gang

(Released Nov. 19, 1932)

BASED ON THE AUTOBIOGRAPHY *I Am a Fugitive from a Georgia Chain Gang* by Robert E. Burns. Adaptation by Sheridan Gibney and Brown Holmes. Cameraman, Sol Polito. Editor, William Holmes. Art director, Jack Okey. Assistant director, Al Aborn. Directed by Mervyn Le Roy. Produced by Warner Brothers. Running time, 93 minutes.

James Allen	PAUL MUNI
Marie, his wife	GLENDA FARRELL
Helen	HELEN VINSON
Pete	PRESTON FOSTER
Second Warden	EDWARD J. MC NAMARA
Allen's Secretary	SHEILA TERRY
Barney	ALLEN JENKINS
The Warden	DAVID LANDAU
The Judge	BERTON CHURCHILL
The Bomber, life prisoner	EDWARD ELLIS
Alice	SALLY BLANE
Red	JAMES BELL
Nordine	JOHN WRAY
Rev. Robert Allen, brother of James	
	HALE HAMILTON
District Attorney	DOUGLASS DUMBRILLE
Chairman, Chamber of Commerce	
	EDWARD LE SAINT
Steve	ROSCOE KARNS
Fuller	ROBERT WARWICK
Linda	NOEL FRANCIS
Mrs. Allen	LOUISE CARTER
Prison Commissioner	WILLARD ROBERTSON
Ramsey	ROBERT MC WADE
Parker	REGINALD BARLOW
Hot Dog Stand Owner	CHARLES SELLON
Chief of Police	ERVILLE ALDERSON
Guard	HARRY WOODS

Paul Muni, playing a convict hunted by police, comes out of hiding one night to see his sweetheart, Helen.

"It's been almost a year since you've escaped," she says, staring at his hollow, ravaged face. They are standing together in the shadows outside her home.

"I haven't escaped," Muni says, an edge to his voice. "They're still after me. They'll always be after me. . . . I hide in rooms all day and travel by night. No friends. No rest. No peace. . . . Forgive me, Helen. I had to see you tonight. Just to say good-by."

"It was all going to be so different."

"It is different," says Muni, his voice rising in anger. "They've made it different." Suddenly there is a sound in the background. "I've got to go," he says hurriedly.

"Can't you tell me where you're going?" she pleads. He shakes his head, retreating slowly into the blackness. "Will you write?" He shakes his head again. "How do you live?" she asks.

Now his body has vanished in the shadows. All that can be seen is his face, haunted, terrified. The eyes are sunken and open wide like a cornered cat.

"I steal," he says.

This is the unforgettable ending of *I Am a Fugitive from a Chain Gang*, a chilling episode that critic Pauline Kael has called "one of the great closing scenes in the history of films." As a grim, stark document of social injustice, the movie had no peers in its day. Based on a true story, it awakened the nation to the brutal conditions of Southern prison camps. Probably no other actor could have played the sensitive role of the harried fugitive better than Muni.

213

He was the master character actor. Others achieved stardom by projecting their strong personalities onto the screen. Muni turned the procedure around. He erased his identity. He transformed the character into the actor.

Hollywood called him the "man of a thousand faces." His gallery of biographical roles included Pasteur, Zola and Juarez. He threw himself into each part, spending endless hours painstakingly studying each character. A perfectionist, he researched the figure's speech, his background, his habits, his mannerisms.

So consumed was he with his art that on his wedding day he rushed off from the ceremony to do a matinee. His wife was the former Bella Finkel, slender, dark-haired daughter of the Tomashevsky theatre clan.

Despite his dedication and acting success, he was in private life a shy and retiring person. "I hate being on the stage," Muni once said. "All the things that usually appeal to the actor make me shrivel inside."

When fans spotted him in public, he appeared uncomfortable. His mouth stretched into a grimace. His eyes appealed for privacy. During the run of a play on Broadway, he was considered the least bohemian of any actor. By day, he walked in Central Park or read. By night, he would be at the theatre at least an hour before curtain time, getting ready for his performance. After the play, he would have a snack with his wife and turn in.

Although he led a quiet life off stage, he was firm on matters of principle. He tore up his $800,000 screen contract because he considered the parts offered him poor choices. Recalling his decision, Mrs. Muni said: "That night, he did somersaults in the living room. Believe me. He jumped up and down yelling, 'No one owns me. I'm a free man.'"

Born Muni Weisenfreund in Lemberg, Austria, now part of Poland, in 1895, he was the son of strolling actors who played in the ghettos in Yiddish, their native tongue. When Muni was seven they took him to America, where the family trouped in Yiddish variety theatres. Muni spoke no English on stage until he made his Broadway debut in 1926. At thirty-one, he played an old Orthodox Jewish father in We Americans. One critic, unaware of his age, was so taken by his performance he wrote that it was tragic that "this old man should have spent a lifetime waiting for a chance to appear on Broadway."

When talking pictures arrived, Hollywood summoned Muni. His first movies were not successful, and he returned to Broadway, where he scored a personal triumph in Counsellor-at-Law. So the movies lured him back. This time he came through with a winner. He played Tony Camonte, the tough mobster with the ugly gash down his cheek in Scarface (1932). That same year he starred in Fugitive, which he would call his favorite screen role. Some film historians credit the movie as being Hollywood's first drama to urge social reforms.

The film opens as James Allen (Muni) returns from World War I and quits his old job in a factory. He wants to build bridges. But he can't find work and so he takes to the road. In the South—the movie never specifically mentions Georgia—he innocently becomes involved in a robbery. At gunpoint, another drifter (Preston Foster) forces him to rifle a cash register as the drifter holds up a diner. Police crash in, shoot down the gunman and catch the fleeing Allen with the cash. A judge sentences him to ten years at hard labor.

In the prison camp his life becomes a nightmare. The men are shackled at the ankles. When they sleep, guards run a chain through the shackles linking everyone in the bunk room. The chains make an indelible mark. When a long-term prisoner gets out, he can only shuffle from the camp in the short, faltering gait of the chain gang.

But Allen perseveres. He learns to eat the tasteless food. He endures the floggings and the blazing sun that beats mercilessly down during rock-splitting details in the hills. Finally he manages to slip his shackles and escape. In a gripping chase scene, he lies underwater in a swamp, breathing through a hollow reed as the guards and bloodhounds go by.

Allen goes north to Chicago, where over the passing years he works himself up to become president of his own construction firm. But a scheming blonde slattern (Glenda Farrell) learns his secret and uses it to force him to marry her. "I wouldn't tell," she says, "if I had a reason to protect you."

When Allen falls in love with a society girl (Helen Vinson) and asks for a divorce, his wife cruelly informs on him. At first Allen fights extradition. But a representative of the state tells him he will be pardoned if he returns and serves ninety days as trusty. He goes back to wipe the slate clean. The state reneges and he is sent to the chain gang.

Allen flees again. He and another convict steal a truck carrying dynamite and blow up a bridge to cut off the pursuing guards.

This time he becomes a harried, frightened fugitive on the run. At the end he meets his sweetheart for a brief farewell, fading into the black abyss of night. It is a moving finale, reportedly conceived by both Muni and director Mervyn Le Roy.

The film is generally faithful to the book *I Am a Fugitive from a Georgia Chain Gang*. The author was Robert Elliott Burns, who had been sentenced to serve on a Georgia chain gang for a five-dollar holdup. Burns said he was a hungry, jobless World War I veteran and he had merely gone with an acquaintance to the robbery of a grocery.

Burns escaped in 1922 after serving two months of a six- to ten-year sentence. He became a writer. Seven years later he was a $20,000-a-year editor of a magazine in Chicago. But his first wife disclosed his identity. And despite pleas from many prominent people, he was returned to Georgia.

Prison authorities sent him back to the chain gang. A year later he escaped again, wrote his book and became a tax consultant in New Jersey. Again Georgia asked for him back. However, three New Jersey governors refused to extradite him.

Finally Governor Ellis Arnall of Georgia, who did away with chain gangs in his state, volunteered to be Burns's lawyer if he would return. Despite the anxiety of his second wife, Burns went back in 1945. "In all people's lives there comes a time when one must show courage," Burns said. ". . . This is the time for us." The Georgia Pardon and Parole Board erased Burns's sentence and restored his civil rights. But it refused a full pardon because he

had admitted his role in the holdup. Burns, who met Muni once backstage in a New York theatre, died in 1955.

After *Fugitive*, an also-ran in the Oscar derby behind *Cavalcade*, Muni's Hollywood career soared. He won an Academy Award for his performance in *The Story of Louis Pasteur* (1936). He received critical acclaim for his part as a Chinese peasant in *The Good Earth* (1937) and for the title role in *The Life of Emile Zola* (1937). After this movie, which many consider his most successful, Warner Brothers billed him with "Mr." in front of his name, a rare cinematic honor.

In 1939 he played Mexican President Benito Juarez in *Juarez*. But his box office appeal slipped in the 1940s and, dissatisfied with the roles he was offered, Muni left the movies. His penchant for perfection also prompted him to turn down offers to appear in Broadway plays. And so he went into semi-retirement.

However, in 1955 he returned to do a brilliant stage portrayal of Clarence Darrow in *Inherit the Wind*. Critics hailed the sixty-year-old actor. Mrs. Muni said this success vindicated him after a decade of being considered finished.

The same year, he lost his left eye to surgery because of a tumor. He left the play. But he returned in 1959 to make *The Last Angry Man*, which was to be his last movie. He died in 1967, leaving virtually his entire estate of $1,100,000 to his wife. They had no children.

A tough guard (Harry Woods) yanks Allen up from his cot after Allen protests against the brutal treatment.

The camp warden (David Landau), right, gets ready to give Allen the feel of his lash.

Allen, at first, has no stomach for the food. But after days splitting rocks under the blistering sun, he gets used to it. That's character actor Edward Ellis, extreme right, playing a life prisoner. Looking on are Allen Jenkins, extreme left, and John Wray, next to Muni.

After his escape, Allen puts in long hours of studying and his career begins rising.

A scheming slattern (Glenda Farrell) learns Allen's secret and blackmails him into marrying her.

Allen, the successful engineer, shares a brief moment of happiness with the woman he really loves (Helen Vinson).

Alfred Hitchcock, master of suspense. *(Copyright 1958 by Paramount Pictures Corp.)*

VIII

DIRECTORS

ALFRED HITCHCOCK • THE 39 STEPS
FRANK CAPRA • MEET JOHN DOE
PRESTON STURGES • HAIL THE CONQUERING HERO
ORSON WELLES • CITIZEN KANE
BUSBY BERKELEY • 42nd STREET

Alfred Hitchcock

The 39 Steps

(U.S. Release August 1, 1935)

ADAPTED by Charles Bennett from the novel by John Buchan. Dialogue, Ian Hay. Continuity, Alma Reville. Editor, D. N. Twist. Art director, W. Werndorff. Photography, Bernard Knowles. Musical director, Louis Levy. Directed by Alfred Hitchcock. Produced by Michael Balcon. Associate producer, Ivor Montagu. A Gaumont-British Picture Corp. production. Running time, 85 minutes. (Hitchcock's walk-on is as a passer-by.)

Hannay	ROBERT DONAT
Pamela	MADELEINE CARROLL
Miss Smith	LUCIE MANNHEIM
Professor Jordan	GODFREY TEARLE
Crofter's Wife	PEGGY ASHCROFT
Crofter	JOHN LAURIE
Mrs. Jordan	HELEN HAYE
The Sheriff	FRANK CELLIER
Memory	WYLIE WATSON
Commercial Travelers	GUS MAC NAUGHTON, JERRY VERNO
Maid	PEGGY SIMPSON

In *The 39 Steps,* a woman opens her mouth to scream. The next instant the camera flashes to a locomotive and we hear its shrill whistle.

In *Psycho,* Janet Leigh is soaping herself in a shower. She sees something moving on the other side of the curtain. Someone pulls it open. A butcher knife flashes. Blood and water swirl round and round, emptying down the drain.

In *The Man Who Knew Too Much,* an assassin sights his human target in a concert hall. At the moment he pulls the trigger, the cymbals clash.

This is the film magic of director Alfred Hitchcock. Not a word has been spoken in these three spine-tingling scenes. There is too much talk in pictures, Hitchcock once said. Instead of speech, he uses motion or sound to make a point. Wherever he can, he stresses the camera rather than the actor.

And so his films, at their best, are pure moving pictures, total cinema, what he has called "pictorial storytelling." Says Hitchcock, "In a good movie, the sound could go off and the audience would still have a perfectly clear idea of what was going on."

A short, fat, penguin-like man, Hitchcock has been called Hollywood's master of suspense. He is careful to point out the difference between suspense and terror. "On the screen, terror is induced by surprise," he says. "Suspense by forewarning."

Hitchcock once gave this illustration: If three men are sitting in an office and a time bomb goes off, the audience is surprised. However, their surprise lasts only a second or two. But if that same audience knows there is a bomb planted and set to go off in two minutes, it is charged with excitement, hoping the men leave. They start to go. But one says, "No, wait a minute." The audience holds its breath, agonizing while the seconds tick by. "That's suspense."

In Hitchcock thrillers there has always been an odd mixture of suspense and humor. Hitchcock injects comedy to relieve tension. It establishes a pause, a chance for the moviegoer to catch his breath before the next attack of gooseflesh.

The light touch also has allowed him to indulge

his favorite pastime of squeezing himself into every movie. He usually sneaks on as an extra. One time it looked like it would be impossible. In *Lifeboat,* the cast consisted of Tallulah Bankhead and eight others marooned on the high seas. But he found a way. Near the end of the movie, an actor picks up an old newspaper. It has a before-and-after ad for a reducing medicine. Hitchcock is the subject.

Hitchcock was born in London in 1899, the son of a wholesale poultry dealer. A Catholic, he went to Jesuit schools as a boy, then studied science and engineering at London University. But he had become intrigued with cinema from watching American movies. When the predecessor of Paramount Pictures opened a London studio, the twenty-year-old Hitchcock got a job.

He apprenticed in every role from art director to script editor. He won his first directorial assignment in 1926 in a movie called *The Lodger,* a story of Jack the Ripper's exploits. It was so well done, critics hailed it as one of the finest films made in London. More pictures followed. By the end of the 1930s he had turned out such classics as *The 39 Steps, The Lady Vanishes* and *Sabotage,* establishing himself as England's top director.

The 39 Steps, based on a novel by John Buchan (later to become Canada's Governor-General), firmly established Hitchcock's thematic trademark of tossing an innocent, average man into a web of intrigue. The picture opens in the London Palladium during the act of a vaudevillian named Mr. Memory (Wylie Watson), a performer with a photographic mind who challenges the audience to stump him with any question of fact.

Richard Hannay (Robert Donat), a Canadian recently arrived in London, is watching the performance. Suddenly a shot rings out. In the crush for the exits, he chivalrously helps a girl (Lucie Mannheim) who seems unduly alarmed.

At his flat, she discloses that she is a counteragent on the trail of a master criminal who is trying to smuggle vital military secrets out of the country. She doesn't know the master spy's name but his little finger is amputated at the first joint. The woman mentions "the 39 Steps" but mysteriously doesn't tell him what they are.

Hannay, discovering that the flat is being watched, lets her stay. At dawn he is awakened by a commotion and finds she has been stabbed. With her dying breath she tells him that his own

life is now in danger. She clutches in her hand a map with a circle drawn around a hamlet in Scotland.

Hannay eludes his pursuers and takes a train to Scotland. At Edinburgh, he reads a newspaper account of the girl's slaying. He is astounded to learn he is the prime suspect because he has run away. As the train pulls out, police start searching the cars. Hannay ducks into a compartment and embraces its sole occupant, a lovely blonde (Madeleine Carroll), hoping the police won't question them. But she gives him away and he has to jump from the train to escape.

He flees through the Scottish highlands, stealing clothes to disguise himself. Finally he reaches the home of a Professor Jordan (Godfrey Tearle) who, unknown to Hannay, is the spy chief. Hannay tells him the girl's story, then, too late, notices the joint of his little finger is missing. Jordan shoots him and leaves him for dead.

But a Bible in the stolen overcoat has stopped the bullet. With police in hot pursuit, Hannay takes refuge in a political meeting where he is mistaken as the keynote speaker. Forced onto the platform, he bumbles along in generalities until he spots the girl whom he had kissed on the train. She gets him arrested, but not by the police. Unwittingly, she summons the professor's gang, who handcuff her to Hannay and put the pair in a car.

When the car stops on a moor, Hannay leaps out, pulls the girl with him. They find a lonely inn and, still handcuffed, spend a quarrelsome night. When Hannay sleeps, she slips free, but she sees two gang members arrive and overhears their conversation. Now she realizes Hannay has been telling the truth.

When Hannay awakes, she tells him what she has heard. He tells her he must go back to the London Palladium. Meanwhile, she goes to the police. But they don't believe her.

The Palladium is full and Hannay scans the theatre with binoculars. There, in a box, is Professor Jordan. The girl joins Hannay. However, the police, who have followed her, start closing in to arrest him.

Mr. Memory is on stage. All at once, Hannay bolts up and asks, "What are the 39 Steps?" Memory says nothing. "Come on! Answer up," Hannay shouts. "The 39 Steps," Memory blurts out, trapped by his professional pride, "is the name of an organization of spies collecting information on behalf of the foreign office of . . ." A shot suddenly rings out and Memory goes down. Jordan, who fired the bullet, leaps to the stage to try to escape. But police swarm from every exit and quickly disarm him.

Backstage, Memory discloses that the gang had made him use his photographic mind to memorize plans for a secret airplane engine. Instead of photographing the plans, the spies were going to use Memory's brains to get it out of the country. Hannay at last is cleared.

Hitchcock came to the United States in 1939, succumbing to the lure of Hollywood's big money. *Rebecca*, his first picture, won the Academy Award for best picture that year although the director's award went to John Ford for *The Grapes of Wrath*.

Nevertheless, he turned out a remarkable array of movies over the next three decades that made him one of the few directors whose name on a theatre marquee virtually guaranteed a box office success. Some of his most popular films include: *Foreign Correspondent* (1940), *Suspicion* (1941),

Spellbound (1945), *Rope* (1948), *Dial M for Murder* (1954), *Rear Window* (1954), *Vertigo* (1958), *North by Northwest* (1959), *Psycho* (1960), and *The Birds* (1963).

Ironically, it was television, not the movies, that made his double chin, jutting lower lip, droopy nose and bald dome a household image. In 1955 he introduced his own half-hour dramatic show, *Alfred Hitchcock Presents*. The show was an instant hit and his wry humor became as compelling to viewers as the story that followed. Commercials were his pet spoof. "Now my sponsor would like to bring you an important message," he once said. "I needn't tell you to whom it is important."

Would he consider doing any other kind of movie but melodrama? A comedy? A musical, a children's story, perhaps? "No, I'm a typed director," says the master of skulduggery. "If I made *Cinderella*, the audience would immediately be looking for a body in the coach."

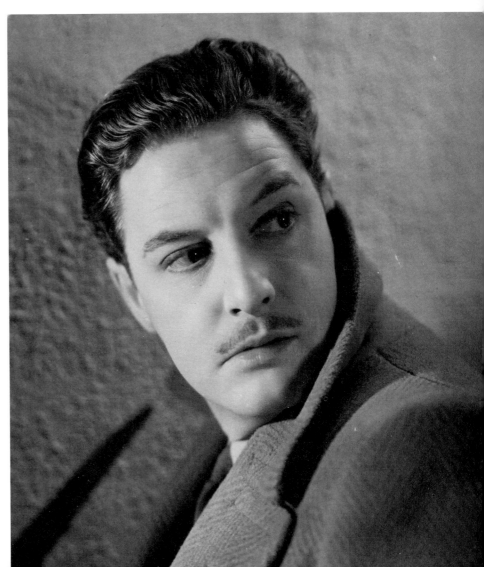

Robert Donat playing the Canadian Richard Hannay, who blunders into a network of intrigue in England.

(*Photos by Gaumont-British Picture Corp. Ltd.*)

Hannay, eluding the police, asks for a night's shelter from a Scottish farmer (John Laurie) and his wife (Peggy Ashcroft).

Hannay spots the missing little finger of Professor Jordan (Godfrey Tearle) and realizes the professor is the spy leader Hannay has been tracking.

Hannay shows to a skeptical police officer the Bible that stopped a bullet and saved his life.

Handcuffed to a strange girl (Madeleine Carroll), Hannay bluffs her into thinking he has a gun in his coat pocket and convinces the maid (Peggy Simpson) they're husband and wife.

Director Frank Capra enjoys a joke on the set with Barbara Stanwyck and Gary Cooper.

(*Photos by Warner Bros.*)

Frank Capra

Meet John Doe

(Released May 3, 1941)

SCREEN PLAY by Robert Riskin from an original story by Richard Connell and Robert Presnell. Art director, Stephen Goosson. Music, Dimitri Tiomkin. Music director, Leo F. Forbstein. Photography, George Barnes. Editor, Daniel Mandell. Special effects, Jack Cosgrove. Montage effects, Slavko Vorkapich. Produced and directed by Frank Capra in association with Riskin. Released through Warner Brothers. Running time, 135 minutes.

Long John Willoughby (John Doe)	GARY COOPER
Ann Mitchell	BARBARA STANWYCK
D. B. Norton	EDWARD ARNOLD
Colonel	WALTER BRENNAN
Connell	JAMES GLEASON
Mayor Lovett	GENE LOCKHART
Beany	IRVING BACON
Bert Hansen	REGIS TOOMEY
Mrs. Hansen	ANN DORAN
Tim Sheldon	ROD LA ROCQUE
Mrs. Mitchell	SPRING BYINGTON
Hammett	PIERRE WATKIN
Barrington	WALTER SODERLING
Weston	STANLEY ANDREWS
Spencer	ANDREW TOMBES
Sourpuss Smithers	J. FARRELL MAC DONALD
Angelface	WARREN HYMER
Mayor Hawkins	HARRY HOLMAN
Mike	PAT FLAHERTY
Mug	GENE MORGAN
Mrs. Brewster	MRS. GARDNER CRANE
Mayor's Wife	SARAH EDWARDS
Pop Dwyer	ALDRICH BOWKER
Political Manager	ED STANLEY
Red	BENNIE BARTLETT
Mattie	BESS FLOWERS
Dan	STERLING HOLLOWAY
Radio Announcers at Convention	KNOX MANNING, SELMER JACKSON, JOHN B. HUGHES
Mr. Delaney	LAFE MC KEE
Mrs. Delaney	EMMA TANSEY
Governor	VAUGHAN GLASER
Bennett	MITCHELL LEWIS

He is very quiet on the set, almost inconspicuous, and he never shouts. When he wants to criticize an actor he takes him off on the side and has a chat with him.

He casts his movies with people who look and act like the parts they're playing. Then he tells them to forget about acting and just be themselves. Instead of long rehearsals, he likes to discuss a scene with his players. Often he leaves to them the final decision on how a sequence will be done.

And so they have dubbed Frank Capra—the actor's director.

They have also called him a social moralist; the deflater of the rich; the champion of the common man, the dope and the punk; the apostle of good cheer, optimism and happy endings. Others have called him a sentimentalist and his movies pure "Capracorn."

"My whole philosophy is in my films," Capra once said, answering his critics. "People are basically good or can be made good. Sentimental? Of course, but so what? Let's not be hard-boiled about this. Happy endings—life is full of them."

In fact, Capra can point to one in his own life that had the bonus of giving him an instant education. He once worked as a writer for the great Mack Sennett, father of the Keystone Cops. One of Capra's early gags put Ben Turpin in a cart with a loose wheel. The wheel would work away from its hub, then waver back, finally dump Turpin in a ditch.

"Junk it," said Sennett. He said the audience wouldn't even snicker. Capra told the director to shoot it anyway. When Sennett found out, he was furious. "To teach you a lesson, I'm going to leave that scene in the picture and watch you squirm when it lays the biggest egg in history."

Both Sennett and Capra were at the preview. But the audience howled at the wavering wheel. Afterward, Capra patted Sennett on the back. "Some lesson, eh, Mr. Sennett?" Snapped Sennett: "Here's your lesson, Capra. You're fired!"

Capra has never crowed over a boss since. Still, he didn't let Sennett's temper faze him. He walked up and down outside the studio for three days. Finally Sennett looked out the window and took him back. Thereafter the two formed a close working relationship and Capra learned his comedy at the feet of the old master.

A native of Sicily, Capra came to the United States in 1903 when he was six. His family was poor, and young Capra sold newspapers in Los Angeles, teaching himself to read from his unsold stock. A brilliant student, he graduated from high school at sixteen, got a scholarship to the California Institute of Technology, where he majored in chemical engineering.

But after serving in World War I, jobs for engineers were scarce and Capra spent the next six years as a salesman, selling anything that came along. Then in 1924, broke and sleeping in flophouses, he spotted a newspaper item about a new movie studio starting in an old San Francisco gymnasium. He showed up and announced he was from Hollywood, which so impressed the pioneer studio head, a Shakespearean actor named Walter Montague, that he gave Capra a two-reeler to direct. Capra immediately hired assorted amateurs who had never faced a camera—"I didn't want real actors who might show me up," he said—called in a professional cameraman, and made the silent film in two days. It cost $1,700. The studio sold it to Pathé for $3,500. Capra got $75 for the job.

Capra went on to work for Hal Roach as a gag man for the *Our Gang* comedies, later joining Sennett's studio in the same capacity. After a while he moved up to director. One day he got a call from Harry Cohn, chief of Columbia Pictures. Cohn was looking for a director who would work cheap. He reached Capra simply by going through a directory list alphabetically. Capra was the first available man. "How much do you want?" Cohn asked. "Never mind," Capra said. "What kind of story have you got for me to do?"

In the next ten years Capra's income from Columbia soared from $1,000 for that first film (*That Certain Thing*) to $200,000 a year. His pictures became so popular, exhibitors bought them sight unseen on the strength of his name alone. They included *It Happened One Night* (which won Capra his first directing Oscar in 1934), *Mr. Deeds Goes to Town* (which gave Capra another directing Oscar in 1936), *Lost Horizon* (1937), *You Can't Take It With You* (his third directing Oscar in 1938) and *Mr. Smith Goes to Washington* (1939).

When his contract ended at Columbia in 1939, Capra left to form his own production company with writer Robert Riskin, who had collaborated with him on most of his successes. Their first picture was *Meet John Doe*, a film in which Capra brought to maturity his almost mystical faith in the little guys and their potential to become an important force for good if they band together.

Actually, Doe was the same hayseed knight as his predecessors, Deeds and Smith, only this time he faced a bigger dragon. In *Mr. Deeds*, he was a simple small-town bumpkin who inherited a fortune and was considered a screwball for wanting to carve up his estate to give to out-of-work farmers. In *Mr. Smith*, he was the same homespun idealist but he was aroused by something tangible—a corrupt bill in the Senate. Still, his impassioned filibuster was directed at a narrow target—a single bill which affected only a single dam project in one state.

As John Doe, Capra's hero leads a national movement for brotherhood, then strikes out against a publisher-politician who wants to manipulate the movement to sweep himself into the White House. The evil is broader, the stakes are higher, and so the impact is more intense.

John Doe opens as columnist Ann Mitchell (Barbara Stanwyck) is fired from her newspaper. She ends her last piece with a letter from an imaginary John Doe, railing about the injustice being heaped against the little men. As a dramatic protest, Doe says he's going to jump off City Hall on Christmas Eve.

What started off as a whimsical item creates such a stir that managing editor Henry Connell (James Gleason) demands the letter. Ann admits it was a phony. But she suggests that they find some down-

and-outer to play the bogus hero and milk the story to boost circulation. When the rival paper calls Doe a fake, Connell buys her idea. They pick a hobo, Long John Willoughby (Gary Cooper), a former bush-league pitcher with a sore arm. He goes along with the scheme to get the money to have his ailing wing doctored.

At first Doe and his tramp cohort, called "Colonel" (Walter Brennan), loll in the luxury of a fine hotel while Ann cranks out dozens of articles. The stories become so popular, the public clamors to see Doe.

Editor Connell thinks it's time for Doe to disappear. But Ann convinces tycoon publisher D. B. Norton (Edward Arnold) to put Doe on the radio. "If he made a hit around here," Ann tells Norton, "he can do it every place else in the country. And you'll be pulling the strings."

Doe goes on the radio. Reading a speech Ann has ghost-written, he makes a simple appeal for brotherly love. "To most of you, your neighbor is a stranger, a guy with a barking dog and a fence around him," Doe says. "Now you can't be a stranger to any guy that's on your own team. So tear down the fence that separates you. . . . You'll tear down a lot of hates and prejudices."

Doe isn't saying anything that the Scriptures haven't already set down. But he's got a straightforward delivery and his words have a sincere ring. "I know a lot of you are saying to yourself, 'He's asking for a miracle.' . . . Well, you're wrong. It's no miracle. . . . I see it happen once every year. . . . At Christmastime. . . . Why can't that spirit last the whole year round? Gosh, if it ever did—we'd develop such a strength that no human force could stand against us."

The speech creates a sensation. But when John Doe Clubs spring up all over the country, Doe thinks the fraud has gone far enough and walks out. However, when he reaches a little Midwestern town, people recognize him and flock around him like he was a celebrity. One of them, a soda jerk named Bert Hansen (Regis Toomey), tells Doe his speech has inspired him to become pals with his grouchy neighbor, Sourpuss Smithers (J. Farrell MacDonald). Sourpuss has suddenly become so friendly he's been elected president of the town's John Doe Club. Scores of people, just plain folks, come up to shake Doe's hand.

Who could fight against those odds? So Doe relents and stumps the country as the leader of the National John Doe Movement.

Now publisher Norton steps in. At the upcoming National John Doe Clubs' convention, he tells his cronies, he plans to launch a drive for a third party with Doe backing him for President. "That practically means 90 per cent of the voters," Norton beams. Just before the convention, editor Connell gets to Doe and warns him that Norton is simply using Doe to further Norton's own political ambitions. The publisher's vast, fascist-like power already includes control of the police.

Enraged, Doe bursts in on Norton and announces he won't read the nominating speech. "And what's more," Doe adds, "I'm going down to that convention and I'm going to tell those people exactly what you and your fine feathered friends are trying to cook up for them."

Norton counters by threatening to expose Doe as a fake and kill the John Doe Movement the moment Doe steps out of line. Doe won't back down and storms out to the convention. Once there, Doe mounts the platform, but the Norton-controlled cops pull him back. Norton seizes the microphone and accuses Doe of pocketing the collection dues from John Doe Clubs. He says Doe never wrote the suicide letter, got paid to pose as John Doe, and has no intention of jumping off City Hall.

Broken and discredited, Doe decides the only way he can keep his new movement alive is to become a martyr. On Christmas Eve he goes to the tower atop City Hall. Snow is falling and it's bitter cold. (To add realism, the scene was shot in a rented icehouse—with temperature at 12 degrees—so that the actors' breath would smoke when they spoke.) Norton and his politicos are there to tell Doe it will do him no good. But they can't change his mind.

As he's about to jump, Ann runs out. She throws her arms around him, says she loves him and begs him not to take his life. Somebody has already died to keep the John Doe idea alive, she says. He was the first John Doe. "And he has kept that idea alive for almost two thousand years. . . . If it's [an ideal] worth dying for, it's worth living for. . . . This is no time to give up," Ann says, sobbing hysterically, then fainting in Doe's arms.

(At this point, Capra was on the horns of a dilemma. He felt Ann had not quite talked Doe out of jumping. Nor had Doe put suicide out of his mind. So, after the picture had already been released, he inserted "the people" into the scene.)

Hansen, the soda jerk, and his wife, drive through the snow. With other friends, they rush up to the tower. "Mr. Doe, we're with you," Hansen says.

227

"We need you," Mrs. Hansen (Ann Doran) adds. "There were a lot of us who didn't believe what that man [Norton] said. We were going to start our own John Doe Club again whether we saw you or not . . . And there were a lot of others going to do the same thing. . . . Only it'd be a lot easier with you. Please, please, come with us, Mr. Doe."

Doe is motionless. Then, turning away from the ledge and holding Ann in his arms, he walks toward the Hansens and his supporters. Norton and his politicos look on silently, their eyes glistening. Finally, in a touch reminiscent of Ma Joad's curtain line in *The Grapes of Wrath*, editor Connell looks at the jowly publisher. "There you are, Norton—the people. Try and lick that." As the scene dissolves, the joyful choral finale of Beethoven's Ninth Symphony swells in the background.

Long John Willoughby (Cooper), a former bush-league pitcher, has his first meal in days with his tramp cohort pal the Colonel (Walter Brennan) as reporter Ann Mitchell (Miss Stanwyck) watches. Willoughby, who has agreed to pose as protester John Doe, strikes up on his harmonica while the Colonel plays his ocarina ("sweet potato").

Angelface (Warren Hymer) lights up a cigar for Doe, lolling in his new-found luxurious quarters while Beany (Irving Bacon), a news photographer, hands him a paper. The Colonel, holding his duds in a strap pack, is unhappy about the whole thing.

228

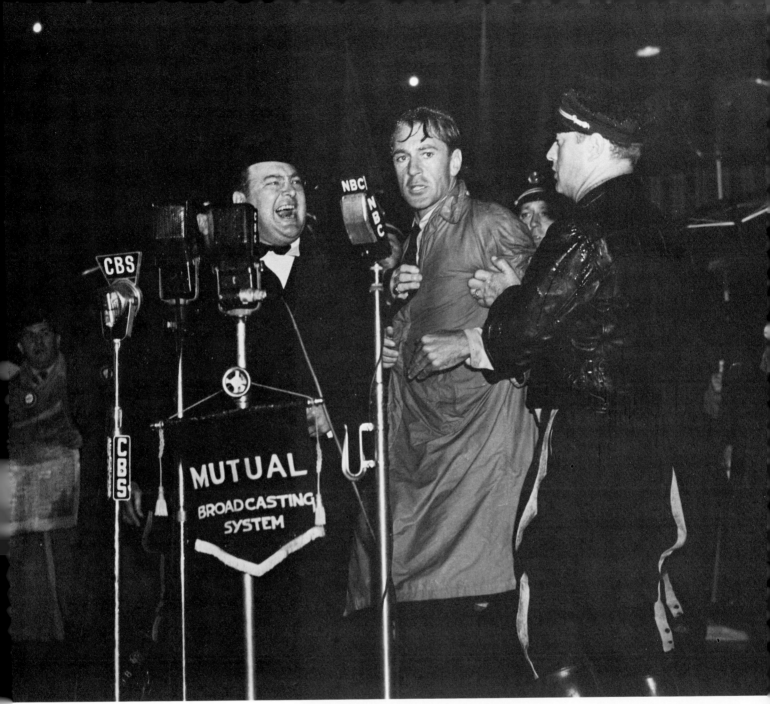

Doe tries to tell his followers that Norton is a crooked politician trying to use the Doe Movement for a White House bid. But police pull him back and Norton takes the microphone to denounce Doe as a fake.

Newspaper tycoon D. B. Norton (Edward Arnold) decides to finance the John Doe Brotherhood Movement which Ann has mastered-minded. But the Colonel has misgivings.

Writer-director Preston Sturges, Hollywood's eccentric wonder boy. *(Copyright 1940, Paramount Pictures Inc.)*

(Photos by Paramount)

Marine corporal (Jimmie Dundee) hands a reluctant Woodrow some hash marks for his uniform.

Preston Sturges

Hail the Conquering Hero

(New York Premiere, August 9, 1944)

WRITTEN AND DIRECTED by Preston Sturges. Music written by Werner Heymann. Musical director, Sigmund Krumgold. Photography, John Seitz. Editor, Stuart Gilmore. Art directors, Hans Dreier and Haldane Douglas. Song: "Home to the Arms of Mother" by Sturges. Released by Paramount. Running time, 101 minutes.

Woodrow Truesmith	EDDIE BRACKEN
Libby	ELLA RAINES
Forrest Noble	BILL EDWARDS
Mayor Noble	RAYMOND WALBURN
Sergeant	WILLIAM DEMAREST
Corporal	JIMMIE DUNDEE
Mrs. Truesmith	GEORGIA CAINE
Political Boss	ALAN BRIDGE
Jonesy	JAMES DAMORE
Bugsy	FREDDIE STEELE
Bill	STEPHEN GREGORY
Juke	LEN HENDRY
Mrs. Noble	ESTHER HOWARD
Libby's Aunt	ELIZABETH PATTERSON
Judge Dennis	JIMMY CONLIN
Rev. Upperman	ARTHUR HOYT
Doc Bissell	HARRY HAYDEN
Committee Chairman	FRANKLIN PANGBORN
Progressive Band Leader	VICTOR POTEL
Mr. Schultz	TORBEN MEYER
Regular Band Leader	JACK NORTON

His car was a midget roadster, not much bigger than his three-year-old's express wagon. His office chair had a sloping back, a back so low he was actually in a reclining position when he got behind his desk and—instead of sitting down—lay down. For an intercom system, he used an auto beep horn. His Oscar was pushed off on a table. In its place on his desk, he had a foot-tall statue of a horse's backside.

Writers used the adjectives "eccentric, madcap, screwball" to describe Preston Sturges. But when they talked about the movies he wrote and directed, they added the word "genius."

Sturges came to Hollywood as a wonder boy in the 1930s. Although he left it as a bad boy ("bad" because he refused to work for any of the studios) in the 1940s, he left behind a body of work perhaps unequaled for its modern satire. Hollywood had done satires on contemporary America before Sturges appeared. But no one had picked for his target such sacred idols as matrimony, Mom and the war hero.

Sturges did. And he did it so cleverly, his efforts offended no one. More important, his comedy had style and wit and flair. He created memorable minor characters (played by William Demarest, Freddie Steele, Raymond Walburn, Franklin Pangborn, Jimmy Conlin, Victor Potel) and heroes who were bumblers and simpletons—but sympathetic, all the same. His comedies at their best—as in *Hail the Conquering Hero*—evoked genuinely touching moments, drama juxtaposed with humor à la Chaplin.

Sturges, son of a wealthy stockbroker and a much-married mother who was the best friend of barefoot modern dancer Isadora Duncan, achieved his first fame in 1929 with his play *Strictly Dishonorable*. It ran on Broadway for two years, earned him $300,000 and a subsequent contract as a Hollywood screen writer.

Universal started him at $1,000 a week. His first assignment was to do an adaptation of H. G. Wells's *The Invisible Man*. Nine writers had tried it without luck. Sturges became the tenth. Instead of despairing, he worked harder. He turned out a succession of successful scenarios and original screen plays, moving from MGM to RKO to Fox and finally to Paramount until his salary soared to $2,500 a week.

During his climb up the ladder, Sturges once wrote down what he considered the eleven keys to box office success. As they appeared in *Variety*, they are: "1. A pretty girl is better than an ugly one. 2. A leg is better than an arm. 3. A bedroom is better than a living room. 4. An arrival is better than a departure. 5. A birth is better than a death. 6. A chase is better than a chat. 7. A dog is better than a landscape. 8. A kitten is better than a dog. 9. A baby is better than a kitten. 10. A kiss is better than a baby. 11. A pratfall is better than anything."

Despite his success, Sturges wasn't satisfied. His stories didn't turn out on the screen the way he wanted them to. The actors weren't speaking his lines right, or at least as he felt they should be spoken. The scenes weren't played as he had meant them to be. It was the old Hollywood story. Pictures were turned out by writers whose scripts were then subject to the interpretation of directors. In turn, their product was subject to revision by any number of producers. Sturges felt that a movie, instead of being the product of a team tinkering job, should be the product of one mind. So he decided to make his own pictures.

In 1940 he wrote *The Great McGinty*, a story of a crooked politician whose downfall came when he performed one honest deed. He sold the script to Paramount for ten dollars but with one proviso—that he could direct it. Paramount agreed. The movie was a hit and Sturges won the Academy Award for best original screen play.

Sturges had made his point. Paramount upped his salary to $3,250 a week and gave him the rare freedom to write and direct his own movies. Over the next four years came a string of seven Sturges movies. One memorable film was *Sullivan's Travels* (1941), about a Hollywood director who goes on an odyssey to find out what poverty is all about. Another offbeat comedy was *The Miracle of Morgan's Creek* (1944), about a girl who gets pregnant after marrying an unknown GI during a wild farewell party and suffers humiliation in her small town until she bears sextuplets and becomes a national heroine. Other pictures were: *Christmas in July* (1940), *The Lady Eve* (1941), *The Palm Beach Story* (1942)

and *The Great Moment* (1944). But *Hail the Conquering Hero*, which spoofs the American penchant for hero-worship (the hero in this case being a dope who comes home with a chestful of medals), is Sturges at his satirical best.

Woodrow Lafayette Pershing Truesmith (Eddie Bracken), son of a World War I leatherneck who died heroically at Belleau Wood, joins the Marine Corps at the start of World War II. To his chagrin, he is discharged a month later because, of all things, he has chronic hay fever. Ashamed to go home, he takes a shipyard job and has Marines post his letters to his mother from the South Pacific. He writes his best girl (Ella Raines) that he has fallen in love with someone else.

Then one day six Marines back from Gaudalcanal bump into Woodrow in a bar and learn about his pitiful deception. One of them, called Bugsy (played by Freddie Steele, a former middleweight boxing champion), suffers from shell shock and psychopathic reverence for mothers. Bugsy phones Truesmith's mother (Georgia Caine), tells her that her son has returned from the war a hero. The Marines put the reluctant Woodrow in a uniform and drag him aboard a train. Their hard-boiled but sentimental sergeant (William Demarest) convinces Woodrow that they can sneak him into town and give his mother the joy of seeing him as a hero. Then he can peel off his uniform and put it in mothballs.

But when Woodrow and his honor guard step off the train at Oakridge, the whole town is there to hail their conquering hero. In one of the film's funniest scenes, windbag Mayor Noble (Raymond Walburn) launches into his welcoming speech. But he keeps getting drowned out by two bands, much to the mortification of the prissy, whistle-blowing master of ceremonies (Franklin Pangborn). "Nonono," the harassed M.C. screams. ". . . will you please wait until I give you the signal."

Within hours, the townspeople burn the mortgage on his mother's home, propose a monument to Woodrow's honor, start booming him for mayor. Woodrow, agonizing over the deception, tries to tell them it's all a mistake. In his speech, he tells them he did what he did only because he loves his mother. One of the city fathers whispers, "He has a natural flair for politics."

"The medals that you saw pinned on me, you could say were practically pinned by mistake. . . . I'm no hero," Woodrow insists. It's all in vain. The crowd cheers him even louder. "After that he could become President," one old crony says. Says another: "Finest political speech I heard since Bryan and the crown of thorns."

That night Woodrow tries to sneak away. But Bugsy has posted himself outside his room. Woodrow then stages a fake call ordering him back to duty. But the Marines foil this attempt too. "See that look in your mother's eyes," Bugsy says. "That's what we're working for."

Finally the mayor learns of Woodrow's deception. But before he can expose him, the bogus hero makes a clean breast of his fraud at a town meeting. It is a poignant moment, made even more moving because it comes as a sharp contrast to the fast-paced, rollicking slapstick humor. Bracken, who up to this point has turned in a hilarious performance as the befuddled Woodrow, proves himself to be a comedian of wide-ranging ability as he makes this scene the dramatic highlight of the movie.

"This should have been the happiest day of my life. Instead, it's the bitterest," Woodrow says. "If I could reach as high as my father's shoestrings, my whole life would be justified. And I would stand before you proudly, instead of as the thief and coward that I am. A coward because I postponed until now what I should have told you a year ago when I was discharged from the Marine Corps for medical unfitness. A coward because I didn't want my mother to know it. . . . A thief because I stole your admiration. I stole the ribbons I've worn. I

stole this nomination. . . ."

Woodrow goes home to pack his bags. But Sarge strides to the podium and tells the crowd that Woodrow's confession took more courage than any battlefield deed. Then he discloses that the hoax was not Woodrow's idea but the Marines'.

The crowd marches to the train station, looking like a lynch mob. They catch Woodrow just as his train pulls in. "If to act out a little lie to save one mother humiliation was a fault," Doc Bissell (Harry Hayden) tells Woodrow, "it was a fault any man could be proud of." Oakridge has found an honest and courageous man, the townsfolk tell the bewildered Woodrow. They ask him to stay, after all, and run for mayor.

The picture won accolades from the critics. But when Sturges' long-term contract with Paramount expired, he refused to renew. Every other studio courted him. He turned them all down in favor of a partnership with millionaire Howard Hughes. It came to nought. Something happened to his talent and his pictures lost their unique style. Even later, when he moved to France, his lone picture there emerged flat and punchless.

Sturges died in 1959 at the age of sixty. He was survived by his fourth wife, the former actress Anne Nagel, three sons and a string of earthy, human comedies that held a mirror up to small-town America and let it reflect on what a farce it sometimes made of itself.

Marine reject Woodrow Lafayette Pershing Truesmith (Eddie Bracken) is literally carried back home by six leatherneck veterans of Guadalcanal. At right, holding his leg, is Bugsy (Freddie Steele, former middleweight boxing champion).

Poor Woodrow is stunned to find the whole town has turned out to greet him, thinking he's a hero. The reception committee chairman (Franklin Pangborn) and the Marine sergeant (William Demerest) are alongside.

Woodrow listens to welcoming speeches, standing between his mother (Georgia Caine) and his former girl, Libby (Ella Raines). At right is Libby's aunt (Elizabeth Patterson).

The chagrined Woodrow can barely manage to raise a finger to acknowledge his nomination for mayor.

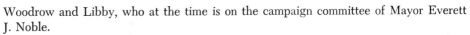

Woodrow and Libby, who at the time is on the campaign committee of Mayor Everett J. Noble.

Idealistic newspaper publisher Charles Foster Kane (Orson Welles) writes his Declaration of Principles. Joseph Cotten, left, and Everette Sloane look on. *(Courtesy WOR-TV)*

Circulation booms as Kane's paper features colorful crime stories, firsthand accounts of the war. That's Welles and Cotten atop a pile of newspapers.

(Photos by RKO)

Orson Welles

Citizen Kane

(Released September 5, 1941)

An original screen play by Orson Welles * and Herman J. Mankiewicz.* Produced and directed by Welles. Photography by Gregg Toland. Music composed and conducted by Bernard Herrmann. Art director, Van Nest Polglase. Editor, Robert Wise. Special effects, Vernon L. Walker. A Mercury Production released through RKO Radio Pictures. Running time, 119 minutes.

Charles Foster Kane	ORSON WELLES
Jedediah Leland	JOSEPH COTTEN
Susan Alexander	DOROTHY COMINGORE
Mr. Bernstein	EVERETT SLOANE
J. W. Gettys	RAY COLLINS
Walter Parks Thatcher	GEORGE COULOURIS
Mrs. Kane (Mother)	AGNES MOOREHEAD
Raymond	PAUL STEWART
Emily Norton	RUTH WARRICK
Herbert Carter	ERSKINE SANFORD
Thompson	WILLIAM ALLAND
Matiste	FORTUNIO BONANOVA
Headwaiter	GUS SCHILLING
Mr. Rawlston	PHILIP VAN ZANDT
Miss Anderson	GEORGIA BACKUS
Kane's Father	HARRY SHANNON
Kane III	SONNY BUPP
Kane (age 8)	BUDDY SWAN

(The movie was the screen debut of Welles, Cotten, Collins, Moorehead, Stewart and Warrick.)

A "No Trespassing" sign hangs from a fence. The camera pans along the misty landscape. We see a gate with the giant initial *K*. Beyond it, perched

---

* Academy Award winner.

high on a hill, a castle looms in the night. The camera takes us closer. A single light is on in one of the towers.

Suddenly the scene shifts and we see snowflakes swirling around a house. The camera sweeps back and we see the scene is actually taking place in a crystal glass ball an old man is holding. "R-o-s-e-b-u-d," he says. Just the one word. Slowly. The sound comes out blurred and distant, an echo in an undersea chamber.

The camera retreats again and we see the man is in bed. His hand relaxes and the crystal falls, smashing to bits on the floor. A nurse rushes into the room. Her reflection flashes across a mirror. She puts her hand over the old man's heart, then covers his face with a sheet.

And so begins the movie many critics rank with the best ten films of all time. A few have called it the finest picture to come out of Hollywood. Ironically, hindsight suggests the movie was too far ahead of its time to be fully appreciated in its day. *How Green Was My Valley* outpolled it in the 1941 Oscar derby. It won no prize for acting or directing. The sole Academy Award Orson Welles took home was a co-prize shared with Herman J. Mankiewicz for best original screen play.

But if the Academy was not generous in its balloting, the critics were intrigued by the picture's fast, fluid motion and bold cinematic techniques. Breaking Hollywood taboos, cameraman Gregg Toland shot flush into bright lights (an opera is seen from behind the singer). For the first time, lenses lingered in dark corners (a projection room conference is held in semi darkness) and angled up at low ceilings (unlike other Hollywood sets, which replaced ceilings with overhead lights, Welles used ceilings to add realism). Indeed, the movie had a fresh and exciting look like you were seeing something that had never been done before.

Master-minding all this was a bass-voiced, cocksure showman, a twenty-five-year-old *enfant terrible* whom newspapermen were calling "the boy wonder." Welles came to Hollywood in August 1939, fresh from triumphs in radio and the theatre. He had won headlines by staging a Negro version of *Macbeth,* a stirring labor opera called *The Cradle Will Rock* and a modern-dress *Julius Caesar.* On radio, he had a meteoric rise from a role as "The Shadow" to producer of his own Mercury Theatre of the Air. On October 30, 1938, he gave his listeners a coast-to-coast scare with his famous "Martians" broadcast. Thousands panicked when they heard that men from Mars had landed at Grovers Mill, New Jersey.

Welles sprang full-fledged upon the screen. *Citizen Kane* was his first picture. For his cast, he brought his talented Mercury Players from New York. But it was clear who the boss was. Welles was producer, director, star and co-author.

Some Hollywood veterans, used to seeing a film made through the collaboration of many minds, were skeptical that he could pull it off. For a while it looked like there might be some foundation to their doubts. Months went by without anything in production. But Welles was learning his trade, passing up parties to work late into the night on the RKO lot. He thought about his picture for a full year. Then he filmed it—in four months.

The shooting was done in tight secrecy. Welles was leery that studio executives would balk at releasing a picture showing the emptiness of a contemporary American success story. But even after it was finished (at a cost of only $800,000), Welles's worries weren't over. William Randolph Hearst, the chain newspaper publisher, demanded that it be suppressed. Hearst's representatives claimed the picture was based on the publishing czar's life. They said it painted an unfair and uncomplimentary picture.

Although he said he drew on history for his story, Welles insisted *Citizen Kane* was not biographical. "It is not based upon the life of Mr. Hearst or anyone else," Welles said. "On the other hand, had Mr. Hearst and similar financial barons not lived during the period we discuss, *Citizen Kane* could not have been made."

No lawsuit was filed. But Hearst retaliated by banning all ads of the film and Welles's name from his vast newspaper empire. His efforts backfired. It only served to touch off more interest in the movie.

When *Citizen Kane* started its New York run at the RKO Palace on May 1, 1941, it played to capacity audiences.

The film opens with the death of Charles Foster Kane, a newspaper tycoon secluded in a fabulous Florida palace called Xanadu. In its great halls he has accumulated the paintings and statues of Europe, art treasures to fill ten museums. As the breath of life passes from his body, he says the word "Rosebud."

Suddenly a newsreel reminiscent of *The March of Time,* flashes on with the highlights of Kane's life. It shows how Kane rose from humble beginnings to amass the world's sixth largest private fortune. It tells how he became a successful newspaper publisher, made a losing run for governor, married and divorced twice, then ended his life in the solitary splendor of Xanadu.

The newsreel goes off with a whir. And we find we are in a projection room, illuminated by the beam from the camera to the screen. Rawlston (Philip Van Zandt), the newsreel editor, isn't satisfied. This is only Kane's public life. What was he really like? "It's not enough to tell us what a man did," the editor says. "You've got to tell us who he was. . . . Maybe he told us all about himself on his deathbed. When Kane died, he said just one word—'Rosebud.' . . . Now what does that mean?"

Thompson (William Alland), the newsreel reporter assigned to find out the meaning of "Rosebud," reads the memoirs of Kane's guardian and interviews two newspaper associates, his second wife and his butler. All agree he is a megalomaniac. But each has seen a different part of his character.

Now the threads of Kane's private life are spun out in flashbacks. Through the memoirs of banker Walter Parks Thatcher (George Coulouris), we first see young Kane frolicking in the snow with his sled in Colorado. Inside his meager home a grim scene is being played out. His mother (Agnes Moorehead) has come into a large sum of money through some landholdings. She has decided to spare the child from a brutal father and signs him and his inheritance over to Thatcher, a Wall Street financier, who is to be the boy's guardian. Young Kane strikes at Thatcher with his sled when he learns what is in store for him.

Years pass. Kane has reached his twenty-fifth birthday and is eligible to take full control of his estate, now worth $60,000,000. On a whim, he decides to take personal charge of one of his failing holdings—the New York *Enquirer.* Much to Thatcher's displeasure, Kane ends up taking his job seriously. He campaigns successfully to clear slums and becomes a vigorous social reformer. Irritated, the ultraconservative Thatcher ends up calling Kane a "Communist."

"It wasn't money he wanted," says Mr. Bernstein (Everett Sloane), Kane's loyal general manager. "Thatcher couldn't figure that out. Sometimes even I couldn't." Bernstein's narrative shows us the triumphant moments of Kane's early career. At the outset he publishes a front-page Declaration of Principles. He vows his paper will tell all the truth honestly, become the people's champion. But to win a circulation war he goes after juicy crime stories, buys the cream of his competitor's staff and prods the U.S. into the Spanish-American War.

He marries the socially prominent Emily Norton (Ruth Warrick), the President's niece. There's talk that one day she might be the next President's wife. But, Bernstein sadly tells us, she turns out to be no rosebud. "Rosebud . . . ," Bernstein says. "Maybe that was something he lost. Kane was a man who lost almost everything he had."

Jedediah Leland (Joseph Cotten), theatre critic for Kane's paper, was his college chum. "I was his oldest friend," Leland says. "And as far as I was concerned, he behaved like a swine." Leland's flashback shows Kane as the new father of a baby boy. But bored and repelled by his wife's prim, blueblooded ways, he finds solace with a young mistress. She is Susan Alexander (Dorothy Comingore), a pretty but shallow salesgirl whose second-rate voice brings him pleasure.

Kane runs for governor, promising to send his opponent, a crooked political boss named J. W. Gettys (Ray Collins), to Sing Sing. However, Gettys learns of Kane's affair and threatens to expose the love nest unless Kane drops out of the race. Kane's wife, shocked, urges him to quit. Kane stubbornly refuses. Gettys wins in a landslide, leaving Kane's public image in ruins.

Shortly afterward, Kane's wife and son are killed in a car accident. Kane marries the singer. To forget his sorrows and restore his ego, he devotes himself to building her career. He puts up a $3,000,000 opera house for her, tries to make her into a diva. But she has little talent. After opening night, Leland returns to Kane's paper and starts typing an unfavorable review. "Miss Susan Alexander, a pretty but hopelessly incompetent amateur, last night opened the new Chicago Opera House. . . ." The task proves too painful and he drinks himself into a stupor. Kane finishes the review himself, calling her performance a fiasco. Then he fires Leland.

"He [Kane] thought that by finishing that notice he could show me he was an honest man," Leland says. "He was always trying to prove something. . . . Love. That's all he really wanted out of life. . . . That's Charlie's story. You see, he didn't have any to give."

The second Mrs. Kane, who has become an alcoholic, tells how Kane took her to his 50,000-acre estate, Xanadu. There, echoes rebound as they shout to one another across a long dinner table. She turns to giant jigsaw puzzles as loneliness and boredom assail her. Finally she rebels. "You don't love me," she screeches. "You want me to love you. 'Sure, I'm Charles Foster Kane. Whatever you want, just name it and it's yours. But you gotta love me.'" He slaps her. And she walks out.

Raymond (Paul Stewart), the butler, takes up the tale, describing how, when Kane's wife leaves, Kane smashes everything in her room. Suddenly Kane comes upon a crystal ball showing a pretty snow scene. He stops and looks at it. "Rosebud," he says in a hoarse whisper. The butler says he heard Kane mutter the word a few more times—even before he said it on his deathbed. But Raymond thinks it has no significance. "He said all kinds of things that didn't mean anything," the butler tells the reporter.

Other newsreel people join Thompson at Xanadu to take pictures of the castle. Has he found out what "Rosebud" means? "No," Thompson says. If he did, a woman reporter says, it probably would have explained everything. "No, I don't think so," Thompson says. ". . . I don't think any word could explain a man's life. I guess Rosebud is just a piece in a jigsaw puzzle—a missing piece."

That piece is filled in. But only for us. After the reporters leave, the camera sweeps slowly over the vast pile of objects Kane has collected over a lifetime. Workmen are throwing some of it into a furnace. One of them picks up a sled and tosses it in. The camera comes closer and picks out the faded letters written across the wooden slats. "Rosebud," the name on the sled Kane played with before he was called away to his inheritance, fills the screen as the flames devour it.

The camera now moves outside Xanadu, tracing back over the path it took at the beginning. We see smoke trailing into a somber sky. There is the "No Trespassing" sign and the initial K on the gate. Far away, the window behind which Kane lay dead is now dark. The faint light of dawn shimmers from behind clouds into which the rising smoke plume fades.

Kane and his first wife Emily Norton (Ruth Warrick), the President's niece, at their White House reception following their marriage. (*Courtesy WOR-TV*)

As the years go by, the Kanes become bored with each other. Mrs. Kane even reads a rival paper at breakfast. Photo shows Welles's pioneering use of sets with ceilings to add realism.

On the stump in the unsuccessful race for governor. *(Courtesy WOR-TV)*

The first Mrs. Kane meets her husband's mistress (Dorothy Comingore). In the background is Kane's opponent who arranged the confrontation—political boss Gettys (Ray Collins, who would become best known in the role of Lieutenant Tragg in the Perry Mason TV series). (*Courtesy WOR-TV*)

Kane's second wife turns to gigantic jigsaw puzzles to fight boredom in their huge estate, Xanadu. *(Courtesy WOR-TV)*

Busby Berkeley, dance master extraordinaire, who was the architect of the musical spectacular of the 1930s. (The montage shows the "Remember My Forgotten Man" number from *Gold Diggers of 1933*).

Cuties from the chorus wearing derbies and polka-dot shirts. Sitting, second from left, is Toby Wing to whom Dick Powell croons "I'm Young and Healthy."

(Photos by Warner Bros.)
(Courtesy United Artists)

Busby Berkeley

42nd Street

(Released March 11, 1933)

A SCREEN MUSICAL COMEDY based on the novel by Bradford Ropes. Adapted by Rian James and James Seymour. Songs by Al Dubin and Harry M. Warren: "I'm Young and Healthy," "Shuffle Off to Buffalo," "You're Getting to Be a Habit with Me," "It Must Be June" and "42nd Street." Dances created and staged by Busby Berkeley. Editor, Thomas Pratt. Art director, Jack Okey. Cameraman, Sol Polito. Directed by Lloyd Bacon and presented by Warner Brothers. Running time, 89 minutes.

Julian Marsh	WARNER BAXTER
Dorothy Brock	BEBE DANIELS
Pat Denning	GEORGE BRENT
Peggy Sawyer	RUBY KEELER
Lorraine Fleming	UNA MERKEL
Ann (Anytime Annie)	GINGER ROGERS
Abner Dillon	GUY KIBBEE
Barry	NED SPARKS
Billy Lawler	DICK POWELL
MacElroy	ALLEN JENKINS
The Actor	HENRY B. WALTHALL
Terry	EDWARD J. NUGENT
Jerry	HARRY AKST
Leading Man	CLARENCE NORDSTROM
Jones	ROBERT MC WADE
Andy Lee	GEORGE E. STONE
Song Writers	AL DUBIN, HARRY M. WARREN
"Young and Healthy" Girl	TOBY WING

One hundred girls playing one hundred lighted violins. Or, if you prefer, pounding away on one hundred baby grand pianos. One hundred dolls splashing away to the tune of "By a Waterfall." One hundred babes dancing on a giant revolving turntable.

Girls as human harps. Girls on roller skates. Girls twirling hoops. Girls reflected by huge mirrors in an endless array of patterns. Who dreamed up these fantastic sequences? Who else but Busby Berkeley?

He was king of Hollywood's musical spectaculars of the 1930s. He could take a song and dance and give it wings, dishing it up as movie audiences had never seen it dished up before. One girl dancing alone was peanuts. But one hundred girls dancing in unison—ah, that's what movies were all about, feller.

Anyway, that was Berkeley's theory. And, as *Newsweek* once put it, for a decade Hollywood lived through a "commercial opium dream . . . songs were sung and dances danced on a scale later reserved for wars and traffic jams."

A bargain basement Berkeley wasn't. But no one, not even Agnes de Mille, ever topped him in his greatest asset—flamboyance. "My philosophy," said Berkeley, "call it gigantic entertainment."

Born William Berkeley Enos in 1895, he was the son of touring actors. Berkeley made his stage debut at five. Later, after time out for the army in World War I (during which he became an expert in drilling troops), he made the transition from acting and dancing to directing straight plays and musicals.

Berkeley had worked in twenty-one Broadway musicals when Hollywood imported him as a dance director in the early 1930s. He was hired to create the production numbers only. Directing was to come later.

During the early years of the talkies—they began in 1927—studios flooded movie houses with gaudy backstage musicals. Each film company ground out about half a dozen a month. It was too much too soon. The musicals quickly wore out their welcome. In fact, the public stayed away in such large numbers that some theatres put signs outside reading, "This Show Is Not a Musical."

It took Berkeley just three years in Hollywood and seven pictures—including *Whoopee* (1930) and *Palmy Days* (1931)—to figure out what was wrong. Berkeley thought the problem was that the studios had depended too much on routines borrowed from the stage. In film after film, chorus girls danced in a single line before uninspired cameras. Musicals needed a whole new approach. They needed fresh and original productions that would let audiences see things that could only be seen in movies. The way to do this was (1) by creating massive song and dance sequences on sets too lavish for a Broadway show. Then (2) shooting the numbers from all angles with a mobile camera.

It was in Berkeley's eighth picture—*42nd Street* —that his talent sprang forth in full bloom. The movie had an all-star cast. And Darryl Zanuck, Berkeley's boss at Warner Brothers, gave him carte blanche to mount four productions and hire a big chorus.

The studio said Berkeley screened 5,000 girls. There were conflicting reports as to just how he arrived at his final chorus. At the time, Warner Brothers gave this account of the Berkeley method: He picked 300 girls with pretty faces. From there, he chose 200 who also had pretty ankles. He arranged this group in size places, the tallest to the shortest. Then he went down the line and, without looking at faces, picked the 100 prettiest sets of knees. So in the end the knees had it.

However, in 1965, the London *Evening Standard's* Alexander Walker quoted Berkeley as saying: "I picked the girls for their eyes. Their eyes must talk to me, not flirt with me. I don't need to see girls in bathing costumes to judge them."

So were the knees or the eyes really the final arbiter of Berkeley's taste? I wrote him about the puzzle in 1969. He responded with one sentence: "Yes, I do pick beauty through a girl's eyes—because the eyes mirror the soul."

Nevertheless, even though he looked into his girls' souls, in the end he was just as concerned about their bodies. He watched over his chorines like a mother hen. He put them on a football-like training schedule. He insisted on regular sleeping hours and supervised meals. Pastry was out. So were candy, doughnuts, all between-meals snacks. It paid off. When a flu epidemic hit Hollywood

during the filming, stars dropped like flies. But as far as Berkeley's girls were concerned, there wasn't a cough in a carload.

Berkeley dreamed up his grandiose production numbers as he meditated in his studio office. "I don't know where my ideas came from," he said. "But I never did the same thing twice."

He constructed a swimming pool in a lake in Cypress Gardens, Florida, for an Esther Williams movie. He punched holes through a floor and had violinists raise their instruments over their heads so leggy Ann Miller could dance through a bodiless battalion of arms. For *42nd Street* he built three enormous turntables, pyramided them one above the other, then spun them slowly in different directions while girls tap-danced on them. "All I could do was try to top myself," Berkeley said. "I always came through." Berkeley couldn't have cared less about the plot. But audiences of today, for whom his extravaganzas have become high camp, get just as much tongue-in-cheek fun out of seeing their dated story lines unfold.

42nd Street, which started the era of opulent film musicals, tells the classic backstage story of the chorus girl who substitutes for the injured star on opening night and stops the show. As the movie opens, a couple of producers hire the famous Julian Marsh (Warner Baxter) to direct a new musical that will star Dorothy Brock (Bebe Daniels).

She's good. But the real sweetener is her sugar daddy's bankroll (Guy Kibbee), which is financing the show. Baxter, known as a slave driver because he works his chorus girls until they drop, has been told he's a sick man. But he is broke. So he vows to make his last show a smash hit.

When auditions start, backstage romances start too. Bebe Daniels plays up to the angel, Kibbee, to keep his mind off production costs. However, she's really in love with Pat Denning (George Brent), her former vaudeville partner who hasn't made the big time. Peggy Sawyer (Ruby Keeler), a wide-eyed, ambitious chorine, becomes the apple of singer Billy Lawler's eye (Dick Powell). Ruby, who was Mrs. Al Jolson in real life, is strictly from down on the farm. So two veteran showgirls—Ann (Ginger Rogers) and Lorraine (Una Merkel)—take her under their wing. Ginger, by the way, sports a monocle and affects an English accent at the audition.

Meanwhile, Baxter relentlessly puts his chorus through their paces, getting their timing honed to precision in the show's dance sequences. There's a bevy of tap-dancing prostitutes and hoods in the big production scene, "42nd Street." There is a Pullman car set for the "Shuffle Off to Buffalo" scene and some saucy lyrics. Bebe Daniels sings the catchy tune, "You're Getting To Be a Habit with Me," as she dances with chorus boys. And Dick Powell croons "I'm Young and Healthy" to blonde Toby Wing in a turntable sequence where girls are transformed into designs of living geometry.

Even with the hectic rehearsal schedule, fun and games aren't totally absent. In one production sequence, as chorus boys are swinging Una Merkel, she chirps to one, "You've got the busiest hands."

But a crisis looms on the eve of the opening. Miss Daniels spots boy friend George Brent with Ruby Keeler. It's really all very innocent. But Miss Daniels, suspecting the worst, gets potted and insults Guy Kibbee. He, in turn, threatens to withdraw his backing. While the fight goes on, Miss Keeler and Brent blunder in. Bebe flies into another rage, falls and breaks her ankle. So with opening curtain less than twenty-fours off, the show is minus its leading lady.

Someone says Ginger Rogers can do the part. Instead, she passes and tells Baxter that Ruby Keeler is the one to save the day. Baxter is unconvinced. "She's just a raw kid out of the chorus," he says.

"I've been waiting years for a chance like this," Ginger snaps. "If I give it up for somebody else, she's got to be good."

"Send her in," Baxter orders. (The audience laughed and cheered when I saw the movie in 1969.)

Miss Keeler walks in uncertainly, sporting one of her two expressions—bewilderment. (The other is a smile.)

"You think you can play the lead tonight?" Baxter asks.

"The lead?" she gasps.

Baxter, exasperated, looks heavenward, rolls his eyes and walks off. (This piece of business, probably taken as straight acting in 1933, brought down the house at the show I saw.) But Baxter is a realist. He knows Ruby is their only chance. So he takes her through a fast rehearsal. ("I'll either have a live leading lady, or a dead chorus girl," he snarls.) Then, as she waits in the wings for her big moment, Baxter sidles up.

"You're going out a youngster," he says. "But you've *got* to come back a star." (This abbreviated pep talk has become the movie's most quoted line —although usually not in those exact words. The lines are now usually quoted as: "You're going out a chorus girl, but you're coming back a star!")

Ruby is frightened but she knows the numbers. She goes out and wows 'em. And the show comes home a winner. In a final touch of irony, Baxter overhears the audience berating him as it files out. "All those directors make me sick," one man says. "Take Marsh (Baxter), he puts his name all over the program. Gets all the credit. Except for kids like Sawyer (Ruby Keeler), he wouldn't have a show. . . . Some guys get all the breaks."

After *42nd Street*, Berkeley had a stormy private life. Married six times. Object of an alienation suit pressed without success by Carole Landis' first husband, Irving Wheeler. Involved in a fatal car collision that led to his trial and acquittal on a second-degree murder charge.

But when it came to movie musicals, it was smooth sailing through the 1930s and early 1940s. He did production numbers for the *Gold Digger* series and *Footlight Parade* (1933). Among many other films, he later directed *Babes in Arms* (1939), *Strike Up the Band* (1940), and *For Me and My Gal* (1942). In his long career, he directed such stars as Al Jolson, Eddie Cantor, Judy Garland, Mickey Rooney, James Cagney and Joan Blondell.

Production costs, television and the demise of the big studios eventually changed the face of Hollywood. The musical spectacular faded. And so did Busby Berkeley.

In 1969 he lived quietly with his wife, Etta, in a modest ranch house in Palm Desert, California. When the camp cult movement revived his movies in the mid-1960s, he became a celebrity to a new generation. He appeared at Busby Berkeley Festivals in New York and Europe. However, the hip crowd saw his work through different eyes. They dubbed him the King of Camp, a term he did not understand.

Still, it must have been refreshing for him to see live audiences enjoying his fantasies again and to be applauded when the lights went up. In 1969, at the age of seventy-four, he was gray-haired and deeply lined but still hale and hearty. "You have no idea of the enthusiasm everywhere we go," Mrs. Berkeley told a writer. "People just stand up and cheer." *

---

* In 1970, Berkeley signed to direct a Broadway revival of the 1925 musical "No, No Nanette." The production, which was to have twenty-five gorgeous dancing girls, was to mark his return to the New York stage after a thirty-five-year absence.

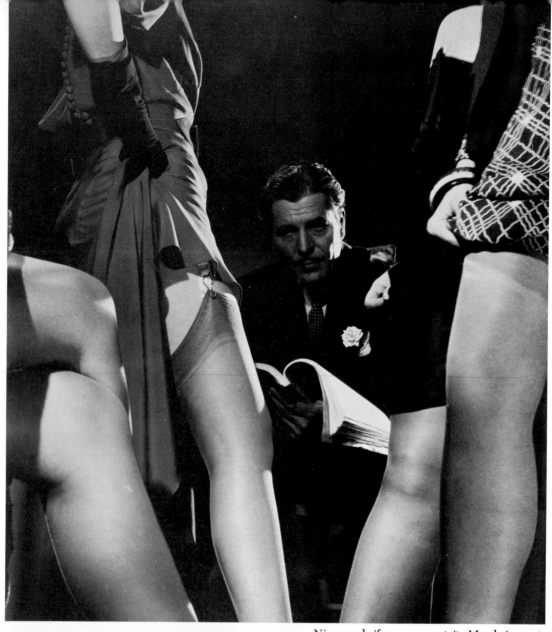

Nice work if you can get it. Marsh inspects gams belonging to some would-be chorus girls.

Andy Lee (George E. Stone) has a quizzical expression as he talks to new dancer Peggy Sawyer (Ruby Keeler) and her girl friend Lorraine Fleming (Una Merkel).

"We don't need dancers with two left feet," dance director Julian Marsh (Warner Baxter) seems to be telling Peggy, who appears to be looking for a deep hole to crawl in. That's Ginger Rogers, right, playing Ann Lowell. Lorraine, next to Peggy, and Andy, next to Marsh, look on.

Leading lady Dorothy Brock (Bebe Daniels) rehearsing with Billy Lawler (Dick Powell) as Andy and Marsh watch.

Wow! If kisses were dollar bills, Billy Lawler would be on easy street.

249

Reporter Peter Warne (Gable) shows his disdain for city editors after he has been fired in a telephone argument over drinking on assignment. The crowd, surrounding the booth, has overheard his side of the tiff and thinks he has won.

IX

THE LOVE GAME

The Greyhound bus that starts Pete and society damsel Ellie Andrews (Claudette Colbert) on their hilarious trek. Ward Bond, at the wheel, plays the driver.

**IT HAPPENED ONE NIGHT
GRAND HOTEL
DEATH TAKES A HOLIDAY
MAYTIME**

(Photos by Columbia)

It Happened One Night*

(Released February 23, 1934)

SCREEN PLAY by Robert Riskin* based on the *Cosmopolitan* magazine short story "Night Bus" by Samuel Hopkins Adams. Art director, Stephen Goosson. Photography, Joseph Walker. Editor, Gene Havlick. Music director, Louis Silvers. Assistant director, C. C. Coleman. Produced by Harry Cohn. A Columbia Picture. Directed by Frank Capra.* Running time, 105 minutes.

Peter Warne	CLARK GABLE *
Ellie Andrews	CLAUDETTE COLBERT *
Alexander Andrews	WALTER CONNOLLY
Mr. Shapeley	ROSCOE KARNS
King Westley	JAMESON THOMAS
Bus Driver	WARD BOND
Danker	ALAN HALE
Lovington	WALLIS CLARK
Henderson	HARRY C. BRADLEY
Zeke	ARTHUR HOYT
Zeke's Wife	BLANCHE FREDERICI
Joe Gordon	CHARLES C. WILSON
Reporter	CHARLES D. BROWN
Auto Camp Manager	HARRY HOLMAN
Manager's Wife	MAIDEL TURNER
Station Attendant	IRVING BACON
Flag Man	HARRY TODD

(Columbia did two remakes—*Eve Knew Her Apples* (1945), a musical with Ann Miller and William Wright, and *You Can't Run Away from It* (1956), a romantic comedy with June Allyson and Jack Lemmon.)

There were no lavish newspaper ads, no big billboards proclaiming the comedy of the year had

---

* Academy Award winner.

arrived. No great beating of the drums about the sparkling performances of Clark Gable and Claudette Colbert. No advance publicity about Frank Capra's craftsmanlike direction or Robert Riskin's inspired screen play.

It Happened One Night was a sleeper. It came to the movie-going public without any of the usual superlatives that Hollywood publicists crank out to ballyhoo a would-be classic. And so the public's overwhelming acceptance of this zany comedy-romance was spontaneous, a response based on the picture's merits alone.

The truth is, Columbia's executives had badly underrated this lighthearted film, totally misgauging the impact it would have on a Depression-mired nation eager to laugh. When you stop to think, it was all about a lot of nonsense. It was completely unrealistic. But who wanted sense? And who wanted realism? The public simply wanted to forget its troubles.

The movie, which launched a parade of so-called screwball comedies, rejected romance as a delicate, polite ritual. Instead, with witty dialogue and hilariously contrived situations, it showed two young people—a brash newspaperman and a spoiled society girl—squabbling like cats and dogs. Like so many real-life couples, this engaging twosome barked and howled at each other before they eventually billed and cooed.

If the studio moguls underrated the movie's potential, it also eluded its stars and even Louis B. Mayer, production chief of Metro-Goldwyn-Mayer. His film company had first rights to "Night Bus," the Samuel Hopkins Adams *Cosmopolitan* magazine story on which the picture was based. But Mayer turned it down because he felt the heroine's tycoon daddy was shown in an unfavorable light.

Gable was originally reluctant to do the film.* In fact, his casting in the movie was supposed to be a punishment. He had been hospitalized in 1933—Gable said he was overworked—but MGM, his studio, thought he was goldbricking. When he got out, the studio sent him to Columbia on loan as a disciplinary measure for what MGM thought would be just a routine film. Only after Gable actually went before the cameras did he see its bright humor and warm to the part.

It took Miss Colbert even longer to understand that she had helped create a whole new style of romantic humor. The actress, who had refused to play the part until Columbia doubled her salary for the picture ($50,000), was so sure she hadn't a chance for an Oscar that she didn't bother to attend the Academy Awards banquet. She was boarding a train to New York when officials reached her and brought her back to receive her award.

It was one of five Oscars for the movie. The picture itself won the coveted prize, the first comedy to be so honored. Other Academy Awards went to Gable (best actor), Capra (best director) and Riskin (best scenario). It was the only movie ever to win all five major Oscars.

The movie opens with Ellie Andrews (Miss Colbert) embroiled in a tiff with her millionaire father (Walter Connolly). A headstrong, impetuous girl, she has married, in a rash moment, King Westley (Jameson Thomas), a fortune-hunting aviator. Her father, who dislikes Westley intensely, dispatches private detectives to yank her home after the wedding. Then old man Andrews spirits Ellie off to Miami aboard his yacht. As soon as it anchors, she swims ashore and buys a Greyhound bus ticket to New York to join her husband, hoping to evade her dad's army of private eyes.

On the same bus is Pete Warne (Gable), a hard-boiled, outspoken reporter from the feet-on-the-desk, liquor-in-the-drawer school of journalism. Warne has just lost a phone hassle with his editor (over drinking on assignment) and his job to boot. Boiling, Warne bids his boss a fond farewell. "When you fired me, you fired the best newshound your filthy scandal sheet ever had. . . . You gashouse palooka!"

The newsman and the runaway heiress hit it off from the start—with jabs and uppercuts. They share the same tiny seat. When the bus lurches, Warne tells her, "Next time you drop in, bring your folks." But at a rest stop Pete discovers who she is from a newspaper story that says her father has offered a $10,000 reward to anyone reporting her whereabouts. He uses his discovery to force her to stick with him so he can get a scoop.

However, things don't go too smoothly. Their temperaments clash. Ellie is flippant, petulant and stubborn. Pete is hot-tempered, sulphur-tongued, and cave-mannish. She's the immovable object. He's the irresistible force.

Their first bump occurs when the bus runs into a storm and has to stop in an auto camp for the night. For financial reasons, Pete registers them as man and wife and discreetly hangs a blanket across their room.

"Behold the Walls of Jericho," he says with a flourish. "Maybe not as thick as the one that Joshua blew down with his trumpet. But a lot safer. You see I have no trumpet."

When Ellie seems reluctant to budge—even though they have twin beds—Pete simply starts peeling. No two men undress alike, he says, demonstrating his own socks-before-pants style. When he gets to his belt buckle he says, "Now it's every man for himself." She bolts to her side of the Wall.

(When Gable took off his shirt, moviegoers were shocked to see he wore nothing but his bare skin. The phenomenon that ensued became an object lesson in the entertainment world's potential for changing social customs. Following Gable's lead, millions of men quit wearing undershirts. Gable later said he was just doing what came naturally. "That was just the way I lived," he said. "I hadn't worn an undershirt since I started to school.")

Another crisis develops the next morning, even before Pete can finish teaching Ellie the art of dunking doughnuts at breakfast. Two detectives pound at the door. When they start asking pointed questions, quick-witted Pete draws Ellie into a make-believe domestic donnybrook.

"You don't have to lose your temper," she snaps.

"That's what you said the other night at the Elks Dance when that big Swede made a pass at you," Pete snarls. ". . . Kept pawin' you all over the dance floor."

"He didn't," she yells. "You were drunk."

"Aw nuts," Pete roars. "You're just like your old man. Once a plumber's daughter, always a plumber's daughter. . . ."

When Ellie bursts out crying, the flabbergasted

---

* Robert Montgomery and Myrna Loy had originally been picked for the leads. They turned out to be unavailable because of prior contract commitments.

dicks beat a hasty retreat. "I told you they were a happily married couple," the auto court manager says.

But the twosome's troubles aren't over. Back on the bus, Oscar Shapeley (Roscoe Karns), a traveling salesman, learns Ellie's identity and tries to horn in on the reward. Gable scares him off, pretending he's part of an underworld ring that have kidnaped Ellie. "I got a couple of machine guns in my suitcase," Pete says as Shapeley gulps. "I'll let you have one. May have a little trouble up North. Have to shoot it out with the cops."

Pete knows it's only a matter of time before the other riders recognize Ellie. So they take to the road. When their feet start aching, Pete gives her a lecture on hitchhiking, then watches a half dozen cars leave him in their dust. So Ellie tries her luck. Pete chuckles loudly until she raises her skirt, exposing a shapely stockinged leg. The next car screeches to a halt.

Except for their starvation diet of raw carrots, Ellie is enjoying their adventures and, when they stop at another roadside camp just outside New York City, the Walls of Jericho begin to crumble. She knows she has really fallen in love. And so does Pete.

When Ellie falls asleep, he drives to the city to sell his exclusive story to his editor for $1,000, enough to marry Ellie. But when he is gone, Ellie is awakened, thinks Pete has deserted her and calls her father. As Pete is driving back to the camp, he passes Ellie on the way to New York in a limousine.

He thinks she's played him for a sap.

Ellie's father reluctantly arranges a formal remarriage for Ellie and King. Even so, Ellie is thoroughly miserable. However, when her father shows her a letter from Pete asking for a financial interview, Ellie thinks Pete has been after the reward all the time.

A few minutes before the wedding, Pete shows up and surprises Ellie's father with a bill for only $39.60—just what he spent on Ellie. As her father escorts her down the aisle during a crowded lawn ceremony, he tells her what Pete came for. "You're a sucker to go through with this," he whispers. "He loves you, Ellie. . . . If you change your mind, your car's waiting at the gate." In the middle of the nuptials, she hikes up her wedding gown and dashes off.

Several days, or weeks, later, we see her father, who has just arranged the annulment, reading a telegram from Pete and Ellie. "What's holding up the annulment, you slowpoke? The Walls of Jericho are toppling." Says Dad: "Send them a telegram right away. Just say, 'Let 'em topple.'"

In the last scene at an auto camp, the manager's wife wonders why a new young couple have asked for a rope and blanket. "Blamed if I know," the manager says. "I just brung 'em a trumpet. One of them toy things. They sent me to the store to get it." What in the world do they want a trumpet for? she asks, more puzzled than ever. "Dunno," he says. And as they look toward the cabin, the trumpet's tinny blast echoes through the auto court.

Ellie puts on an iceberg look after she has to share cramped bus quarters with Pete. He isn't exactly overjoyed either.

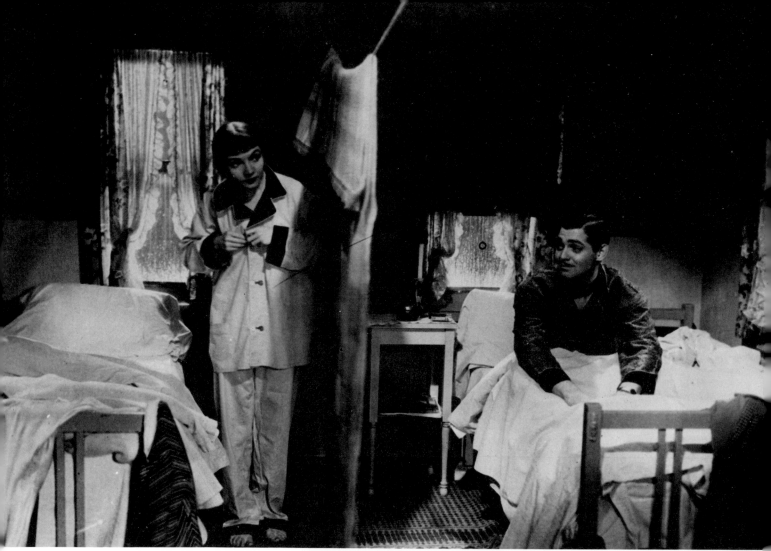

The celebrated "Walls of Jericho" that Pete erects between their beds to keep things proper. Ellie, wearing Pete's pajamas, peeks warily from her side.

The scene that startled a nation. When Gable peeled off his shirt and audiences saw nothing under it but himself, millions of men stopped buying undershirts.

254

Ellie changes her mind just a little about Peter after a traveling salesman (Roscoe Karns) tries to pick her up. Pete comes to her rescue.

In a hayfield where they spend a night, Peter and Ellie find they really don't hate each other that much.

Greta Garbo, playing a distinguished but
aging ballerina, sweeps into the lobby of the
Grand Hotel with her entourage. Other actors, from left, are Frank Conroy, Ferdinand
Gottschalk, John Davidson, Robert McWade
and Rafaela Ottiano.

Grand Hotel*

(Released September 11, 1932)

SCENARIO by William A. Drake from Vicki Baum's play, *Menschen im Hotel*. Film editor, Blanche Sewell. Art director, Cedric Gibbons. Camera, William Daniels, Costumes by Adrian. Directed by Edmund Goulding. Produced by Irving Thalberg for Metro-Goldwyn-Mayer. Running time, 115 minutes.

Grusinskaya	GRETA GARBO
Baron von Gaigern	JOHN BARRYMORE
Flaemmchen	JOAN CRAWFORD
Preysing	WALLACE BEERY
Kringelein	LIONEL BARRYMORE
Dr. Otternschlag	LEWIS STONE
Senf	JEAN HERSHOLT
Zinnowitz	PURNELL PRATT
Pimenov	FERDINAND GOTTSCHALK
Suzette	RAFAELA OTTIANO
Chauffeur	MORGAN WALLACE
Gerstenkorn	TULLY MARSHALL
Rohna	FRANK CONROY
Schweimann	MURRAY KINNELL
Dr. Waitz	EDWIN MAXWELL
Meierheim	ROBERT MC WADE
Hotel Manager	JOHN DAVIDSON

(Remade as *Weekend at the Waldorf* [1945].)

Garbo was terrified that the ambitious Crawford would steal the picture. Crawford thought Garbo had the sexiest love scenes. The Barrymores failed to see the play's movie potential. Even after filming started, Beery went on a two-day strike because he thought he had been miscast as the unsympathetic tycoon.

Grand Hotel. No other movie of its time had such an all-star cast. None started production with so much misgiving. Few finished with so many memorable performances. From the moment producer Irving Thalberg showed it to an unsuspecting audience at a sneak preview, it was obvious that MGM had made a classic.

The story was written by Vicki Baum, a Berlin author and wife of an operatic conductor. She had done *Grand Hotel* as a serial for a popular German magazine. It created wide interest and Max Reinhardt, the German producer, adapted it for the stage.

Again, it was an immediate hit and, after a successful four-month run in Berlin, the play swept triumphantly across the capitals of Europe. In the United States, MGM financed the Broadway production in return for the movie rights. Eugenie Leontovich played Grusinskaya in the 1930 New York opening and Sam Jaffe was Kringelein.

The unenviable job of controlling the galaxy of clashing Hollywood temperaments fell to Edmund Goulding. He was picked partly because of his ability to handle the most volatile stars and partly because he was adept enough to squash scene stealing. And the cast was filled with notorious scene stealers.

Beery's favorite trick was to ad-lib or read his lines differently from the way they were in the script. Taken by surprise, the actor playing opposite him would concentrate so hard on listening for his cue, he would forget about acting. John Barrymore's ploy was the fixed stare. Lionel would often bound onto the set bubbling with vitality.

But these problems paled next to the anticipated Garbo-Crawford feud. Each felt her career was at stake. Each thought she was putting her beauty and her dramatic ability on the line. Yet, as it turned out, there were no hysterics, no embarrassing confrontations. Goulding was astute enough to see

---

* Academy Award winner.

257

that neither played in the same scene.

Moreover, the great array of talent had its own inhibiting effect. It was one thing to throw a fit when you were the key performer on the set. But a star looked childish tossing a tantrum in the midst of her peers.

In fact, Garbo worked like a trouper. She had never before rehearsed with a co-star. But in *Grand Hotel* she frequently went over her lines with John Barrymore. She came to the studio early, left late. She looked at rushes, made suggestions about changes. When the picture was finished after forty-eight days, movie writers dubbed Goulding "the lion tamer."

Grand Hotel is the story of how five people's lives are affected when they cross briefly at a cosmopolitan hotel. As the movie opens, the hotel's revolving doors spin around and into its magnificent lobby come:

• Grusinskaya (Garbo), an aging ballerina suffering from a dwindling public and an unfathomable malaise.

• Kringelein (Lionel Barrymore), a dying factory clerk determined to have one last fling.

• Baron von Gaigern (John Barrymore), a dashing, handsome nobleman desperately in need of money.

• Herr General Director Preysing (Beery), an arrogant textile magnate who faces ruin unless he can negotiate a merger for his failing company.

• And Flaemmchen (Crawford), a lovely young stenographer seeking the good life.

Already at the hotel is Dr. Otternschlag (Lewis Stone), a war-scarred physician who asks for messages at the desk and, because there are never any, thinks that nothing ever happens at the Grand Hotel.

That evening Grusinskaya is so upset she refuses to dance. It is only when she is told the theatre is crowded—although it is really half empty—that she consents to go. In the hall where he has been waiting for the dancer to pass, the baron meets Flaemmchen. He flirts with her and makes a date to meet her at a dance the next day. She leaves to take dictation from Preysing, who also becomes smitten with her good looks and youthful charm.

But Flaemmchen is repelled by the rough-mannered Preysing when he insults the retiring old Kringelein at the hotel bar. However, as the story unfolds, the two men's lives take a sudden turn. Kringelein gambles in a card game and wins a small fortune. Preysing fails to pull off the crucial business deal and faces bankruptcy.

Meanwhile, the baron has slipped into Grusinskaya's suite and found her pearls. But as he is about to leave, Grusinskaya returns in tears. She has left the ballet after the first act, crushed by the sparse turnout. From behind a curtain, the baron watches while she prepares to go to bed. In utter despair, she picks up a bottle of poison. The baron suddenly reveals himself, explaining that he is a secret admirer. "Who are you?" she asks. "Someone who loves you," says Barrymore. And Garbo replies with a line that will haunt her thereafter: "I want to be alone."

But the baron won't go. He confesses his theft and, overwhelmed by her ethereal beauty, pours out his soul. "I'd like to take you in my arms. I've never seen anything in my life as beautiful as you are. . . . Let me stay for just a little while." The doleful dancer, whose life is suddenly warmed by a ray of sunshine, does.

The next night the baron ransacks Preysing's room while the general director is preparing to seduce Flaemmchen in an adjoining room. But Preysing hears a noise. He bounds in, catches the baron, and strikes him on the head with the telephone. The blow kills the baron. Flaemmchen runs to Kringelein and the lowly clerks turns in the mighty capitalist to the police.

Thrown together, Kringelein and Flaemmchen decide to go to Paris and enjoy life and Kringelein's sudden wealth. As they leave, so does Grusinskaya. She must go on to Vienna for her next performance. Suzette (Rafaela Ottiano), her maid, convinces her that the baron will be on the train and Grusinskaya sweeps happily through the lobby followed by her adoring retinue.

Lewis Stone watches the passing parade, but without perceiving that their lives have been changed in their brief stay. "Grand Hotel," he mutters. "Always the same. People come. People go. Nothing ever happens."

The question on every moviegoer's lips was—who would the critics say stole the show? There was no unanimity. Richard Watts of the New York *Herald Tribune* said Garbo ran away with the picture. So did John S. Cohen of the New York *Sun*. Matthew Johnson of *New Republic* gave his award to Crawford. So did Ed Sullivan. William Boehnel of the New York *World-Telegram* nominated Lionel Barrymore. The Des Moines *Register*'s critic picked Beery. Some contended that all came out even. There was honor for everyone.

I had my own impressions after seeing the movie in 1969. Admittedly, it may have been quite different had I seen it when it opened in 1932. But from this point in time, Garbo appeared miscast. She looked long-legged and gawky, at times even absurd in her part of a great ballet dancer. In the close-ups when the camera brought out her mystical eyes, her expressive lips, her exquisite profile, she captured the part. But again, in full figure, she had neither the grace nor the air of a dancer. Nor could she manage the mercurial peaks and valleys from despair to exuberance implicit in the Russian artist's temperament.

John Barrymore was suave and charming, but his performance in the crucial scene with Garbo was overdone, and therefore a disappointment. Lionel Barrymore nearly pulled off a tour de force. But he was a bit too petulant and whining. Kringelein should have been pathetic and blighted, a doomed man. Despite his bluntness, Beery turned in a surprisingly forceful characterization that brought out the Prussian officiousness of Preysing.

Curiously, he was the only actor to use a German accent.

But the prize has to go to Crawford. Her moving and eloquent performance gave depth and pathos to a part that could easily have just passed for that of a simple trollop. And never was she more beautiful. Her dark eyes sparkled in a fresh, young, radiantly lovely face.

Grand Hotel won the Academy Award for best production, beating out *The Champ* (which won an acting Oscar for Beery), *Arrowsmith* and *Shanghai Express*. The National Board of Review picked *I Am a Fugitive from a Chain Gang* and curiously failed even to rate *Grand Hotel* in its top ten choices.

Nevertheless, the film was so successful that its basic idea—that of bringing together a cross section of strangers for a short time on a single set—has been repeated many times. *Separate Tables, Bus Stop* and *The V.I.P.s* are three recent examples. And the device has become known as the *Grand Hotel* formula.

The famed dancer, suffering malaise, is unable to perform and languishes in her hotel suite.

603-37

Preysing (Wallace Beery), the German industrialist who has hired Flaemmchen, rudely stops her in the hotel bar as she walks with the baron.

Kringelein (Lionel Barrymore), the timid clerk, kneels over the body of the baron as Preysing, who has just killed him with a blow to the head, looks over his shoulder.

The dashing Baron von Gaigern (John Barrymore) comes to rob the dancer of her jewels and stays to make love to her.

The suave baron tries to cheer up Flaemmchen (Joan Crawford), an ambitious secretary in search of the good life.

Death in the guise of the monocled Prince
Sirki (Fredric March) with Grazia (Evelyn
Venable), the girl with whom he falls in
love.

(Photos by Paramount)

Death Takes a Holiday

(Released March 30, 1934)

SCREEN PLAY by Maxwell Anderson and Gladys Lehman from the play by Alberto Casella as adapted by Walter Ferris. Photography by Charles Lang. Recording engineer, Harold Lewis. Directed by Mitchell Leisen. Produced by E. Lloyd Sheldon. Presented by Paramount. Running time, 78 minutes.

Prince Sirki	FREDRIC MARCH
Grazia	EVELYN VENABLE
Duke Lambert	SIR GUY STANDING
Alda	KATHERINE ALEXANDER
Rhoda	GAIL PATRICK
Stephanie	HELEN WESTLEY
Princess Maria	KATHLEEN HOWARD
Corrado	KENT TAYLOR
Baron Cesaria	HENRY TRAVERS
Eric	G. P. HUNTLEY, JR.
Fedele	OTTO HOFFMAN
Dr. Valle	EDWARD VAN SLOAN
Pietro	HECTOR SARNO
Vendor	FRANK YACONELLI
Maid	ANNA DE LINSKY

At the height of one of the bloodiest battles in World War I, an Italian soldier wondered what would happen if Death suddenly were to quit his work and go on vacation. Alberto Casella, a young writer, became so taken with the idea he began writing a play as soon as the Armistice was signed.

Casella, who called his fanciful work *Death Takes a Holiday*, opened his story with Death wearying of his isolation and loneliness. He is curious to know why men fear him, why they cling to life so tenaciously and shrink in terror when he comes for them. To find out, Death visits an Italian duke in his luxurious villa and announces that he plans to spend a three-day holiday as his guest. He wants to experience life as a man, and so he will come in the guise of a prince who has just died.

Casella came to a kind of literary crossroad here. If he took one approach, he could consider the impact of Death's holiday on the world. What would it mean to us? What would happen in a world free from death? Would we find we had lost a friend as well as an enemy? Or if Casella took the other path, he could examine the effect of the holiday on Death himself, suddenly made mortal.

It was the latter idea that intrigued Casella and so his play, instead of being a broadly based drama, focused on a single character. The original version, which played in Italy and then in leading European cities, was in the nature of a comedy. The Italians were apparently more apt to take a lighthearted view of Death rattling around as the bony Grim Reaper.

But the play assumed a darker character when it came to this country. Lee Shubert contracted for the script and assigned Walter Ferris, a playwright and educator, to revise it. Ferris took Death more seriously and presented him as the fearful messenger come to take man to an unknown world. In its more sober form, it opened on Broadway in 1929 with Philip Merivale as Death and Rose Hobart as Grazia, the girl with whom he falls in love. Critics received the play favorably but not enthusiastically. Still, public interest grew steadily and it

263

became one of the season's popular successes.

When Paramount decided to make the film in 1934, it chose a director with only one full directing credit. He was Mitchell Leisen (*Cradle Song*, 1933), a former set designer for De Mille. Despite his lack of seasoning, Leisen had already shown talent and imagination as an associate director. And so the studio gave him a chance to make the most of the fantasy and opulent scenery inherent in the scenario.

Leisen, who later directed *Hold Back the Dawn* (1941) and *Lady in the Dark* (1944), created a sumptuous villa. Frescoes decorated huge, high-ceilinged rooms. French doors opened onto sunken gardens, palatial fountains and black pools. During the duke's party, the haunting "Valse Triste" played in the background, lending poetic, melancholy undertones to the romantic story.

The role of Death went to Fredric March, who was looked on then as something of an oddity in Hollywood. He was one of the few stars with a college degree (University of Wisconsin). Nevertheless, two years earlier, he had won an Oscar for his performance in *Dr. Jekyll and Mr. Hyde*.* Affecting an accent and wearing a monocle, he played Death with hauteur and arrogance, adding a touch of ironic humor.

His eyes were the most fascinating thing about his characterization. In close-up, they were piercing, darting, transfixing. "The special distinction of Mr. March's eyes," newspaperman Melvin Maddocks once wrote, "is that they are not simply an efficient signaling system. They are part of the man. They burn from within."

March's co-star was twenty-one-year-old Evelyn Venable, a Virginia girl from an old American family. Miss Venable, a dark-haired beauty who had won Hollywood attention while touring with Walter Hampden's company, had appeared in only one previous picture, *Cradle Song*. But her performance as the girl vulnerable to Death's fatal charm was done with sensitivity. Still, she would always have to live down a clause put in her contract by her father, a college professor who had mixed feelings about his daughter in Hollywood. It prohibited kissing in love scenes.

As the story opens, Death comes to the Villa Felicita (Villa of Contentment) of Duke Lambert (Sir Guy Standing) to experience life for the first time. "There is something here to be known and

---

* He got a second Oscar in 1946 for *The Best Years of Our Lives*.

felt," he tells the duke, "something desirable that makes men fear me and cling to their life. I must know what it is." Death, who appears as a transparent figure in black cape and cowl, says he will come to the duke's home for three days in the guise of an expected guest, Prince Sirki of Vitalbla, Alexandri. Death has already met the prince professionally and knows he won't be coming.

"No one under this roof shall show repulsion or fear on pain of my instant displeasure," Death warns. "If my secret is divulged, I shall leave instantly as Sirki and return in my proper person." He gives his word, no one will be harmed if they obey.

Death vanishes and the terrified duke steels himself for the arrival of this mysterious visitor. All that day, he and his house guests have felt a strange presence. The car of the duke's son, Corrado (Kent Taylor), has miraculously escaped driving off a cliff. The duke's own car has crashed into a flower vendor's wagon, demolishing it without injuring a soul. That evening in the garden, Grazia (Miss Venable), Corrado's fiancée, has seen a huge shadow and fainted.

At midnight Prince Sirki arrives. Dressed in the splendid white tunic of a Russian grand duke, he presents a dashing figure. He clicks his heels and bows. The men return his bow. The women curtsy.

In a memorable scene, the duke introduces his guests. To the old statesman, Baron Cesarea (Henry Travers), Sirki, speaking with slow, mannered tones, says, "Considering your distinction and age, it is surprising that fate has not introduced us before." To lovely Countess Alda di Parma (Katherine Alexander), he says graciously, "I wish that we may never meet when you are less beautiful and I must be less kind." When the duke offers him some refreshment, the prince says, "I have never tasted wine —of your country." Then he proposes a toast: "To life and to all brave illusion."

As Sirki is about to retire, Grazia comes down the broad marble stairway to be introduced. There is a strange attraction and they stand and look at each other as if no one else were there. As she watches him, he ascends the stairs, slowly turning twice to look at her. When he reaches the top, he turns once more and bows. Grazia curtsies.

The next day the duke and his guests are amazed to read in the newspapers that a man has jumped off the Eiffel Tower and landed unhurt. An orphanage has burned to the ground with no fatalities. And a steamship has sunk with no loss of life.

Grazia's mother takes her home. And so Sirki starts his holiday with Alda and her American friend Rhoda (Gail Patrick). They take him to all the area's amusement centers. He wins a fortune at Monte Carlo but is bored. They go to the horse races but he is still bored. Sirki feels that what humans do with themselves is futile and empty. However, the old baron tells him that he has overlooked one thing. "One never gets tired of love," the baron says. "One pair of lips will change your mind.".

Sirki decides to test the baron's wisdom. Rhoda, fascinated by the prince, is delighted to be his accomplice. But she finds his conversation unsettling. "If the rest of your life were only a few days or a few hours, would that be enough to justify love?" he asks. "What a macabre thought," she replies. "Did you bring me here to analyze me?" When she finds he seems to be only experimenting with his emotions—and hers—she becomes piqued and leaves.

At a party on the last night of his stay, Alda goes to Sirki and tells him of her love. Sirki says superficial love isn't enough for him. A woman must give him her very soul.

"Look into my eyes," he tells her. "What do you see?"

"Shadows," she says, suddenly fearful.

"Look into those shadows. . . . I *will* you to know who I am."

She sees Death. "No," she shrieks. "I want to live."

Just then, Grazia returns and she and Sirki go into the garden. They dance to the music from the party and both realize they are in love. Grazia tells him she knows he is from another world. So deep is her love, she wants to go with him. "Now suddenly I know for the first time that men bear a dream within them," says Sirki, "a dream that lifts them above their dust and their little days."

A few minutes before midnight Sirki returns alone to say good-by and to tell everyone that Grazia is going with him. The duke's guests, who have now been let in on the secret of Sirki's identity, are horrified and beg the prince not to take her. The duke implores him to honor his word not to harm anyone. Torn by conflicting emotions, Sirki relents and calls Grazia back.

When she insists on going with him, Sirki tells her he made love to her only as a jest. He insists she stay with her loved ones. As the clock tolls twelve, Sirki changes into the shrouded figure of Death.

"Good-by, Grazia. Now you see me as I am."

Her expression remains the same. "But I have always seen you like that. You haven't changed."

"You have seen me like this?" Death asks, astonished.

"Yes," says Grazia, walking toward him. "Always."

"Then there *is* a love which casts out fear. And I have found it," Death says triumphantly. "And love *is* greater than illusion, and as strong as death."

Death sweeps Grazia into his cloak, and at the last stroke of midnight they disappear into eternity together.

Prince Corrado (Kent Taylor), Grazia's earthbound lover, comes to take her home from church. The movie was only the second for Miss Venable, whose father put a clause in her contract prohibiting kissing scenes. *(Photo by MCA-TV)*

Prince Sirki with Grazia's mother, Princess Maria (Kathleen Howard).

Prince Sirki plays roulette at Monte Carlo and amasses a small fortune. But gambling and all other mortal diversions bore him until an old baron tells him about love. Alongside Sirki are, left, Rhoda (Gail Patrick) and, right, Alda (Katherine Alexander).

Prince Sirki has breakfast with Rhoda.

Rhoda walks by on the arms of two escorts as Prince Sirki watches during a party on the last night of his holiday.

Paul Allison (Nelson Eddy) and Marcia Mornay (Jeanette MacDonald) have a one-day fling together on a blossom-filled May Day. But before the day ends she tells him she is already engaged.

Maytime

(Released March 26, 1937)

SCREEN PLAY by Noel Langley based on the operetta by Rida Johnson Young (book and lyrics) and Sigmund Romberg (music). Photography, Oliver T. Marsh. Editor, Conrad A. Nervig. Music adapted and directed by Herbert Stothart. Songs: "Will You Remember (Sweetheart)?" and "Maytime Finale" by Romberg and Young; "Virginia Ham and Eggs," "Vive l'Opéra" by Stothart, Bob Wright and Chet Forrest; "Student Drinking Song" by Stothart; "Carry Me Back to Ole Virginny" by James A. Bland; "Czaritza" based on Tchaikovsky's Fifth Symphony, libretto by Wright and Forrest; "Reverie" based on Romberg airs; "Jump Jim Crow," "Road to Paradise," and "Dancing Will Keep You Young" by Young, Romberg and Cyrus Wood. "Maypole" by Ed Ward; "Street Singer" by Wright, Forrest and Stothart. Vocal arrangements, Leo Arnaud. Opera sequences, William Von Wymetal. Produced by Hunt Stromberg. Directed by Robert Z. Leonard. Running time, 132 minutes.

Marcia Mornay	JEANETTE MAC DONALD
Paul Allison	NELSON EDDY
Nicolai Nazaroff	JOHN BARRYMORE
Archipenko	HERMAN BING
Kip	TOM BROWN
Barbara	LYNNE CARVER
Ellen	RAFAELA OTTIANO
Cabby	CHARLES JUDELS
Trentini	PAUL PORCASI
Fanchon	SIG RUMANN
Secretary	EDGAR NORTON
Louis Napoleon	GUY BATES POST
Madame Fanchon	ANNA DEMETRIO
Rudyard	WALTER KINGSFORD

Sweetheart, sweetheart, sweetheart . . .
Will you remember the day
When we were happy in May
  —"Will You Remember" * from *Maytime*

In the mid-1930s director Robert Z. Leonard compiled a fanciful list of Hollywood couples—his rating of the all-time best screen teams.

As "Mr. and Mrs. America, happily married," he picked Myrna Loy and William Powell. "The irresistible love force meets the immovable love body" were Robert Taylor and Greta Garbo. At the top of the score card of movie mates were "The Princess and Prince Charming"—Jeanette MacDonald and Nelson Eddy.

In the weary Depression years when millions flocked to the dreamlands a couple of times a week, the buttermilk-complexioned, red-haired soprano and the strapping, wavy-blond baritone put a song in America's heart. Remember "Ah, Sweet Mystery of Life," "Indian Love Call" and "Rose Marie"?

Miss MacDonald and Eddy sang so well together, many assumed they were husband and wife. They starred in eight musical films. They began with *Naughty Marietta* in 1935 and ended with *I Married an Angel* in 1942.† And in those seven years their earnings climbed well into the millions.

Yet despite the fortune they made, their real interests lay in other directions. Her burning ambition

---

* Copyright © 1917 by G. Schirmer, Inc.

---

† Other MacDonald-Eddy films were: *Rose Marie* (1936), *Maytime* (1937), *The Girl of the Golden West* (1938), *Sweethearts* (1938), *New Moon* (1940) and *Bitter Sweet* (1940).

was to sing grand opera. He didn't like his screen image. He wanted instead to be a comedian.

Miss MacDonald trained arduously, hired the best coaches. She made her operatic debut in Montreal in 1943, singing in *Romeo and Juliet* with Ezio Pinza. Soon afterward she made her American debut as Marguerite in *Faust* with the Chicago Civic Opera.

But critical acclaim eluded her. Movie reviewers described her screen voice—whose volume could be opulently enhanced by sound-track technicians—as rich and melodious. However, music critics said it was small and not particularly distinguished on stage.

Eddy, who was sometimes as wooden on the screen as Miss MacDonald was expressive, tried his best to forget his movies. "I never saw any of my pictures," he said. "Back in those days, actors used to run them over and over to study themselves." Once when one of his old films turned up on television, he saw it by chance. "I was all dressed up in one of those silly suits with frills at the cuffs," he said. "My reaction was simple and direct. I whistled and said—'Get him! Ain't he pretty?'"

Nevertheless, even though they never fulfilled their private desires, their love songs won them screen immortality. No team has ever topped them in appeal, drawing power or just plain schmaltz.

As might be expected, America's celluloid sweethearts both got started in show business at an early age. Born in Providence, Rhode Island, in 1901, Eddy came from a family whose lineage, he said, traced back to colonial days. When his parents moved to Philadelphia in 1915, he had to go to work and dropped out of high school. Eddy became a police reporter, then an ad salesman and copywriter with Philadelphia newspapers.

But music was an important part of his home life and after work he took voice lessons and later sang with the Philadelphia Civic Opera. When his boss found he was more interested in singing than in writing ads, he fired Eddy.

It turned out to be the best thing that could have happened to him. Forced into music full time, he became an opera singer and made his debut with the Metropolitan Opera in 1924 as Tonio in *Pagliacci*. Eddy, whose repertoire eventually embraced thirty-two parts in seven languages, also went on the concert stage.

When he made a substitute appearance in Los Angeles in 1933, movie moguls heard him and signed him to a long-term contract. Two years later he was cast opposite Miss MacDonald in *Naughty Marietta* and screen romance turned a corner.

Born in 1907 * to a Philadelphia contractor and politician, Miss MacDonald started working toward a music career at a tender age. She sang her first song in public—at a benefit performance when she was three years old. Before she was nine, she was singing arias from recordings. At fifteen, she was appearing on stage, singing and dancing. By the time she was in her late teens she was getting secondary roles in Broadway musicals.

In 1929, Ernst Lubitsch saw a screen test she made and signed her to play opposite Maurice Chevalier in *The Love Parade*. It was a hit and so began her Hollywood career. The slight, vibrant soprano, one of the first film stars whose success was built around her voice, was not in the ranks of the divas of her day. Yet when studio technicians amplified her songs, some critics said her voice sounded better than the sound-track efforts of Lily Pons and Grace Moore.

Miss MacDonald made twenty-eight movies through 1949, bringing light opera to thousands of small towns whose musical experiences had mainly centered around square dances or hillbilly bands.

It was in her thirteenth film, *Naughty Marietta*, that she first teamed with Eddy. Although she did some non-Eddy movies such as *San Francisco* and *The Firefly*, her most distinctive films remain the ones she did with him. They hit just the right note of escapism during the economically lean pre-World War II years. Of them all, her favorite, the one that gave her the widest variety of songs and the one many of her fans remember most fondly, was *Maytime*.

The movie opens with a prologue showing a young couple quarreling after a May Day celebration. The girl (Lynne Carver) doesn't want to give up her singing career to marry. She confides in her neighbor, a lonely old woman, who, it turns out, also was a singer. And the elderly lady tells the story of her own great love.

The camera fades in on Marcia Mornay (Miss MacDonald) as she sings gloriously for Emperor Louis Napoleon in Paris. She is a glittering tri-

---

* This is the date that appeared in her obituary. Since then, some writers have used 1903, basing their revision on her school records.

umph, the toast of all Europe. Composers begin writing operas for her. Marcia's fame has been due, in part, to her skillful teacher, Nicolai (John Barrymore), who now asks her to marry him. Because of her gratitude for the fame he has helped bring her, she accepts.

Excited and unable to sleep that night, Marcia takes a carriage to the Left Bank where students are having a rollicking songfest. She goes to a café to hear the strong, masculine voice of the student leader. The dashing young man is, of course, Eddy, playing Paul Allison. (At the picture's New York premiere women in the audience greeted Eddy's entrance with a rousing cheer.)

When Paul discovers Marcia is also an American, he asks her to a lunch of Virginia ham and eggs and then to a May Day festival. Against her better judgment, she accepts. They go to a country fair and the day turns out to be one of those perfect, once-in-a-lifetime experiences. They sing and stroll and fall in love. But as the day draws to a close she tells Paul the bitter truth. She has promised to marry her maestro and she can't break her word. Then comes a sad parting. They say good-by singing the lilting, bittersweet theme song.

So they go their separate ways—she to a distinguished career in Europe, he to sing in America. Seven years later she comes to New York for her American debut.* Who is to be the baritone lead? Aha, you guessed it—Paul.

After a brilliant opening night, he tells Marcia they can never part again. However, their new-found happiness is short-lived. When she asks Nicolai for a divorce, he promises to give Marcia her freedom. But not the way she thinks. The fiercely jealous maestro takes his pistol from its velvet case, goes to Paul's apartment and kills him.

At this dramatic point the story shifts to Marcia

---

* The opera, based on Tchaikovsky's Fifth Symphony, was a fictional work called *Czaritza*, created for the film. Other "shadow operas" written for movies include *Carnival* in *Charlie Chan at the Opera* (1936) and *Salammbô* in *Citizen Kane* (1941).

as an old woman. The moral of her story is clear: there can be no choice between love and a career. And the young girl accepts the advice.

In the moving ending, the aged Marcia dies, but her spirit—as a young lady—is reunited with Paul's. They walk as ghostly figures down a blossom-strewn path singing "Will You Remember?"

The same year that *Maytime* scored its triumph —the New York *Times* called it a "picture to treasure" and *Time* said it might well be the "best entertainment of 1937"—Miss MacDonald married actor Gene Raymond. Two years later Eddy married Anne Denitz Franklin, ex-wife of producer Sidney Franklin. The marriages were both childless.

After their last movie in 1942 there were many attempts to bring them back. They were together again in 1959 but only for a record date. "We've been asked to do what might be called B-pictures," Eddy said. "Rather than do that, we decided we'd like to leave it on a high note."

After she made her last picture in 1949, Miss MacDonald toured with musical productions and did concerts that drew packed houses. But she later developed a heart condition and underwent treatment from Dr. Michael DeBakey, the renowned Houston heart surgeon. Then in 1965, at the age of fifty-seven, she suffered a seizure at her Beverly Hills, California, home and was flown to Houston. While doctors were considering open heart surgery, she turned to Raymond at her bedside. "I love you," she said. "I love you," her husband of twenty-seven years replied. She turned her head and died.

Eddy stopped making movies in 1947. But he had also established a popular radio career—his trademark was "Short'nin' Bread," always a target for joshing when he was with Charlie McCarthy—and also did well on concert tours. Later he put together a night club act with Gale Sherwood. One night Eddy began faltering while on stage at the San Souci Hotel in Miami Beach. "Will you bear with me," Eddy asked his audience. "I can't seem to get the words out." Then he collapsed. He was rushed to a hospital but he died a few hours later. It was 1967. Eddy, sixty-five, had outlived his movie sweetheart by a little more than two years.

A classic photograph of what many consider
Hollywood's greatest musical duo.

Children dancing around the Maypole during the festive celebration.

Paul and Marcia join in an impromptu duet as a gypsy strums his guitar.

Marcia's husband, Nicolai (John Barrymore), observes her coldly as she stands alongside Paul, whom she hasn't seen for seven long years. Holding Marcia's hand is Archipenko (Herman Bing), Paul's music teacher. At left is Rudyard (Walter Kingsford), opera impresario.

Marcia asks Nicolai for a divorce so she can marry Paul. He promises to give her one, but not in the way she imagines. (*Courtesy Eleanor Knowles*)

American adventurer Rick Blaine (Bogart) in his salad days in Paris with his sweetheart, Ilsa Lund Laszlo (Ingrid Bergman).

After his café has closed, Rick gets drunk to try to forget Ilsa, an old flame. He insults her when she comes to him.

X

INTRIGUE

CASABLANCA
NIGHTMARE ALLEY
THE INFORMER
THE THIRD MAN
CHARLIE CHAN AT THE OPERA

(Photos by Warner Bros.)
(Courtesy, United Artists)

Casablanca *

(Released January 23, 1943)

BASED ON *Everybody Comes to Rick's,* an unproduced play by Murray Burnett and Joan Alison. Screenplay by Julius J. Epstein,* Philip G. Epstein * and Howard Koch.* Music, Max Steiner. Music director, Leo Forbstein. Editor, Owen Marks. Photography, Arthur Edeson. Art director, Carl Jules Weyl. Montages, Don Siegel and James Leicester. Songs by M. K. Jerome and Jack Scholl: "Knock on Wood," "That's What Noah Done," "Muse's Call"; by Herman Hupfeld: "As Time Goes By." Produced by Hal B. Wallis. Directed by Michael Curtiz.* Released by Warner Brothers. Running time, 102 minutes.

Rick	HUMPHREY BOGART
Ilsa Lund Laszlo	INGRID BERGMAN
Victor Laszlo	PAUL HENREID
Captain Louis Renault	CLAUDE RAINS
Major Heinrich Strasser	CONRAD VEIDT
Señor Ferrari	SYDNEY GREENSTREET
Ugarte	PETER LORRE
Carl, a waiter	S. Z. SAKALL
Yvonne	MADELEINE LE BEAU
Sam	DOOLEY WILSON
Annina Brandel	JOY PAGE
Berger	JOHN QUALEN
Jan Brandel	HELMUT DANTINE
Croupier	MARCEL DALIO
Sascha, a bartender	LEONID KINSKEY
Dark European	CURT BOIS
Singer	CORINNA MURA
Mr. Leuchtag	LUDWIG STOSSEL
Mrs. Leuchtag	ILKA GRUNING
Arab Vendor	FRANK PUGLIA
Abdul	DAN SEYMOUR
German Banker	GREGORY GAY
Heinz	RICHARD RYAN

---

* Academy Award winner.

"I've often speculated on why you don't return to America," Claude Rains says to Humphrey Bogart in *Casablanca.* "Did you run off with a senator's wife? Did you abscond with the church funds? I like to think you killed a man. That's the romantic in me."

"It's a combination of all three," says Bogart, not about to let the conversation turn on his personal life.

Rains persists. "What in heaven's name brought you to Casablanca?"

"My health," Bogie says. "I came to Casablanca for the waters."

"The waters?" Rains repeats, puzzled. "What waters? We're in the desert."

"I was misinformed," Bogie answers wryly. Rains laughs. But Bogie's face remains unsmiling, inscrutable, a frozen mask.

Hollywood remembers *Casablanca* as the film that won three Oscars in the midst of World War II. But it has more meaning to the new generation, some of whom were not yet born then. To them, it is the picture that most perfectly delineates the Bogart mystique.

To the world, American expatriate Rick Blaine is the cynical café boss, the uncommitted guy who doesn't give a damn about anything but himself. Inwardly, he's an idealist, a sentimentalist motivated by a deep-seated honesty. Although he puts on the cool front, he's really a good guy committed to doing the right thing in the end.

"That's one reason he's got such an appeal today," said a Harvard law student who has seen the film six times. "Most kids like to think of themselves this way."

At Harvard, the Brattle Street Theatre holds a Bogart Festival twice a year. The films are shown during exam week and the festival highlight is always *Casablanca.* When Paul Henreid leads the café in the "Marseillaise," drowning out a Gestapo gang singing "Watch on the Rhine," Harvard men and their dates stand and join in.

And there is applause for such immortal Bogart lines as: "I stick my neck out for nobody. . . . You want my advice, go back to Bulgaria. . . . Here's looking at you, kid. . . ." And the famous curtain line, "Louie, I think this is the beginning of a beautiful friendship."

(Bogiephiles will also tell you that he never said, "Play it again, Sam." It was Ingrid Bergman who came closest to that erroneous quote when she said simply, "Play it, Sam." The song was, of course, "As Time Goes By." Later Bogie, drinking alone after hours, testily grumps: "You played it for her. You can play it for me. If she can stand it, I can. Play it.")

According to Bogart's biographer, Joel Hyams, when Warner Brothers started filming, everyone, including Bogie, thought the picture was going to be awful. But the film got an unexpected publicity windfall. Just before its New York premiere on Thanksgiving Day, 1942, the Allies launched the invasion of French North Africa, scoring a key victory at Casablanca. Two months later President Roosevelt held a historic conference in the French Moroccan capital. He met with Churchill, De Gaulle and French General Henri Giraud, and made "Casablanca" a household word. "Without this handy coincidence," John McManus wrote in the now defunct *PM*, "a lot of moviegoers might have figured *Casablanca* to be a movie about a chess player, maybe." *

But that's overstating the case. Even discounting the war publicity, the film would have attracted attention, because, for one thing, it got excellent reviews. It also gave Bogart his first chance at a romantic part since he achieved stardom in his own right in *The Maltese Falcon* one year earlier. It added dimension to his tough personality. It showed the couldn't-care-less guy had an Achilles' heel. In the *Falcon*, he cold-bloodedly ditched Mary Astor. Now, for the first time, Bogie found out what it felt like to be a reject in the game of love.

Casablanca opens with a globe spinning and stopping at French Morocco. Here is the coastal city of Casablanca, a World War II way station to freedom. For those refugees from Nazi persecution with money or influence, there are exit visas to Lisbon and then the clipper to America. For others, Casablanca is a prison. And so it has become a city of corruption and intrigue.

---

* He had in mind Capablanca, one of the great chess masters.

It is in this alien atmosphere that Rick Blaine (Bogart), soldier of fortune, has come to live. He has set up a fancy lounge and gambling house called Rick's Café Américain, and to it sooner or later comes every visitor to Casablanca.

One day Nazi Major Heinrich Strasser (Conrad Veidt) arrives to investigate the murder of two German couriers. The couriers carried two letters of transit providing visas that cannot be rescinded. What has been done in the matter? Veidt asks as soon as he has stepped off the plane.

"Because of the importance of the case," says French Police Captain Louis Renault (Claude Rains), "our men are rounding up twice the number of suspects." A Vichy flunky adds that the cops already know the murderer. Is he in custody? Veidt asks. "Oh, there's no hurry," Renault says. "Tonight, he'll be at Rick's. Everybody comes to Rick's."

And so do we. The camera shows a moderately posh club with a roulette wheel, a Negro singer at an upright piano, a bar, and tables crowded with a motley collection of people. We pick up a few threads of conversations. "Waiting, waiting, waiting, I'll never get out of here. . . ." "But can't you make it a little more [money]?" "Surely, madame. But diamonds are a drag on the market. There are diamonds everywhere."

Into Rick's comes Ugarte (Peter Lorre), a little weasel who makes his living providing exit visas for refugees. He tries to make small talk with Rick. But Rick has no stomach for his business. Think of all those poor devils who can't pay the going rate, Ugarte says. "I get it for them for half. Is that so parasitic?"

"I don't mind a parasite," says Rick. "I object to a cut-rate one."

"You despise me, don't you?" says Ugarte.

"Oh, if I gave you any thought I probably would," says Rick.

Nevertheless, it's just because Rick despises him, Ugarte says, that he can trust Rick. Ugarte asks Rick to hide two letters of transit, obviously stolen from the slain couriers. Rick puts them in the café piano. "I'm a little more impressed with you," he adds, mellowing just for the instant.

Captain Renault shows up and tells Rick that Victor Laszlo (Henreid), head of the European underground movement, is expected at the café tonight. Laszlo, who has escaped from a concentration camp, is trying to get to America. Rick bets ten thousand francs he'll make it. "Under that cynical shell," says Renault, "you are a sentimentalist at heart."

Now comes Major Strasser. Intent on impressing his Nazi boss, Renault signals his gendarmes to arrest Ugarte. As they close in, Ugarte makes a break for it, stumbles into Rick and pleads for help. Rick does nothing. As the police lead the screaming Ugarte away, Rick mutters, "I stick my neck out for nobody."

Strasser summons Rick to his table and tries to find out whose side he is on. Is Rick one of those people who can't imagine the Germans in their beloved Paris? "It's not my beloved Paris." Can he imagine them in London? "When you get there, ask me." Well, who does he think will win the war? "I haven't the slightest idea."

Ruffled, the major points out he has a full dossier on Rick. "Age thirty-seven. Cannot return to his country. The reason is a little vague. We also know what you did in Paris and why you left Paris." Rick apparently worked for the French underground. (Renault has told us earlier that Rick ran guns to the Ethiopians in 1935—and fought on the Loyalist side in Spain in 1936—and, of course, got well paid both times.)

The conversation has become heated. So Rick discreetly takes his leave. "Forgive me, gentlemen. Your business is politics. Mine is running a saloon."

Now enter Laszlo escorting a Scandinavian beauty (Bergman). When he leaves the table to do a little business with a contact, she persuades Sam the pianist (Dooley Wilson) to play a favorite old love song. That immediately brings Rick over in a nasty mood. "I thought I told you never to play it," he snaps. Then he sees Bergman, his old flame. Bogie, the master of rapier repartee, for once is at a loss for words.

After the café has closed, Rick reminisces alone. In a flashback, we learn that he and the girl, Ilsa Lund Laszlo, were sweethearts in Paris before the Nazis came. They were to have met at the train station, run off and gotten married the day the Germans occupied the city. But she never showed up. Now, as Rick gets drunk, she comes to him to explain. She tells him that Laszlo is her husband and was even when she knew Rick in Paris. Embittered, he insults her and she leaves in tears.

The next night another piece of Rick's jigsaw-puzzle personality shows through. A pretty young Bulgarian fugitive (Joy Page) comes to him. Earnestly and pathetically, she tells him she and her husband are broke. Renault has promised two visas to Lisbon if she'll sleep with him. Will Renault keep his word? Will her husband forgive her? "You want my advice," Rick says, "go back to Bulgaria."

Outwardly, Rick seems gruff. But what he is trying to get across is that the girl is too naïve to be in Renault's league. And he doesn't want her to get hurt. Rick solves the couple's dilemma in his own fashion. He rigs the roulette game so her husband can buy the visas. ("Have you tried 22 tonight?")

When Laszlo learns Rick has the letters of transit, he appeals to him to sell them. Laszlo says he must get to America to help the underground cause. Rick turns him down flat. "The problems of the world are not my department," Rick says. "I'm a saloon-keeper."

Later Ilsa returns, begging Rick to change his mind. "One woman has hurt you," she tells him scornfully, "and you take your revenge on the whole world." When she sees it's useless she pulls a gun. But Rick walks straight toward her, dares her to shoot him and she breaks down.

Finally touched, he takes her in his arms. Then Ilsa tells him she left him because she had learned Laszlo, whom she thought dead, was alive. Now she is at a loss about what to do. "You'll have to think for both of us," she says.

Rick does. He tells Ilsa they're going to Lisbon together. Then he quickly arranges to have Renault and Laszlo meet him at the café. When they show up, he orders Renault at gunpoint to call the airport and give instructions for safe passage for two on the Lisbon plane. Instead, Renault calls Major Strasser.

At the airport, Rick suddenly tells Ilsa she is going with Laszlo. First, deep down they both know she belongs with Laszlo. Second, if she doesn't go with Laszlo, she'll regret it the rest of her life.

"What about us?" Ilsa asks.

"We'll always have Paris . . . ," Rick says.

"And I said I'd never leave you," she half says to herself.

"And you never will," Rick says. ". . . it doesn't take much to see that the problems of three little people don't amount to a hill of beans in this crazy world. Someday you'll understand that. Here's looking at you, kid."

As they board the plane, Strasser dashes up, sizes up the situation and picks up the phone to the control tower. Bogart warns him to stop, then shoots him. Seconds later a carload of Gestapo men screech up. Renault, who has just told Rick he has no choice but to arrest him, suddenly tells the Germans, "Major Strasser has been shot. Round up the usual suspects."

As the plane lifts off the runway for Lisbon and freedom, Renault suggests it might be a good idea if Rick made himself scarce. There is a Free French garrison at Brazzaville, Renault says, and passage could be arranged. And so Renault, who outwardly blows with the wind as much as Rick, has turned out to be made of the same solid stuff.

"I could use a trip," says Rick. He quickly adds, "It doesn't make any difference about the bet. You still owe me ten thousand francs."

"And that ten thousand francs should pay our expenses," adds Renault.

"*Our* expenses?" Rick says and smiles ever so slightly. "Louie, I think this is the beginning of a beautiful friendship." And the two walk off together in the night fog.

Vichy French Police Captain Renault (Claude Rains) greets Nazi Major Heinrich Strasser (Conrad Veidt) as he arrives in French Morocco to investigate the killing of two German couriers.

Underground leader Victor Laszlo (Paul Henreid) and his wife Ilsa appear at police headquarters in Renault's office.

278

Rick stands by as police disarm Ugarte (Peter Lorre), who runs a black market in exit visas in Casablanca. "I stick my neck out for nobody," Rick says.

At first Rick seems to turn a deaf ear to Laszlo when he pleads with Rick to help him escape to America. But later Rick has second thoughts.

Rick, offering Renault a cigarette, bets the French police captain that Laszlo will get out of Casablanca and get to America.

Zeena, "Miracle Woman of the Ages," steps out to answer questions through telepathy as Stan Carlisle (Tyrone Power), barker for her act, introduces her.

Stan nestles up close to Molly (Colleen Gray), a winsome side-show girl, but Bruno the strong man (Mike Mazurki), Molly's protector, doesn't care for the close quarters.

(Photos by 20th Century-Fox)

Nightmare Alley

(New York Premiere, October 9, 1947)

SCREEN PLAY by Jules Furthman. Based on the novel by William Lindsay Gresham. Photography, Lee Garmes. Editor, Barbara McLean. Directed by Edmund Goulding. Produced by George Jessel for 20th Century-Fox. Running time, 111 minutes.

Stan Carlisle	TYRONE POWER
Zeena	JOAN BLONDELL
Molly	COLLEEN GRAY
Lilith Ritter	HELEN WALKER
Ezra Grindle	TAYLOR HOLMES
Bruno	MIKE MAZURKI
Pete	IAN KEITH
Mrs. Peabody	JULIA DEAN
Hoatley	JAMES FLAVIN
McGraw	ROY ROBERTS
Town Marshal	JAMES BURKE
Hobos	EMMETT LYNN, JACK RAYMOND, GEORGE LLOYD, OLIVER BLAKE, GEORGE CHANDLER

Stan Carlisle (Tyrone Power), an ambitious carnival barker, is talking one night with Pete (Ian Keith), an alcoholic who once was a top-billed mind reader. "You should have seen me work," Pete says. And then, suddenly inspired, Pete launches into his old act.

"Throughout the ages, man has sought to look behind the veil that hides him from tomorrow . . . ," Pete says, peering into an imaginary crystal ball. "Wait. The shifting shapes begin to clear. I see fields of grass and rolling hills and a boy—a boy is running barefoot through the hills. A dog is with him."

"His name was Gip," Stan says, mesmerized. There is silence. "Go on," Stan says.

Pete laughs. "See how easy it is to hook 'em? Stock reading. Fits everybody. Every boy has a dog."

What would it be like to be able to see into the future—or to make others think you could? To be held in awe by people who believe you can tell them what lies ahead or bring back their cherished past? Visions whirl in Stan's mind. He is hooked and the course of his life is inevitably set.

Such is the black drama that unfolds in *Nightmare Alley*, a powerful, offbeat film of dark ambition and human gullibility told in the rise and fall of a charlatan. The movie was adapted from William Lindsay Gresham's tawdry potboiler, one of the many examples of how poor books often make exciting movies.

It is true that *Nightmare Alley* failed to attract much attention when it came out in 1947. Its sordid, ruthless plot was nearly devoid of light entertainment and that proved to be an insurmountable box office obstacle. But over the years film buffs have come to admire the unrelenting cynicism of its story line, the craftsmanship of its direction and the excellence of its acting. It was, in fact, Tyrone Power's favorite role. Many think it was his finest screen performance.

Power had already done twenty-nine movies before *Nightmare Alley*. He was darkly handsome, gifted with an ease of manner and a deep vibrant voice. But in most films he came through too stiff and serious, unable to break away from a deadening solemnity that kept him from delivering fluid, rounded characterizations.

Power, who had three wives,* came from theatrical stock going back over a century. His father and grandfather were Shakespearean actors on both sides of the Atlantic. His great-grandfather Tyrone Power was a popular comedian on the Dublin stage in 1827. (Although the name "Tyrone" came

---

* They were French actress Annabella, actress Linda Christian, and Deborah Minardos, a former Mississippi coed. The latter became Power's widow in 1958 when he died of a heart attack while making *Solomon and Sheba* in Spain.

from County Tyrone in Northern Ireland, the family was Roman Catholic.)

Born in Cincinnati in 1913, Power had his first stage role at seven. After graduating from high school he skipped college and, instead, began preparing for an acting career. He studied Shakespearean drama under his father until the elder Power died in 1931. When Power made the rounds of casting offices, he was hardly noticed at first. But Katharine Cornell gave him his start in the theatre and he played on Broadway in *Romeo and Juliet* and *Saint Joan*, in which she starred. When Power returned to Hollywood in 1936 he scored a success in *Lloyds of London,* one of his first pictures. He went on to establish himself as a matinee idol in such popular movies as *Alexander's Ragtime Band* (1938), *Jesse James* (1939), *The Rains Came* (1939), *The Mark of Zorro* (1940), *Blood and Sand* (1941) and *The Razor's Edge* (1946).

Still, many reviewers thought he did not grow into his full dramatic maturity until 1947 when he starred in *Nightmare Alley.* In it, he captured all the designing evil and cold malevolence inherent in a swindler-mentalist who carries his slick bag of tricks into the world of religion. Commenting on his performance, *Variety* said: "Power's talent hits a new high." Wrote critic James Agee: "Tyrone Power, who asked to be cast in the picture, steps into a new class as an actor."

The movie opens in a canival where Stan Carlisle works as a barker for the mind-reading act of Zeena (Joan Blondell) and Pete. At the end of the alley of side shows is a strange, illegal attraction called the Geek, a creature billed as a half-man, half-beast who lives in a bran pit and eats live chickens. The shaggy-haired Geek draws the wide-eyed hicks by the score. He is really a dipsomaniac who goes through his horrifying act for a quart of rotgut a day and a place to sleep it off. But he holds a strange fascination for Stan. "How do you get a guy to be a Geek?" Stan asks. "I can't understand how anybody can get so low."

Stan's burning ambition is to move up the ladder of success. So he studies Zeena and Pete's act, one of the carnival's top attractions. Zeena, "Miracle Woman of the Ages," steps out on a platform, offering to answer through telepathy any personal questions anyone cares to write. Stan collects the questions and Zeena burns them in an urn. Then she proceeds to astonish the audience by reading the questions in her crystal and answering them. What the spellbound crowd doesn't see is that

Stan, while taking the questions to her, has slipped behind the platform for an instant. He pulls a "gipsy switch"—exchanging the written questions for blank paper. Beneath the stage, Pete quickly reads each question, then chalks it on a small blackboard. When Zeena peers into her crystal, she can see Pete's blackboard.

Molly (Colleen Gray), a pert but dumb side-show gal, tells Stan that, good as the act is, it's a far cry from their big-time days when Pete never came near the stage. He stayed in the audience and tipped Zeena off with a secret word code. But Pete has become a drunken souse and they had to abandon the act and work in the carny.

By her own words, Zeena, a blowzy, earthy blonde, has always been a willing player in the game of sex. ("I have a heart like an artichoke—a leaf for everyone.") Stan has an affair with her and persuades her to teach him the code. Then one night, when Pete shows Stan how he did the act in the old days, Stan gives Pete a bottle. By mistake, he gives him a quart of wood alcohol. Pete dies the next day.

Stan takes Pete's place and he and Zeena draw big crowds with the word code.

"What have I here?"

"A gold earring."

"Can you tell me what this is?"

"A key case."

"What color?"

"Red."

However, Stan's relationship with Zeena ends suddenly when Stan seduces Molly and the carnival people force him to marry her. Undaunted, he leaves the show and starts his own mentalist act with Molly in a plush Chicago night club. He calls himself "The Great Stanton," and he quickly becomes a sensation. Asking a question at his show one night is Lilith Ritter (Helen Walker), a successful psychologist who has the richest families in the city as her patients. Stan goes to her office and makes a deal with her. In return for a percentage of his profits, he gets her to let him use confidential information from her clients to convince them he has spiritual powers.

His new "supernatural" qualities win him a large following. One of his first supporters is Mrs. Peabody (Julia Dean), an elderly socialite who has told psychologist Ritter that she dreams of her dead daughter. When Mrs. Peabody comes to Stan's act and asks if she will ever see her daughter again, he tells her she will if she believes in the hereafter. Suddenly he tears off his blindfold. He says he has a vision of her daughter. "She wants to speak to you," Stan says, then faints.

Mrs. Peabody begins seeing Stan regularly, telling her friends he brings her spiritual comfort. Another prominent person, industrialist Ezra Grindle (Taylor Holmes), gives Stan $150,000 for a spiritual tabernacle so Stan can start a religious cult. Grindle promises much more if Stan can materialize Grindle's long-dead sweetheart.

In a pivotal scene, Stan asks his reluctant wife to pose as the spirit. When Stan argues he's not doing anything that other spook workers don't do, Molly says other spiritualists don't pose as ministers.

"You make it sound so sacred and holy when all the time it's just a gag with you," Molly says. "You're just laughing your head off at those chumps. You think God's going to stand for that?" But in the end she goes through with it.

A few days later Stan and Grindle are talking in the moonlight in Grindle's vast gardens. In the distance Grindle sees the silhouette of a girl dressed in old-fashioned clothes. As the shape comes closer, he thinks he sees the spirit of his dead sweetheart and tries to grab her. Stan holds him back. When the old man falls to his knees and prays, Molly breaks down. "No, no—I can't stand it," she screams. "I'm Stan's wife." Shocked and enraged,

Grindle starts after Stan. "You crook. You dirty sacrilegious thief." Stan knocks him down.

He rushes to psychologist Ritter, who has been holding his cash. But she refuses to give him more than a token payment. She knows he was responsible for Pete's death, she tells Stan. She'll tell the police if he doesn't get out.

Broken and penniless, Stan leaves town, holes up in a cheap hotel and gets drunk. He takes to the bottle and wanders aimlessly through hobo jungles, sinking deeper and deeper into a mindless alcoholic abyss. One day he shows up at a carnival, dirty and hollow-eyed, begging for a job. The manager says he's got nothing open. Wait a minute, he says. He does have one small job. Of course, it's only temporary until we can get a real Geek. "Mister," Stan says, "I was made for it."

In an apparent effort to placate the Hays Office, the studio added a final scene. It shows Stan running hysterically around the carnival after his first day as a Geek. By coincidence, Molly is working in the same show, goes to him and takes him to her trailer. The indication is she will start his regeneration.

"How can a guy get so low?" a carnival hand asks the manager.

"He reached too high," the manager replies.

Pete (Ian Keith), once a first-rate mind reader but now a hopeless lush, tells Stan about the old days when Pete and Zeena had a top-billed vaudeville act.

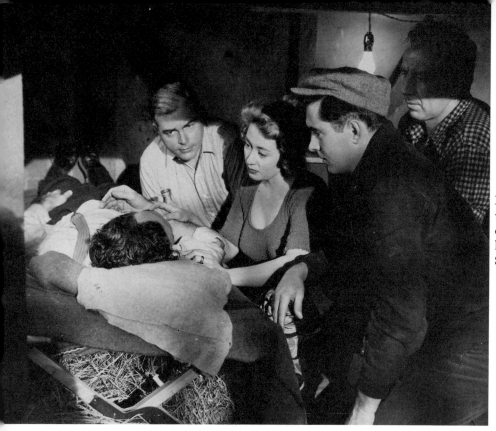

Pete, who has drunk a bottle of wood alcohol which Stan has inadvertently given him, dies on his carnival bunk. Looking on, from left, are Hoatley (James Flavin), Zeena, Stan and Bruno.

Now billed as "The Great Stanton," Carlisle opens a mentalist act with Molly in a plush Chicago night club.

Wealthy industrialist Ezra Grindle (Taylor Holmes) kneels in astonishment as he sees what he believes is the materialization of his long-dead sweetheart. Carlisle restrains him.

Broken and penniless, Carlisle watches a bunch of hobos drain the liquor from his bottle. From left are Emmett Lynn, Jack Raymond, Power, George Lloyd, Oliver Blake (partly obscured) and George Chandler (a president of the Screen Actors Guild).

285

"Frankie. Frankie. Your mother forgives
me." Frankie's mother (Una O'Connor) is
in front pew. *(Courtesy WOR-TV)*

(Photos by RKO)

The Informer

(Released May 19, 1935)

SCREEN PLAY by Dudley Nichols * from the novel by Liam O'Flaherty. Art directors, Van Nest Polglase and Charles Kirk. Cameraman, Joseph H. August. Musical director, Max Steiner.* Editor, George Hively. Directed by John Ford.* Produced by Cliff Reid for RKO Radio Pictures. Running time, 97 minutes.

Gypo Nolan	VICTOR MC LAGLEN *
Katie Madden	MARGOT GRAHAME
Dan Gallagher	PRESTON FOSTER
Mary McPhillip	HEATHER ANGEL
Frankie McPhillip	WALLACE FORD
Mrs. McPhillip	UNA O'CONNOR
Terry	J. M. KERRIGAN
Mulholland	JOSEPH SAUERS (later JOSEPH SAWYER)
Pat Mulligan	DONALD MEEK
Tommy O'Connor	NEIL FITZGERALD
Blind Man	D'ARCY CORRIGAN
Donahue	LEO MC CABE
Flynn	FRANCIS FORD
Madame Betty	MAY BOLEY
The Lady	GRIZELDA HARVEY
Street Singer	DENNIS O'DEA
Man at Wake	JACK MULHALL
Young Soldier	BOB PARRISH

(Other versions: *The Informer*, British, 1929; *Uptight!*, Paramount, 1968, all-Negro.)

Gypo Nolan (Victor McLaglen), his body torn by four bullets, staggers into a church. He weaves down the center aisle and drops to his knees before the front pew where the mother (Una O'Connor) of the slain Frankie McPhillip (Wallace Ford) sits.

---

* Academy Award winner.

Gypo, a modern-day Judas, has turned in his pal for a twenty-pound reward. "'Twas I informed on your son, Mrs. McPhillip," the strapping, bearlike man says meekly. "Forgive me."

Tears stream down the old lady's face. "Ah, Gypo," she replies, "I forgive you. You didn't know what you were doing."

A great weight seems to have lifted from Gypo's shoulders. Rising to the full majestic height of his towering frame, he turns toward the altar. "Frankie. Frankie," he cries in his dying breath. "Your mother forgives me." Stiffly he shuffles to the foot of a great carved Christ and falls before it.

This was Victor McLaglen at the apex of his career. Big, blustery and brawny. He had the shoulders of an ox, a chest like a barrel and a mobile, roughhewn face that resembled a worn-out tire. When he spoke, his voice was a thunderclap, a cannon roar, a kettledrum sweetened by an Irish brogue. He was perfectly cast for Gypo Nolan. And both he and director John Ford won Oscars in 1935 for this tragedy of a stool pigeon in strife-torn Ireland.

Ford, who had been grinding out creditable but generally undistinguished movies * for about twenty years, had been badgering RKO to let him do *The Informer* as far back as 1930. An Irishman, Ford felt that Liam O'Flaherty's searing novel of his troubled homeland would make a film of unusual artistic achievement.

The studio felt the movie would be a box office loser. Its theme was dark, and its hero clumsy and unromantic. But it finally let Ford go ahead on his assurance that he would hold expenses to a mini-

---

* Notable exceptions include *The Iron Horse* (1924) and *The Lost Patrol* (1934).

mum. He kept his word. Ford reportedly waived his salary for a percentage of the profits. The movie is said to have cost just over $200,000 and O'Flaherty was given only $5,000 for the rights. The picture took only three weeks to make. "It was the easiest film I ever directed," Ford said. "I had been dreaming of it for five years."

McLaglen, born a bishop's son in Tunbridge Wells, England, in 1886, had a checkered career before taking to the films. He served in the British Army in World War I, prospected for gold in Canada, ran a physical culture school, wrestled, then boxed. He made his screen debut in 1920 and soon became typed as a brawling, hard-drinking, easy-swearing professional soldier. He was best known for *What Price Glory?*, the 1926 silent film that teamed him as Captain Flagg and Edmund Lowe as Sergeant Quirt. But, in 1934, McLaglen gave promise he was more than just a one-dimensional buffoon and strong man. He turned in a solidly dramatic performance in the Ford-directed movie *The Lost Patrol*.

So Ford picked him for the lead in *The Informer*, a film that would portray not the shimmering Ireland of lilting beauty, poetry and romance but the somber Ireland of bleak slums, foggy lamplit streets and the tensions of men at war.

The movie takes place in the early 1920s when Dublin is in the throes of the Sinn Fein rebellion. (The Gaelic expression means "We Ourselves.") Ireland is under British domination. But Irish patriots have banded together in a guerrilla organization to battle the hated Black and Tans. The undercover army lurks in dank hallways, huddles in hidden meeting places, always on the run from the British.

In this chaotic nightmare world, Gypo Nolan lumbers along the shadowy streets. There is no dialogue as the film opens. Instead, Gypo is seen looking at a poster offering a twenty-pound reward for information about the whereabouts of his fugitive friend Frankie. Gypo, too, has been a member of the Irish Republican Army. But he has been ousted for his softheartedness, which prevented him from carrying out a political assassination.

Gypo angrily tears down the poster. But it catches the wind and pursues him—a dark harbinger—clinging to his feet, then blowing loose until it scuttles along the street, leading us to the feet of Katie (Margot Grahame), Gypo's streetwalker girl friend. Only then does the silence end. "Gypo," Katie says.

As they walk along, they see a sign offering passage to America for ten pounds. Miserable and hungry, she taunts Gypo about their utter poverty. "What chance have we to escape?" Katie says. "Ten pounds to America. Twenty pounds and the world is ours. Twenty pounds. It might as well be a million."

Stung by Katie's bitterness, Gypo, on impulse, goes to the British. He tells them where Frankie is and claims the reward money. In turning informer, he has committed an unforgivable sin in a nation where the government and the police were for centuries the enemies of the people.

But Gypo is a simple-minded bloke whose thoughts are usually of the moment. Only after he leaves the police station does he begin to perceive the enormity of his deed. He thinks a stranger has seen him. Afraid that he will be betrayed, he starts shaking the man, but the man is blind. Gypo passes his hand before the sightless eyes and flees. As Gypo runs down the street, the blind man's tapping cane follows. The cane, a symbol of Gypo's conscience, seems obvious today. But in 1935 it was a fresh and unpretentious device.

Gypo committed his deed about 6:00 P.M. During the next eight hours he squanders his blood money, carousing in an attempt to wipe it from his mind. He is already drunk when he attends Frankie's wake in an agonized attempt to appear innocent. As the women are keening, Gypo sits in the foreground and blusters out, "I'm sorry for your trouble, Mrs. McPhillip." He starts to rise. And as he does, the telltale coins drop from his pocket. All stare at him. The wake suddenly halts. The camera shifts from face to face: Commandant Gallagher (Preston Foster). Frankie's mother, Mary McPhillip. Frankie's sister (Heather Angel). Back to Gypo. No one speaks. Still, Gypo is naïve enough to believe he hasn't given himself away.

Thereafter, while his money lasts, the pathetic lout wanders aimlessly through the slums of Dublin. He treats everyone in a fish and chips shop, visits a brothel and finally ends up before the rebel commandant who has convened a court of justice. Gypo accuses another man. Unluckily he picks Pat Mulligan (Donald Meek), a tailor who has a perfect alibi. Finally Gypo breaks down and confesses. But before he can be executed he escapes and hides in Katie's room. Like a child, he falls asleep before the fire.

Katie goes to Gallagher to plead for Gypo's life but she unwittingly gives him away. Gypo's former comrades corner him and gun him down. Mortally wounded, Gypo manages to stagger to a church. Here Frankie's mother is kneeling before the altar. And here he receives absolution.

The movie, which was shown right after its New York premiere on the maiden voyage of the French liner *Normandie,* received immediate critical acclaim. "As stark and impressive a tragedy as the screen has ever produced," Richard Watts, Jr., wrote in the New York *Herald Tribune.* André Sennwald of the new York *Times* called the film "one of the distinctly memorable events of the season." In London, Campbell Sixon of the *Daily Telegraph* said, "Victor McLaglen's Gypo Nolan could not be bettered by any actor living."

The movie was the turning point of Ford's career. He went on to direct nearly two hundred pictures including the Academy Award winner *Grapes of Wrath* (1940) and such outstanding films as *The Hurricane* (1937), *Stagecoach* (1939) and *The Quiet Man* (1952).

Ironically, McLaglen slipped from stardom. But he made 150 movies, including *Under Two Flags* (1936), *Wee Willie Winkie* (1937) and *Gunga Din* (1939). In fact, McLaglen got a "best supporting" Oscar nomination for his role in *The Quiet Man.* He was the only actor ever to be nominated in this category after winning an Oscar for a starring role.

Gypo Nolan (Victor McLaglen) and his girl, Katie Madden (Margot Grahame).

POLICE NOTICE

£20 REWARD

WANTED FOR MURDER

FRANKIE McPHILLIP

e 26, 5 feet 9 inches in height, light
plexion, light brown hair, grey eyes,
n shaven, weight about 12 stone.

above reward will be paid by the Authorities to any person
Public Service who may give information resulting in his

to be given at any Police Station.

Gypo and the poster with the twenty-pound reward that leads him to his downfall.
(Courtesy WOR-TV)

Gypo drinks to soothe his conscience at rebel headquarters after secretly informing on his pal Frankie. That's a young Preston Foster with the pipe playing the rebel commandant. Joseph Sauers (whose film name later became Joe Sawyer) is in center. *(Courtesy WOR-TV)*

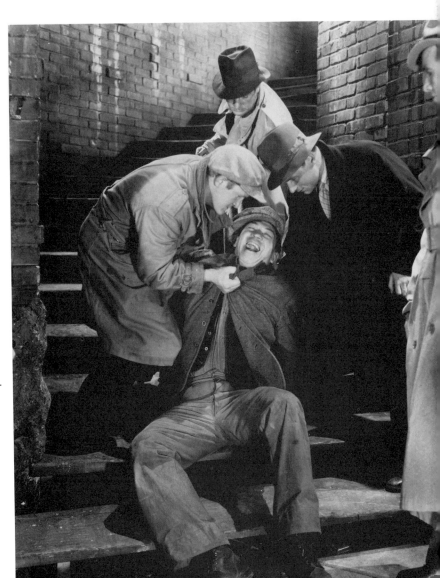

Gypo finally breaks down and confesses before his rebel comrades.

Holly Martins (Joseph Cotten) waits at the
ferris wheel for his dramatic meeting with
his old pal, Harry Lime (Orson Welles),
whom Martins had thought dead.

(Photos by British Lion)

The Third Man

(United States release, February 1950)

SCREEN PLAY by Graham Greene. Music by Anton Karas. Director of photography, Robert Krasker.* Art director, Vincent Korda. Edited by Oswald Hafenrichter. Sound, John Cox. Produced and directed by Carol Reed. A British Lion release of Alexander Korda–David O. Selznick-London Films production. Running time, 104 minutes.

Holly Martins	JOSEPH COTTEN
Anna Schmidt	ALIDA VALLI
Harry Lime	ORSON WELLES
Major Calloway	TREVOR HOWARD
Sergeant Paine	BERNARD LEE
Porter	PAUL HOERBIGER
Porter's Wife	ANNIE ROSAR
"Baron" Kurtz	ERNST DEUTSCH
Dr. Winkel	ERICH PONTO
Mr. Popescu	SIEGFRIED BREUER
Crabbit	WILFRID HYDE-WHITE
Anna's Landlady	HEDWIG BLEIBTREU
Hansl	HERBERT HALBIK
Brodsky	ALEXIS CHESNAKOV
Hall Porter at Sacher's	PAUL HARDTMUTH

(*The Third Man* won the Grand Prix for the best feature film in the 1949 International Film Festival at Cannes. Although it was not released in the United States until 1950, it was filmed and shown in Europe in 1949.)

A zither is singing its sad-sweet melody as Joseph Cotten leans on a cart by the side of a tree-lined cemetery road.

Off in the distance, like a faraway train seen down the ties of a railroad track, Valli approaches head on. She is, at first, a dot, then a pencil shadow, then a lovely young woman. We're set for the conven-

---

* Academy Award winner.

tional Hollywood ending. Cotten will make a gesture, perhaps take a step forward. And she will turn and come toward him. And they will embrace as the humming, pinging music rises and "The End" flashes across the screen.

But in another moment we realize that something odd is happening. Cotten isn't moving. And Valli isn't stopping. On she comes, walking right by him and out of the picture, and we sit there in mild shock as the last frames of *The Third Man* play out.

This is the final irony in a film that is a masterpiece of ironies, a thriller whose intricate plot has as many fascinating twists and turns as the baroque architecture and narrow, winding streets of Vienna, where the picture was made. Running through it all, like an undercurrent, is the pulsing, mesmerizing voice of the zither. The shallow, forty-stringed boxed instrument created movie magic. Not only did it hold the picture in focus, it became an entity unto itself, a kind of cynical commentator on the unfolding drama.

The Third Man had a simple genesis—at a dinner table. After director Carol Reed and writer Graham Greene had finished *The Fallen Idol,* Sir Alexander Korda dined with Greene to ask him to do a screen play for a second joint effort. Greene had no ideas in mind. But he did have an old envelope on which he had scribbled an intriguing opening paragraph some twenty years before. It read: "I had paid my last farewell to Harry a week ago, when his coffin was lowered into the frozen February ground so that it was with incredulity that I saw him pass by, without a sign of recognition, among the host of strangers in the Strand."

Greene had never worked out this old idea of meeting a dead man. But he proposed to do so now. Korda, having full confidence in Greene's talents, let him pursue it to its end. There was a single stipulation. Korda wanted a film about the four-power occupation of Vienna. And so Greene created

Harry out of the rubble of the gloomy, bombed-out Austrian capital.

Actually the script turned out to be a product of a close working relationship between Greene and Reed. They went over and over the manuscript scene by scene, line by line, whipping it into taut shape, resolving all their differences—with one exception.

"One of the very few major disputes between Carol Reed and myself concerned the ending, and he has been proved triumphantly right," Greene said. "I held the view that an entertainment of this kind was too light an affair to carry the weight of an unhappy ending. . . . I was afraid few people would wait in their seats during the girl's long walk from the graveside and that they would leave the cinema under the impression of an ending as conventional as mine. . . . I had not given enough consideration to the mastery of Reed's direction and, at that state, of course, we neither of us could have anticipated Reed's brilliant discovery of Mr. [Anton] Karas, the zither player."

The Karas discovery was one of two intuitive strokes of genius Reed had in making the film. It came about accidentally. After a tiring day touring Vienna for atmospheric backgrounds (which would become an integral part of the story), Reed, Alida Valli and Cotten drifted into one of the wine cellars that gave the city so much of its prewar *Gemütlichkeit*. There he heard Karas, a bespectacled, forty-year-old musician, filling the café with bizarre, jangling sounds from his zither.

Reed knew immediately that this was exactly the right background music for his movie. His friends thought he was way off base. They argued that film music had to have body, that it could not be confined to a single instrument. But Reed was adamant. He took Karas to London and there, over the next six weeks, Karas composed the score. He had no idea then that his "Third Man Theme" would become world famous. And so would he.

The second Reed inspiration was putting Orson Welles in the picture. At first Welles did not want to play Harry Lime because the part was a small one. When Welles came to Vienna, he said it was only to explain why he had decided against appearing in the movie. But Reed had his cameras set and implored him to at least do one scene—the memorable chase through the sewers.

"Reluctantly, he agreed," Reed said. " 'Those sewers will give me pneumonia,' he [Welles] grumbled, as he descended the iron steps. We shot the scene.

Then Orson asked us to shoot it again although I was satisfied with the first take. He had some idea of how to play the scene more dramatically. He talked with the cameraman, made some suggestions, and did the chase again. Then again. The upshot was that Orson did that scene ten times, became enthusiastic about the story—and stayed in Vienna to finish the picture. And, of course, he gave a miraculous performance."

The film is essentially the story of a naïve American who tries to unravel the mystery of his friend's death. Holly Martins (Cotten), a writer of western pulp novels, comes to bleak, postwar Vienna to take a job promised by an old pal, Harry Lime (Welles). When he arrives he is stunned to find that his friend has been killed in a street accident. He is to be buried in an hour or so.

Martins hurries to the cemetery in time to see Lime's coffin lowered into the ground. A girl—we shall know her later as Anna Schmidt (Valli), Harry's girl friend—covers her tearful eyes. Nearby, two men watch Martins closely.

When Martins leaves, a British military officer, Major Calloway (Trevor Howard), offers him a ride. They stop at a bar and when Martins says he was Lime's friend Calloway tells him that Lime was a crook and a murderer. Martins tries to slug him and they exchange bitter words. Refusing to believe Lime was corrupt, Martins sets out on his own investigation.

At the Café Mozart he meets "Baron" Kurtz (Ernst Deutsch), a seedy aristocrat who takes him to the accident scene outside Lime's apartment. Kurtz says Lime wasn't looking where he was going. A truck hit him as he stepped from the sidewalk. Kurtz and Mr. Popescu (Siegfried Breuer), a Romanian friend of Lime's, carried him to a statue in the middle of the square where he died.

Martins wants to talk to the girl who was at the cemetery. Kurtz says he doesn't know her name. However, when pressed, he tells Martin she is a showgirl at the Josefstadt Theatre. "But I don't think it will do Harry any good," Kurtz adds cryptically.

Anna, a graceful, dark-haired girl shattered by Lime's sudden death, goes over the details of the accident. She says Harry's doctor was there and it was Harry's driver who hit him. But, she adds, they said at the inquest it wasn't the driver's fault.

"I don't get this," Martins says. "All of them there. Kurtz, this Romanian Popescu. His own driver knocking him over, his own doctor passing by. No strangers there at all?"

"I wondered about it a hundred times," Anna says, "if it really was an accident."

Together they go to Lime's apartment and find an old porter (Paul Hoerbiger) who was an eyewitness. He says he saw the body carried by three men. Kurtz and the Romanian, Martins says. "There was a third man," the porter says. "He didn't give evidence." "You don't mean the doctor?" Martins asks. No, he came later, the porter says. But who was he? "I didn't see his face." The porter shrugs.

The next day the porter is found dead. Now that Cotten's curiosity is aroused, two thugs come after him at night. But he manages to lose them, hiding in the debris of a ruined building. Frustrated and confused, he gets drunk, then goes to Anna's flat after midnight, trying to sort out the pieces of this strange puzzle. He has fallen in love with her and he takes her in his arms. But she doesn't respond. "Wouldn't stand a chance?" he says. She doesn't answer, and Martins leaves.

However, just as he steps into the street, he spots a figure hiding in a doorway. Except for his shoes, the figure is in shadows. When an apartment light goes on, it shines across the smiling face of Harry Lime.

A car darts down the street, coming between them. By the time it has passed the figure is gone. But Martins tells Major Calloway what he has seen. And when they dig up Lime's coffin, they find the body of Joseph Harbin, a medical orderly who had acted as a police informer against Lime. So Lime had arranged his own death to throw police off his trail. Lime was the third man.

Now Martins secretly arranges a meeting with Lime at the lonely Prater, Vienna's once gay amusement park. In an unforgettable scene, Lime shows up with a glad hand and a hearty greeting. Martins replies coldly and they go up in a ferris wheel for privacy. Martins knows now that Lime is trafficking in diluted penicillin. In this deprived city its sale has brought black market prices, but it has also brought agonizing death to scores of children.

"Have you ever seen one of your victims?" Martins asks.

Lime looks out of the window of the swaying, rising car. Below the figures have shrunk to forms unrecognizable as humans.

"Would you really feel any pity if one of those dots stopped moving forever?" Lime asks. "If I offered you twenty thousand pounds for every dot that stops, would you really, old man, tell me to keep my money? Or would you calculate how many dots you could afford to spare? Free of income tax, old man. . . ."

The ferris-wheel car stops at the peak of its ride, high above the park. There's no proof he's alive except for Martins, Lime says. He carries a gun and no one would look for a bullet in a body that hit the ground from so high up. Martins clutches the car railing.

"They dug up your coffin," Martins says.

"And found Harbin?" Lime asks, startled, his voice suddenly drained of all warmth. Then, as the car begins to sail slowly down, Lime chuckles, makes an offer to Martins to go in with him, and promises to meet Martins when he makes up his mind.

As he steps off the car, Lime tries to justify his black market racket. "In Italy for thirty years under the Borgias they had warfare, terror, murder, bloodshed. They produced Michelangelo, Leonardo da Vinci and the Renaissance. In Switzerland they had brotherly love, five hundred years of democracy and peace. And what did that produce—the cuckoo clock. So long, Holly."

Meanwhile, the British police have found that Anna has a forged passport and have taken her into custody. They intend to hand her over to the Russians. But Martins makes a deal. In exchange for Anna's freedom, he agrees to meet Lime with police staked out so they can arrest him.

When Anna learns what Martins has done, she is furious. She tries to warn Lime as he meets Martins at a café. But it is too late. The police close in.

Lime bolts for the sewers and in a chase sequence brilliantly filmed by Robert Krasker (who won an Oscar for his camera work), police of four nations pursue him through the subterranean network, throwing searchlights about the stone walls and dark, rushing waters.

Lime kills one policeman before a bullet brings him down. Struggling futilely to escape, he crawls laboriously up an iron stairway to reach a manhole cover. The camera shows his fingers emerging through a grill, unable to budge it. Then Martins reaches him. They look at each other and Martins, standing in the sewer water with a gun, fires the shot that finishes Lime.

So Lime is buried for a second time and for a second time Martins is driven off from the cemetery by Calloway. But as they go down the dreary, tree-lined road, Martins gets out. "One can't just leave," he says, and stands by the roadside as Anna approaches.

Martins has been Lime's friend for what he imagined him to be. But Anna has loved him for what he was. And she cannot forgive Martins for selling out his friend like a Judas—even if her own freedom has been bought by the thirty pieces of silver. And so she walks past Martins without a word, without a look, without a gesture.

Anton Karas, the Viennese zither player, who composed and played the haunting music of *The Third Man*. It was director Carol Reed's idea to have a single instrument do the background music. A craze for zither music swept Europe and America after the film.

A close-up of the zither. Hands belong to Karas.

Police take Anna (Valli) into custody for having a forged passport as she turns with pleading eyes toward British Major Calloway (Trevor Howard), with beret. Sergeant Paine (Bernard Lee) holds briefcase.

Lime pressed behind an indenture in Vienna's sewer system as police with torches hunt him down.

Eyes wide and gun leveled, Harry Lime awaits his pursuers behind an iron stairway leading to a manhole exit. *(Photo copyright 1956 20th Century-Fox Film Corp.)*

In this famous closing sequence, Anna, Harry Lime's girl, walks down the cemetery road as Martins waits for her. Instead of stopping, as the audience expects, she walks past him without a word.

Gravelle (Boris Karloff), a baritone gone mad, glares menacingly at Charlie (Warner Oland) in *Charlie Chan at the Opera,* made in 1936.

(Photos by Warner Bros.–Seven Arts)

Charlie Chan at the Opera

(Released January 8, 1937)

SCREEN PLAY by Scott Darling and Charles Belden. From a story by Bess Meredyth based on the character "Charlie Chan" created by Earl Derr Biggers. Opera *Carnival* by Oscar Levant. Libretto by William Kernell. Orchestration by Charles Maxwell. Photography by Lucien Andriot. Editor, Alex Troffey. Produced by John Stone. Directed by H. Bruce Humberstone for 20th Century-Fox. Running time, 66 minutes.

Charlie Chan	WARNER OLAND
Gravelle	BORIS KARLOFF
Lee Chan	KEYE LUKE
Mademoiselle Kitty	CHARLOTTE HENRY
Phil Childers	THOMAS BECK
Madame Lilli Rochelle	MARGARET IRVING
Enrico Barelli	GREGORY GAYE
Madame Lucretia Barelli	NEDDA HARRIGAN
Mr. Whitely	FRANK CONROY
Inspector Regan	GUY USHER
Sergeant Kelly	WILLIAM DEMAREST
Mr. Arnold	MAURICE CASS
Morris	TOM MC GUIRE

(Stars who appeared in the series included Rita Hayworth [then billed under her real name, Margarita Cansino], John Hall [also billed under his real name, Charles Locher], Ray Milland, George Brent, Stepin Fetchit, Heather Angel, Lynn Bari, Slim Summerville, Cesar Romero, Bela Lugosi and Boris Karloff.)

To the daredevils of the 1930s, his words of wisdom were: "Man who flirt with dynamite sometimes fly with angels."

To those who would use the power of persuasion, he said: "When money talks, few are deaf." On negotiations, he counseled: "Save football tactics for gridiron."

These pearls of oriental wisdom come from Charlie Chan, the philosophical Chinese detective from Honolulu who was portrayed in more feature-length American films than any other celluloid investigator. From 1926 to 1949, Charlie moved languidly through forty-six pictures and one serial, spouting aphorisms at the drop of a body.

Not everybody was turned on by Charlie's wise sayings and, toward the end of his movie career, they seemed to lose their gentle punch and grow tiresome. Worse, he began to repeat himself. One writer said his aphorisms were "as endless, if more mellow, than Orphan Annie's."

But to say Chan's quotations were not always stimulating or humorous is beside the point. The fact is they made him an original and distinct character. They set him apart from the two-fisted, gun-toting detective who bullied and shot his way through other series films.

Unlike the tough private eyes, Chan was also courteous, soft-spoken and slow-moving. He was heavy-set and somewhat dull and conservative. But when the chips were down, when a baffling murder had to be solved—and solved on the slimmest of evidence—he had no peer. "Insignificant molehill," Charlie astutely observed, "sometimes more important than conspicuous mountain."

The fictional Chinese sleuth was created by Earl Derr Biggers, who serialized his first book in the *Saturday Evening Post* in 1925. He went on to write six books about Chan, creating the prototype for the movie hero.

In the 1930s the Chan movies often premiered at first-run theatres. But as the series grew older, clichés gradually found their way into the scripts and gave them a distinct B-movie flavor. However, these same telltale mystery story trademarks never fail to delight nostalgic Chan buffs.

FIFTY CLASSIC MOTION PICTURES

• First there is the shady character thrust into the picture to draw all suspicion. Everyone is instantly ready to accept him as the culprit—everyone except Chan. And, of course, he invariably turns out to be a red herring. "There is one sure way of telling who is *not* the killer," says Leonard Maltin, editor of *Film Fan Monthly*. "He is the one who, in the middle of the investigation, sputters, 'Haven't we had enough of this foolishness?'"

• There is Charlie's wheel-spinning Number One son (Keye Luke), always saying the wrong thing, always in the way, always gumming up the works. The greatest puzzle is how this scatterbrain could be the offspring of such an intellectually inclined gentleman in the first place. Chan, by the way, had a family of twelve children, and more sons—including Number Two son (Victor Sen Yung)—appeared in later movies. But none inherited their dad's talent for deduction.

• There are the dim-witted cops whom Chan is constantly showing up and with whom, consequently, there is always friction. When the police chief summons Charlie in *Charlie Chan at the Opera*, William Demarest groans, "You're not going to call in Chop Suey."

Oddly enough, Charlie was never played by a Chinese actor. George Kuwa, a Japanese, was the first to portray Charlie in the 1926 serial *The House Without a Key*. Two years later Kamiyama Sojin, another Japanese, took the part in *The Chinese Parrot*. The following year E. L. Park, a British actor, played the role. All these were minor parts.

Then in 1931, Fox did *Charlie Chan Carries On*, the first picture to make Chan the leading character. The Swedish-born Warner Oland played the role so convincingly, he took over the part permanently. Oland, a former Shakespearean actor who had portrayed the insidious Dr. Fu Manchu and other oriental villains in the movies,* made sixteen Chan films until his death in 1938.

Succeeding him was Sidney Toler, a Missouri-born actor of Scottish descent who had been a playwright and Broadway performer earlier in his career. Toler starred in twenty-five Chan pictures until he, too, died in 1947. Character actor Roland Winters finished the series, playing Chan in six more films through 1949. Others who appeared as the

epigrammatic investigator were William Harrigan on the stage, Ed Begley and Walter Connolly on the radio, and J. Carroll Naish on television.

Chan enthusiasts still debate whether Oland or Toler made the best Chan. But since Oland preceded Toler, he must be credited with building up the tremendous public following. One of Oland's most unusual adventures pitted him against Boris Karloff in *Charlie Chan at the Opera*. The 1937 movie included the opera *Carnival*, written especially for the picture by Oscar Levant. So well made was the film—and so much fun does it seem today—that its interest ranges far beyond the usual circle of Chan buffs. In 1967, for instance, it was shown at a special invitational performance at the Metropolitan Opera Festival at Newport, Rhode Island.

As the movie opens, Gravelle (Karloff), once a great operatic baritone, is in a mental asylum. He was believed burned to death in a theatre fire at the height of his career. But he was later admitted to the asylum, crazed, unidentified, his memory gone. Actually, his wife and her lover had set the fire after locking him in his dressing room.

One night he sees a newspaper picture of Lilli Rochelle (Margaret Irving), his wife, still an opera singer but now remarried. The shock of his wife's picture suddenly restores his memory. He escapes after strangling a guard.

Chan, called in on the case, finds the trampled picture and heads for the opera house with Number One son (Luke). A tense atmosphere pervades the theatre. Gravelle has sneaked in and slipped over to Madame Lucretia Barelli (Nedda Harrigan), whose husband Enrico (Gregory Gaye) has been having an affair with the coquettish Lilli. Chan learns that Lilli has gotten a threatening letter. And several singers have seen the shadowy figure of Gravelle lurking around in a Mephistopheles costume similar to the one worn by Enrico Barelli.

A police guard is thrown around the theatre. But just before the performance Gravelle knocks Barelli out and takes over his role. While the opera is on, Barelli is found dead in his dressing room. And Lilli is stabbed to death in her scene with Mephistopheles, whose voice, strangely enough, is noticed to be unlike Barelli's.

Police Sergeant Kelly (William Demarest) assumes that the man who sang Mephistopheles must be the killer. But three others have a motive for murder: (1) Lucretia Barelli, jealous of Lilli's at-

---

* In an off-character part, Oland also played Al Jolson's father, a cantor, in *The Jazz Singer*, the first talking picture, in 1927.

traction for her husband. (2) Whitely (Frank Conroy), Lilli's second husband, who is also insanely jealous and has even threatened Barelli. And (3) Childers (Thomas Beck), who dislikes Lilli because she has refused to let him marry her daughter.

Chan finds Gravelle and suggests running through the opera a second time, hoping to trap the killer. Tension mounts and the singing resumes with Madame Barelli taking Lilli's part.

As Gravelle draws a knife near the climax, an overzealous cop shoots him. Police say he has killed both Barelli and Lilli. But Chan proves Gravelle is innocent and then proceeds to disclose the real murderer.

Gravelle will recover. But that's as much as we can disclose. We can't commit the unpardonable sin of spoiling a Charlie Chan ending. So this is one you'll have to see on the late show. Suffice it to say, the killer learns too late the wisdom of one of honorable Charlie's favorite sayings: "Man who fight law always loses—same as grasshopper is always wrong in argument with chicken."

Charlie (Oland) and his family of twelve. Unfortunately, none of his sons inherited their father's skillful powers of detection.

Ray Milland and Madge Bellamy with Oland in the 1934 *Charlie Chan in London*.

Sidney Toler, who made more pictures (twenty-five) than any of the six actors who played Chan, appears with Victor Sen Yung, left, his Number Two son, and C. Henry Gordon. Scene is from *Charlie Chan at the Wax Museum*, a 1940 film.

Toler leans over a corpse in *Charlie Chan in Murder Over New York*, a 1940 picture, with Sen Yung, left, and Ricardo Cortez.

Keye Luke, as Charlie's Number One son, is on his toes during a phone conversation from *Charlie Chan at Monte Carlo*. Oland eyes Harold Huber.

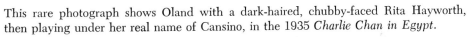

This rare photograph shows Oland with a dark-haired, chubby-faced Rita Hayworth, then playing under her real name of Cansino, in the 1935 *Charlie Chan in Egypt*.

Selected Bibliography

Biography and Autobiography

BAINBRIDGE, JOHN. *Garbo*. Doubleday, 1955.

BARR, CHARLES. *Laurel & Hardy*. University of California Press, 1967.

CHAPLIN, CHARLES. *My Autobiography*. Simon and Schuster, 1964.

COHEN, MORTON. *Rider Haggard*. Walker, 1960.

DESCHNER, DONALD. *The Films of W. C. Fields*. Cadillac, 1966.

EVERSON, WILLIAM K. *The Art of W. C. Fields*. Bobbs-Merrill, 1967.

————. *The Films of Laurel and Hardy*. Cadillac, 1967.

FREWIN, LESLIE. *Dietrich*. Stein and Day, 1967.

HUFF, THEODORE. *Charlie Chaplin*. Pyramid, 1964.

HYAMS, JOEL. *Bogie: The Biography of Humphrey Bogart*. Signet, 1968.

LAMPARSKI, RICHARD. *Whatever Became of . . . ?* 2nd Series. Crown, 1968.

MC CABE, JOHN. *Mr. Laurel and Mr. Hardy*. Signet, 1968.

MC DONALD, GERALD; CONWAY, MICHAEL; and RICCI, MARK. *The Films of Charlie Chaplin*. Cadillac, 1966.

MEYERS, WARREN B. *Who Is That? The Late, Late Viewers Guide to the Old, Old Movies*. Personality Posters, 1967.

MICHAEL, PAUL. *Humphrey Bogart: The Man and His Films*. Bobbs-Merrill, 1965.

SHULMAN, IRVING. *Harlow, an Intimate Biography*. Dell, 1964.

SWINDELL, LARRY. *Spencer Tracy*. World, 1969.

TWOMEY, ALFRED E., and MC CLURE, ARTHUR F. *The Versatiles: Supporting Character Players in the Cinema, 1930–1955*. Barnes, 1969.

WEST, MAE. *Goodness Had Nothing to Do With It*. Prentice-Hall, 1959.

ZIEROLD, NORMAN. *Garbo*. Stein and Day, 1969.

ZIMMERMAN, PAUL D., and GOLDBLATT, BURT. *The Marx Brothers at the Movies*. Putnam, 1968.

History and Criticism

AGEE, JAMES. *Agee on Film*. McDowell, Obolensky, 1958.

BAXTER, JOHN. *Hollywood in the Thirties*. Barnes, 1968.

BUTLER, IVAN. *The Horror Film*. Barnes, 1967.

CLARENS, CARLOS. *Illustrated History of the Horror Films*. Putnam, 1967.

CROWTHER, BOSLEY. *The Great Films: Fifty Golden Years of Motion Pictures*. Putnam, 1967.

DOUGLAS, DRAKE. *Horror!* Macmillan, 1966.

EVERSON, WILLIAM K. *The Bad Guys*. Cadillac, 1964.

FENIN, GEORGE N., and EVERSON, WILLIAM K. *The Western*. Orion, 1962

GOODMAN, EZRA. *The Fifty-Year Decline and Fall of Hollywood*. Simon and Schuster, 1961.

GRIFFITH, RICHARD, and MAYER, ARTHUR. *The Movies*. Simon and Schuster, 1957.

HALLIWELL, LESLIE. *The Filmgoer's Companion: From Nickelodeon to New Wave*. Hill and Wang, 1965.

HIGHAM, CHARLES, and GREENBERG, JOEL. *Hollywood in the Forties*. Barnes, 1968.

JACOBS, LEWIS. *The Rise of the American Film: A Critical History*. Harcourt, Brace, 1939.

KAEL, PAULINE. *Kiss Kiss, Bang Bang*. Little, Brown, 1968.

MICHAEL, PAUL. *The Academy Awards: A Pictorial History*. Crown, 1968.

————, ed. *The American Movies Reference Book: The Sound Era*. Prentice-Hall, 1969.

ROTHA, PAUL, and GRIFFITH, RICHARD. *The Film Till Now*. Funk & Wagnalls, 1950.

SARRIS, ANDREW. *The American Cinema*. Dutton, 1968.

SHICKEL, RICHARD. *The Stars*. Dial, 1962.

SPRINGER, JOHN. *All Talking! All Singing! All Dancing!* Cadillac, 1966.

ZIEROLD, NORMAN. *The Moguls*. Coward-McCann, 1969.

Miscellaneous

BARBOUR, ALAN G. *The Serial*. Vols. I and II. Barbour, 1967 and 1968.

BEAUMONT, CHARLES. *Remember? Remember?* Macmillan, 1963.

CHERTOK, HARVEY, and TORGE, MARTHA. *Quotations from Charlie Chan*. Golden, 1968.

WEINTRAUB, JOSEPH. *The Wit and Wisdom of Mae West*. Putnam, 1967.

Magazines Consulted

Time, Newsweek, Life, The New Yorker, The Nation, The Literary Digest, Reader's Digest, Playboy, The Saturday Evening Post, Collier's, Commonweal, Look, Theatre Arts, Harrison's Reports, Films in Review, Film Culture, Sight and Sound, Screen Facts, Film Fan Monthly.

Index